I0100483

Connecting
&Distancing

The **Singapore Society of Asian Studies (SSAS)** is a local academic association which was established in 1982. Its aims are to promote research on Asian society and culture, focusing on the Southeast Asian region and the ethnic Chinese. It concentrates on organizing talks, seminars, and conferences as well as publishing books, monographs, and a journal *Asian Culture* (*Yazhou Wenhua*) in two languages: Chinese and English. Its objective is to contribute to the academic life in the city-state.

The **Institute of Southeast Asian Studies (ISEAS)** was established as an autonomous organization in 1968. It is a regional centre dedicated to the study of socio-political, security and economic trends and developments in Southeast Asia and its wider geostrategic and economic environment. The Institute's research programmes are the Regional Economic Studies (RES, including ASEAN and APEC), Regional Strategic and Political Studies (RSPS), and Regional Social and Cultural Studies (RSCS).

ISEAS Publishing, an established academic press, has issued almost 2,000 books and journals. It is the largest scholarly publisher of research about Southeast Asia from within the region. ISEAS Publishing works with many other academic and trade publishers and distributors to disseminate important research and analyses from and about Southeast Asia to the rest of the world.

Connecting &Distancing

Southeast Asia and China

EDITED BY Ho Khai Leong

SINGAPORE SOCIETY OF ASIAN STUDIES

INSTITUTE OF SOUTHEAST ASIAN STUDIES
SINGAPORE

First published in Singapore in 2009 by
ISEAS Publishing
Institute of Southeast Asian Studies
30 Heng Mui Keng Terrace
Pasir Panjang
Singapore 119614

E-mail: publish@iseas.edu.sg
Website: <http://bookshop.iseas.edu.sg>

All rights reserved. No part of this publication may be reproduced, stored in a retrieval system, or transmitted in any form or by any means, electronic, mechanical, photocopying, recording or otherwise, without the prior permission of the Institute of Southeast Asian Studies.

© 2009 Institute of Southeast Asian Studies, Singapore

The responsibility for facts and opinions in this publication rests exclusively with the authors and their interpretations do not necessarily reflect the views or the policy of the publisher or its supporters.

ISEAS Library Cataloguing-in-Publication Data

Connecting and distancing : Southeast Asia and China / edited by Ho Khai Leong.
   Papers presented at the International Conference on "Southeast Asia and China: Connecting, Distancing and Positioning", 1 December 2007 in Singapore, organized by the Singapore Society for Asian Studies.
1.   Southeast Asia—Foreign relations—China—Congresses.
2.   China—Foreign relations—Southeast Asia—Congresses.
I.   Ho, Khai Leong, 1954–
II.   Singapore Society for Asian Studies.
III. International Conference on "Southeast Asia and China : Connecting, Distancing and Positioning" (2007 : Singapore)
DS525.9 C5C74   2009

ISBN 978-981-230-856-6 (hard cover)
ISBN 978-981-230-857-3 (E-book PDF)

Typeset by Superskill Graphics Pte Ltd
Printed in Singapore by Utopia Press Pte Ltd

CONTENTS

CONTRIBUTORS

CHAN Yuk Wah is an Assistant Professor at the Department of Asian and International Studies of the City University of Hong Kong. She obtained her Ph.D. from the Department of Anthropology at the Chinese University of Hong Kong, with a fieldwork-based thesis on borderland trade and tourism in Vietnam. Her research interests include: Regional studies: South China and Vietnam; Diaspora and migration studies: Chinese and Vietnamese diaspora; Tourism studies: outbound Chinese tourists.
E-mail: yukchan@cityu.edu.hk

Edgardo E. DAGDAG is Professor, Asian Center, University of the Philippines. His research areas are Philippine foreign relations (including Philippine-China relations), China-Taiwan-ASEAN relations, and security concerns in East Asia.
E-mail: edgardo.dagdag@up.edu.ph

Aimee DAWIS teaches at the Graduate Programme of the University of Indonesia's Department of Communication, School of Social and Political Sciences and the Letters Department, School of Humanities. She obtained her Bachelor of Arts degree in Communication Studies from Loyola Marymount University at Los Angeles, California before pursuing her Master's of Professional degree in Communications from Cornell University at Ithaca, New York. She earned her doctorate in Media Ecology from New York University's Department of Communication in 2005. She has written and presented on Cultural Studies, Research Methods and Methodology, Ethnography, Postmodernism, and Media and Identity. Her book, based on her Ph.D. dissertation, *The Chinese of Indonesia and Their Search for Identity:*

The Relationship between Collective Memory and the Media, has been published by Cambria Press, New York, 2009.
E-mail: canting@hotmail.com

GOH Geok Yian obtained her Doctor of Philosophy in History from the University of Hawai'i at Manoa in August 2007. Born in Singapore, she majored in Southeast Asian Studies and Sociology while she was an undergraduate at the National University of Singapore (1991–95). She worked in the publishing industry for more than 5 years before undertaking postgraduate study. She has interests in the continuities between the ancient and the modern period, with special concentration on Myanmar. Geok is currently working on an English translation of a Myanmar novel by Ma Sandar, a popular novelist of the 1990s, and preparing her dissertation for publication.
E-mail: geok@hawaii.edu

Mike Shi-chi LAN is Assistant Professor and Director of Master of Arts in Contemporary China (MACC) programme, School of Humanities and Social Sciences, at Nanyang Technological University, Singapore. He received his Ph.D. in History from the University of Chicago in 2004. Dr Lan has written on modern Chinese history — particularly Chinese nationalism and China-Taiwan relations, history and international relations of modern East Asia, and the production of national identities, historical knowledge, and memory in China, Taiwan, and Singapore. His recent works include "U.S. Foreign Policy and the Changing Dynamics between China and Taiwan, 1995–2005", in *Ensuring Interests: the Dynamics of China-Taiwan Relations and Southeast Asia*, edited by Ho Kock Chung and Ho Khai Leong (Kuala Lumpur: Institute of China Studies, University of Malaya, 2006), and "Whose War Is Commemorated? History and Memory of the Second World War in Postwar Singapore" (translated into Japanese), in *15ᵗʰ August in Asia*, edited by Kawashima Shin et al. (Tokyo: Yamakawa Publishing Co., forthcoming).
E-mail: SCLan@ntu.edu.sg

Jason LIM graduated with First Class Honours in Asian Studies from Murdoch University in Perth, Western Australia, in 1995. He obtained his Ph.D. from the University of Western Australia in 2007. He has conducted research work in Singapore, Australia, the United Kingdom, China and Taiwan on the Fujian-Singapore tea trade and the political and trading concerns of the Singapore Chinese tea merchants from 1920 to 1960.
E-mail: jasonlim71@yahoo.com

Chin-Ming LIN is currently Assistant Professor and Director of the Graduate Institute of Southeast Asian Studies, Tamkang University in Taiwan. He received his Ph.D. in economics from the University of Wisconsin-Madison. He was a researcher at the Institute of European and American Studies, Academia Sinica and the APEC Study Center, Taiwan Institute of Economic Research. His main fields of research include economic development, international political economy and feminist economics. His recent research works include services trade statistics, remittances of migrant women workers, and East Asian regional integration.
E-mail: 113922@mail.tku.edu.tw

NG Beoy Kui is Assistant Chair/Associate Professor of the School of Humanities and Social Sciences (HSS), Nanyang Technological University, Singapore. Prior to joining academia, he was attached to the Economics Department of Bank Negara Malaysia and the South East Asian Central Banks (SEACEN) Research and Training Centre. His research interest includes macroeconomic management and economic reforms in Southeast Asia and China, international finance and monetary management. He has published research papers on foreign exchange markets, capital markets, ethnic Chinese business as well as financial reforms in Southeast Asia and China.
E-mail: ABKNG@ntu.edu.sg

SHINOZAKI Kaori obtained her Ph.D. at the Department of Area Studies, Graduate School of Arts and Sciences, University of Tokyo in 2007. She is currently Researcher/Advisor, Japan Information Service, Embassy of Japan in Malaysia. She is working on ethnicity and Chinese in Southeast Asia, especially the formation of networks of Chinese communities in the nineteenth and twentieth century, spreading from Penang to cover the northern part of the Malacca Straits and how they established relations with local authorities and other components of the society to participate in construction of social order.
E-mail: shinozaki.kaori@nifty.com

WU Xiao An (Ph.D.) is Professor of History and Director of the Centre for the Study of Chinese Overseas, Peking University. His publications include *Chinese Business in the Making of a Malay State, 1882–1941*.
E-mail: wu2@pku.edu.cn

YOW Cheun Hoe is Assistant Professor in the Division of Chinese, Nanyang Technological University. His academic interests cover Chinese diaspora,

qiaoxiang areas as well as Chinese education and literature in Southeast Asia. His publications include articles in *Modern Asian Studies* and in volumes such as *Demarcating Ethnicity in New Nations: Cases of the Chinese in Singapore, Malaysia, and Indonesia* (edited by Lee Guan Kin), *Nantah tuxiang: lishi heliu zhong de shengshi* [Nantah Images: Looking from Historical Perspective] (edited by Lee Guan Kin), *Ensuring Interests: Dynamics of China-Taiwan Relations* (edited by Ho Khai Leong and Hou Kok Chung), *Chinese Transnational Networks* (edited by Tan Chee Beng), and *Beyond Chinatown: New Chinese Migration: New Chinese Migration and the Global Expansion of China* (edited by Mette Thuno).
E-mail: CHYow@ntu.edu.sg

Editor
HO Khai Leong (Ph.D. Ohio State, 1988) is Associate Professor, School of Humanities and Social Science, Nanyang Technological University, Singapore, and an associate research fellow at the Institute of Southeast Asian Studies, Singapore. His current research interests include Malaysian and Singaporean politics, China-ASEAN relations, corporate governance and administrative reforms. The latest works he has edited are *Reforming Corporate Governance in Southeast Asia: Economics, Politics and Regulations* (Singapore: Institute of Southeast Asian Studies, 2005), *Rethinking Administrative Reforms in Southeast Asia* (Singapore: Marshall Cavendish Academic, 2006), *Ensuring Interests: Dynamics of China-Taiwan Relations and Southeast Asia* (Co-editor) (Kuala Lumpur: Institute of China Studies, 2006), and *ASEAN-Korea Relations: Security, Trade, and Community Building* (Singapore: Institute of Southeast Asian Studies, 2006).
E-mail: klho@ntu.edu.sg

INTRODUCTION

Ho Khai Leong

"Connecting" and "distancing" have been two prominent themes permeating the writings on the historical and contemporary developments of the relationship between Southeast Asia and China. As neighbours, the nation-states in Southeast Asia and the giant political entity in the north communicated with each other through a variety of diplomatic overtures, political agitations, and cultural nuances. The people felt a need to connect even in the worst of times when governments were not on the best of terms. "Connecting" is a two-way street. It denotes a deep influence of Chinese presence in the region since the sixteenth century in the areas of trade, culture and politics, as well as Southeast Asia's enduring bewilderment and perplexity about its giant neighbour. The rise of China and the recent influx of Chinese immigrants in the region added to the already influential and considerable presence of China. In the last two decades with the rise of China as an economic powerhouse in the region, Southeast Asia's need to connect with China has become more urgent and necessary as it attempts to reap the benefit from the successful economic modernization in China.

At the same time, however, there were feelings of ambivalence, hesitation and even suspicions on the part of the Southeast Asian states vis-à-vis the rise of a political power which is so little understood or misunderstood. Much of these negative thoughts admittedly were remnants of historical experiences; some are possibly even related to the growing soft and hard power influence of the People's Republic of China. "Distancing", therefore, refers to the attitudes and policies of these nations' attempts to maintain their sovereign rights as well as political and cultural autonomy in the midst of a rising empire and regional hegemonic power.

To a large extent, the perpetual tensions between idealist expectation and realist necessity have defined Sino-Southeast Asia relations in the last few decades. How Southeast Asia and China should best deal with one another becomes a central question in this complex relationship. Martin Stuart Fox, for example, argues that in deciding how best to deal with China, two factors influencing the countries of Southeast Asia are their own long-standing histories of bilateral relations with China and their own differing conceptions of how foreign relations should be conducted.[1] In other words, a careful appreciation and thoughtful consideration of history and culture are central to any understanding of the likely future shape of China-Southeast Asia relations. An over-simplistic categorization of assigning China to the category of a benign power or that of a rising threat is problematic at best. It is the deeper social memories with which we have to contend; and in so doing, arrive at an understanding as to how China perceives its position in history with respect to the world.

The papers in this volume were presented at a conference organized by the Singapore Society for Asian Studies, in Singapore, on 1 December 2007, with an emphasis on the bilateral relations between Southeast Asia and China. The contributors are authors of various disciplinary backgrounds: history, political science, economics and sociology. They provide a spectrum of perspectives by which the reader can view Sino-Southeast Asia relations.

Wu Xiao An's chapter provides an excellent historical overview of Sino-Southeast Asia relations. He suggests that the tough, complex and multi-faceted historical relationship has been largely shaped by both geo-political dynamics and the internal political forces of individual countries. While the components and the nature of these forces might have presently changed, their impact on the relationship remained very much intact. Undoubtedly inter-state relationships are bound by political circumstances, but the non-governmental interactions in the future will perhaps take central stage as there is now much more room for these actors to manoeuvre. Wu concludes that the social and cultural exchanges at the people-to-people level should be refocused as this may be one area which will be much more meaningful in fostering the China-Southeast Asian rapprochement.

Edgardo Dagdag echoes these arguments in his assessment of Philippine-China connections from the pre-colonial period to post-Cold War era. He is of the view that despite the often tempestuous relations between the two countries, Sino-Philippine relations will continue to prosper in the future. But this is only if they simultaneously rely on both bilateral and multilateral agreements between ASEAN and China. The Philippines cannot hope to connect well with China alone. As a member of ASEAN, the Philippines may pin its hopes on better bilateral ties with China through the concerted efforts of the ten-member organization. Future challenges to the relationship would include the Philippines' close ties with the United States of which the Chinese certainly do not approve.

Mike Lan Shi-chi's paper takes on the issue of memory and commemoration of Singapore's Chinese community towards China at the turn of the twentieth century. His study focuses on the ethnic Chinese in the island-state as they played a major role in shaping the present cultural configuration in the nation-building process. After the British withdrawal in 1942, the ethnic Chinese suffered much hardship under Japanese rule, and many joined the underground forces to fight against the Japanese invaders — in both Singapore and China; their loyalty to the land however was suspected by both the colonial masters and local rulers. Lan argued that these suspicions were unwarranted, as the ethnic Chinese had at that historical point transferred their nationalist loyalty in various ways from China to the new nation.

Kaori Shinozaki's paper is a case study of Penang's Chinese during the period 1911–13 and the community's response in terms of their "revolutionary" and "patriotic" donation campaigns. She argues that the financial support by Penang's Chinese community for the Sun Yat-sen led revolutionary movement in China had grown out of a concern for stability, order and good governance, rather than support for the revolutionary cause of overthrowing the corrupt Ching dynasty. Studying these self-motivating donation campaigns, she saw the nascent emergence of a civil society in colonial Malaya at the beginning of the century.

The commercial connections between the overseas Chinese community and mainland China also grew rapidly after the Republican revolution. Jason Lim gives a detailed study on the Fujian tea merchants in Singapore who imported goods from China and re-exported to local clientele or elsewhere, and then consequently established themselves with branches of their family businesses in Southeast Asia. Lim argued that the sense of patriotism towards China among these wealthy tea merchants was evident in their fervent response to Japanese imperialism as well as their passionate commitment to rebuild a war-torn China. Their attachment to "China" as the motherland, however, quickly dissipated with the proclamation of the People's Republic of China in 1949 as the political loyalty of these merchants mostly rested with the KMT. Subsequently, the dedication and devotion of the second generations of these merchants were transformed very quickly, establishing their cultural and political identities as Singaporeans.

Goh Geok Yian's chapter examines China-Myanmar relations by looking at Burmese sources, a path less taken by scholars in the field, as most tend to view the relationship from the Chinese perspective or from Chinese sources. Her study shows descriptions of Burmese perceptions of their relations with Tarup (China) extracted from indigenous sources which represent invaluable reflections of local views of their foreign neighbour. A more balanced observation of Myanmar-China relations over a period of several centuries from Tagaung (mid-first millennium CE) to Hanthawati-Taungngu of the sixteenth century is presented, and the reader will find the account both refreshing and informative.

Yow Cheun Hoe's paper is a piece of pioneering work on the study of a recent social and migratory phenomenon in Singapore: the influx of a steady and large group of students from the PRC to the island-state. With the arrival of this group of "foreign talents", many issues have since emerged: their adaptation to the local social environment, impact on Singaporean Chinese culture and educational system, and local perceptions of this group. Yow's paper examines these questions pertaining to Chinese students in Singapore, with special focus on the secondary education sector. In examining their migration trajectory, he found that students from China pursuing secondary education in the island-state have the highest tendency to move on to other countries for further studies, making Singapore the "jumping board" of their future life goals. Obviously these findings will have major policy implications.

Aimee Dawis tackles the perennial and difficult issue of cultural identity of the Chinese in Indonesia during the Suharto era (1966–98). Her analysis is based on a study of how the Indonesian Chinese used imported media from Hong Kong, Taiwan and China — places that are simultaneously real and imagined to the Indonesian Chinese — to inform their cultural identity formation and maintenance. Her findings suggest that to the list of agents shaping Chinese identity in Indonesia, one must add the roles of the media and local ethnic organizations.

Beside historical memories, the transforming cultural identities and commercial ties forming the connections between Southeast Asia and China, contemporary economic relations is certainly another major issue. Ng Beoy Kui's paper details the policy responses of individual Southeast Asian countries towards a rising China. Ng contends that, while it is difficult to ascertain whether China poses a threat to the Southeast Asian countries, the complementary economic Sino-Southeast Asia relationship would inevitably benefit Southeast Asia more than China. For the relationship to prosper in the future, Ng suggests that Southeast Asian countries should take a two-track approach, i.e. the first track through the usual export-oriented strategy in manufacturing spearheaded by multinational corporations (MNCs), and the second track augmenting the first by providing additional support to local enterprises dependent on indigenous skills and resources.

Lin Chin-Ming's paper deals with the impact of Asian regionalism on the region as a whole, particularly from Taiwan's perspective. How do countries respond to the changing notions of regionalism — what the author called "old" and "new" regionalism? Looking at China-Taiwan trade relations and patterns of Japanese export and output growth in the pre-Plaza Accord period, Lin argues that "old" regionalism dies hard, and sometimes reappears, intermingled with the "new" regionalism.

Chan Yuk Wah's paper is a study of Vietnam-China relations, focusing on the Vietnamese adeptness in diplomatically pacifying the ambition of its giant neighbour so as to maintain a relatively peaceful and harmonious relationship through "language power" — which comprises both relational rhetoric and historical taciturnity and which the author defines as the language of "routinized intimacy and friendship rhetoric painstakingly displayed by state actors as well as lay people". This tactful approach has enabled Vietnam-China relations to remain stable and secure despite the stress and fault lines in the relationship.

All in all, the volume suggests that history, culture and social memories are some of the main factors influencing Southeast Asian relations with China. Current Southeast Asia relations with a rising China are affected by the Southeast Asian countries' long histories of bilateral relations with China as well as their own differing perceptions as to how bilateral relations have been conducted. At the same time, however, one cannot ignore the fact that commerce and trade, both historical and contemporary, also play an important role in determining their relations. The current pursuit for concluding foreign trade agreements between Southeast Asian states individually and ASEAN as a whole with China is but one indication of the significance of this trade relation.

It is therefore clear that a combination of history, culture and trade affect Southeast Asia's relations with China. The decision to connect or to distance one nation from another has created a type of tension that is both healthy and beneficial. Chinese influence in the region rests on a number of factors: China's restraint in requesting adjustments in Southeast Asian policies to suit her political, economic and strategic interests, her contributions to the political stability of Southeast Asian regimes, and her commitments to continue favourable trade practices. On the other hand, Southeast Asia's anticipation of additional benefits derived from closer relations with China in the future will be contingent upon the pace of economic and political modernization of an ever-changing China.

Note

1. Martin Stuart-Fox, "Southeast Asia and China: The Role of History and Culture in Shaping Future Relations", *Contemporary Southeast Asia* 26, no. 1 (2004): 116–39.

PART I
History and Remembrance

1

CHINA MEETS SOUTHEAST ASIA
A Long-Term Historical Review

Wu Xiao An

This chapter provides a long-term historical and present-day perspective of China-Southeast Asian interactions and their dynamics. In this study of how China-Southeast Asian interactions are shaped, attention is paid not only to the political and economic aspects in terms of so-called "legitimate" institutional relationships from above, but also to the socio-cultural elements in terms of Chinese migration from below. The chapter will explicate these facts in five parts: images of contrasts and contradictions; tributary system and maritime trade, from early time to the mid-nineteenth century; Western expansion and Chinese migration, from the mid-nineteenth century to mid-twentieth century; nation-building and the Cold War, from the mid-twentieth century to early 1990s; and globalization and strategic partnership, from the early 1990s to the present.

I. IMAGES OF CONTRASTS AND CONTRADICTIONS

Chinese language was so badly conserved in Thailand that even he was unable to find a Chinese newspaper to read. A Chinese journalist complained to his Singaporean counterpart upon his return from his golden week holidays in Thailand.

How come? The Singaporean journalist was very suspicious and puzzled. There are six Chinese daily newspapers indeed as far as she knows.

There was no Chinese newspaper available in the flights of the Thai Airline. Their crews even knew no Chinese so that he had to speak English to ask for a cup of water. The Chinese journalist refuted.
Why did you think that the Thai people should speak Chinese? The Singaporean journalist then asked.
This was because China and Thailand are close neighbors geographically and Thailand had been a tributary state to China over centuries in history. Chinese culture supposedly should be better conserved. The Chinese journalist explained.
Do you still think Japanese or American crews should speak Chinese if you take JA or UA flights served on the China route? The Singaporean journalist then asked.
No! The Chinese journalist admitted honestly. (*Lianhe Zaobao*, 13 October 2006)

It is believed that the interesting newspaper report above is not an isolated case. How does China look at Southeast Asia and vice versa? Let me begin by presenting various images of contrasts and contradictions.

First, in the Chinese official and orthodox perception, Nanyang (or "Southeast Asia") had been a peripheral, barbarian and vassal area, which was geographically far away from the Central Kingdom and had been subject to the suzerainty of the Central Kingdom by the tributary system politically and culturally. Such an image contradicts that of the ordinary people in the southern provinces, who looked up to Southeast Asia as a survival "escape" of their impoverishment and a frontier "heaven". If Nanyang has been a popular image among the people in the southern provinces, now they are proudly conscious that their lives are much better off than before, even in comparison with their counterparts in Southeast Asia.

Secondly, Southeast Asian Studies in China are also on the periphery vis-à-vis American, European, Japanese Studies and studies of developed countries. This is in sharp contrast and contradiction with the many realities in China and Southeast Asian relations, such as the fact that Southeast Asia is strategically very significant for China's national interests, that economically ASEAN has now become China's fourth largest trading partner, that socio-culturally there are around 30 million ethnic Chinese living in Southeast Asia, that historically Southeast Asian Chinese were the driving force for Chinese revolution and pioneering agents for Chinese economic modernization, and that academically, China claims to have an impressive 700 Southeast Asianists.

Third, while current China-Southeast Asian relationships are politically and economically driven by governments of both regions, a socio-cultural gap of mutual understanding exists at the level of the different peoples. In the perceptions of Southeast Asian governments, China is a giant shadow and a competitor for foreign direct investment (FDI) and labour-intensive industries and services. Due to China's formidable economic shadow, they are very cautious in dealing with China. On the other hand, Southeast Asia also feels that it would benefit from cultivating relations with China because of its fast growth. However, because of different socio-political systems and ideologies, China is also looked upon with suspicion by Southeast Asian nations even if this view is not publicly expressed. Due to colonial legacy, the Southeast Asian governments and peoples feel somewhat more "superior" and "cosmopolitan" in the international community. The Chinese people, who are very materialistic and look up to the West as a model have a different reaction when meeting Southeast Asians. Their sentiments are mixed with their traditional image of wealthy Nanyang Chinese and they are obviously disappointed with Southeast Asian contemporary realities and have great nationalist pride in China's tremendous progress in the past decades. This is especially true after the mid-1990s when China's economy has grown rapidly.

Last but not least, after World War II, China and Southeast Asia, as newly-independent countries, shared the similar sentiments of anti-colonialism and anti-imperialism and the nation-building projects. This is because of the common historical legacy of the Western colonial and semi-colonial rule. Moreover, because of the Cold War, domestic politics and Southeast Asian ethnic Chinese, Southeast Asian states were much more reserved and therefore sharply divided in opinions as to their foreign relations with China. This is in contrast with present-day China-Southeast Asian relations, which are presently at their historic best. Nevertheless, Southeast Asia is currently trying to engage the big powers such as the United States, European Union, Japan, Australia and even India to balance China as a formidable player. To this end, Lee Kuan Yew said very clearly in 2001 "ASEAN must balance China with Asia" (Lee Kuan Yew 2001, p. 20).

II. TRIBUTARY SYSTEM AND MARITIME TRADE, THE EARLY PERIOD TO THE MID-19TH CENTURY

For centuries, Southeast Asia had been one of the most important regions in Chinese foreign relations and the most popular area for Chinese migration. Without sufficient Chinese records, it would have been impossible to study early Southeast Asian history. Such features were institutionalized through the tributary system from above and the continuous private maritime trade and migration from below. The tributary system paralleled, rivalled, sometimes complemented and even contradicted the private maritime trade and migration. If the tributary system symbolized the loose suzerainty-vassal relationship, then the private maritime trade and migration functioned as routine and substantial interactions between two sides. However, each region cannot be treated as a separate entity, as they could be complementary too. How did two systems work? What were the implications for China-Southeast Asian relationships?

Tributary System

> Until a century ago, China's foreign relations were suzerain-vassal relations conducted through the ancient forms of the tributary system.... The formalities of the tributary system constituted a mechanism by which formerly barbarous regions outside the empire were given their place in the all-embracing sinocentric cosmos. (Fairbank 1942, pp. 129, 133)

Historically, the Chinese domestic power relation and world order were based on cultural superiority, physical and material strength. The tributary system represented an established mechanism and a long-term historical tradition of Sino-centric international relations. The tributary system started in the Chin and Han periods was developed during the Tang dynasty, prospered in the Song and Yuan periods, peaked in the Ming period and declined during the Qing dynasty (Yu Changsen 2000, pp. 55–65). It functioned to demonstrate Chinese cultural dominance in East Asia, served as an ethnical basis of the Emperor' power, a form of the imperial court ritual, a prestige asset, a diplomatic medium, a defence measure, and a cloak for trade (Fairbank and Teng 1941, p. 137; Fairbank 1942, pp. 129–49). However, history has overthrown such exaggerated Sino-centric hegemony over Southeast Asia. On the contrary:

> For centuries the old Southeast Asian kingdoms and principalities regarded powerful imperial China as a source of prosperity and lucrative trade rather than an expansionist threat. Although they bridled at Chinese imperial arrogance and paternalism — the rituals of tribute and recognition ... — countries in the region enjoyed formal relationships with China that generally resulted in commercial gain. (Vatikiotis 2003, p. 66)

Chinese special envoys and Buddhist pilgrims to Southeast Asia featured frequent trade and commercial interactions between two regions. For the Chinese envoys, such well-known examples include Zhu Ying (朱应) and Kang Tai (康泰) who were sent to Champa and Funan by Wu during the period of the Three Kingdoms, Zhou Da-guan (1266–1346) to Zhenla

(真臘) (the Khmer people in Cambodia) in 1295 during the Yuan dynasty, and the impressive Zheng He (鄭和) voyages from 1405 to 1433 during the Ming dynasty. The most prominent Buddhist pilgrims were Fa Xian (法显, 337–422) of the East Jin dynasty and I-Jing (义净, 635–713) of the Tang dynasty. Fa Xian travelled to India overland from China to study Buddhism, but returned from Ceylon by sea in 413–14 AD. After sailing through the Malacca Straits, he landed at the port on the west coast of Borneo, from which he departed for Canton (K. Hall 1984, pp. 58–60). I-Jing was also a zealous Buddhist pilgrim. He left Canton by sea in December 671 and reached Srivijaya within twenty days. After a six-month stay in Malayu [Malaya], I-Jing proceeded to India and returned to Srivijaya between 685 and 689. In 689, I-Jing visited China for three months and again visited Srivijaya, finally leaving in 695. I-Jing wrote three books which provided valuable information on the region (Wolters 1986, pp. 1–41; Zhuo Jianming 1992, pp. 74–79). In addition, there were Chinese envoys who were instructed by Chinese emperors to escort Southeast Asian tributary missions all the way back to their home countries. Such instances were Chinese officials named Zhang Qian (张谦) and Zhou Hang (周航) who accompanied the ruler of Bone in 1408 and Wang Bin (王彬) who escorted the ruler of Champa in 1410 (He Hongyong 2003, p. 87).

Besides indigenous tributary envoys consisting of local rulers and nobles on the Southeast Asian side, there is another interesting category of tributary envoys and interpreters with mixed identity. They were Chinese, but to the high-ranking officials, they were known as the "barbarian vassal state" envoys, or the "Chinese barbarian officials" in imperial Chinese court parlance. These officials were from Siam, Java, Malacca and various other quarters. Such Sino-Southeast Asian "officials" were originally humble natives of the coastal provinces of Fujian, Guangdong and Jiangxi, and they were formerly sailors, fishermen, salt peddlers and the like. Because private overseas trade and emigration were rigorously suppressed, leaving the tributary system as the only legal one, they used different names on the tributary missions and some of them even went on these missions several times. In the fifteenth century Southeast Asian tributary missions alone, fifty-three members were listed as those who bore Chinese names (Hok-Lam Chan 1968, pp. 411–18; Reid 1996, pp. 27–30). Among twenty-five identified Chinese envoys and interpreters from 1392 to 1692 in Southeast Asia there were four from Java, three from Siam and one from Malacca (Li Jinming 1986, pp. 107–18).

The tributary system dates back to the Chin and Han dynasties when the Chinese imperial court started to appoint a governor directly at Tonkin in Vietnam. Tributary envoys from Cambodia in 84 AD and from Java and

Burma in 131 AD went to China (Yu Changsen 2000, p. 56). During the Xi Han period, two routes to Southeast Asia were developed: one by land from the capital Changan via Sichuan province entered into Burma; the other by sea via Guangdong province entered South China Seas states (Zhou Weizhou 2003, pp. 38–44).

The tributary system was further developed during the Tang dynasty. According to Chinese scholars' statistics, the overall number of tributary missions from the South Seas states during the Tang dynasty covered 101 states, including Champa (of Vietnam, 35 times), Khmer (of Cambodia, 16 times), Java (12 times), Tenasserim (of Burma, 8 times including its dependencies), Srivajaya (7 times including its dependencies), Prome (of Burma, 5 times including its dependencies) and other states (Zhou Weizhou 2002, pp. 60–73). During the Song period, there were 26 tributary states and the total number of tributary missions reached 302. While we do not know how many missions came from Southeast Asia, we do know that they visited China 56 times from Champa, 45 times from Cochin, 33 time from Srivijaya, not including other states such as Khmer, Bone and Pugan (Yu Changsen 2000, p. 58; Li Yunquan 2003, p. 102). In the Yuan period, 34 countries sent tributary missions to China, which amounted to over 200 times (Yu Changsen 2000, p. 59).

The Ming dynasty was the most prosperous period for the tributary system. Although we do not have complete statistics of the total missions, a few examples would suffice. Under the reigns of Hongwu Emperor (1368–98) and Yongle Emperor (1402–24), it was listed that there were 129 and 238 tributary missions respectively, of which most were from Southeast Asia: 36 times each from Champa amd Siam, 26 times from Malacca, 24 times from Java, 14 times together from Annam, 13 times from Khmer (Zhenla), 9 times from Bone, 6 times from Srivijaya and 5 times from Sulu. The tributary gifts ranged from local medicine, spices, jewelries and other precious goods, animals, metal tools, cloths, fruits, special servants, maps and so on. The missions were usually large-scale affairs and the tributary goods and gifts especially from China were enormous. For instance, a 540-member mission was led by the ruler of Malacca in 1410, a 340-member mission by the King of Sulu in 1417 who died in Dezhou of Shandong on the way back to the Philippines, and 1,200-member of 16 tributary missions mainly led by Southeast Asian countries such as Borneo, Sumatra and Malacca in 1423 (He Hongyong 2003, pp. 88–89; Tang Kaijian and Peng Hui 2003, pp. 53–54; Li Qingxin 2005, pp. 238–39). Among the tributary goods and gifts from China, there were 37,500 kg pepper from Java (in 1382), 50,000 kg lignum sappan from Siam (in 1387), and 19,000 porcelains to the rulers of Champa, Khmer and

Siam at one time from the Emperor Hongwu (in 1383). It is estimated that at least 61 envoys were sent out to Southeast Asia under the reign of the Emperor Hongwu and 21 envoys overseas under the reign of Emperor Yongle (Peng Hui 2004, pp. 81–82; Zhuang Guotu 2005, p. 4).

Indeed after Zheng He's voyage, the tributary system was on the decline through the Qing dynasty until the mid-nineteenth century when it was eventually replaced by the treaty system imposed by the Western Powers. Over two centuries from 1662 to 1862, according to Fairbank and Teng, the total of recorded tributary embassies to China was about 471: in the first century from 1662 to 1761 it was about 216, while in the following century from 1762 to 1861 it was about 255. During this period in Southeast Asia, the frequencies and total number of recorded tributary embassies can be summarized as follows (Fairbank and Teng 1941, pp. 193–98; Fairbank, 1942, p. 144):

- Annam: sent missions every three, six, or four years, of which, 45 years in the two centuries were mentioned. Among these, 24 were in the second century, a slight increase in the latter part of the period;
- Siam: sent missions every three years, of which 48 years during the two centuries mentioned. Among these, 11 were in the first century and 37 in the period from 1780 to 1860, a marked increase in the latter part of the period;
- Burma: sent missions every ten years, of which 16 years between 1750 to 1853 were recorded. Among these, 12 were after 1789, i.e. chiefly in the nineteenth century;
- Laos: sent missions every ten years for 17 years between 1730 and 1853, rather evenly scattered about 10 years apart;
- Sulu: sent missions every five years, some 7 years between 1726 and 1754.

Maritime Private Trade

At the end of the fourteenth century China began two centuries of expansion in wealth and population. The demand for Southeast Asian products was particularly boosted by six state trading expeditions of the Ming Emperor Yong La (1403–22). They not only brought home enormous quantities of pepper, spice, sappanwood and other forest products, they also stimulated Southeast Asian production, and left a number of crucial communities of Chinese (often Muslim) traders in the bourgeoning entrepots of the region. (Reid 1990, p. 5)

Maritime private trade and the tributary system were, first of all, parallel and contrasting mechanisms where the tributary system manifested official, legitimate and monopoly trade from above, while maritime private trade represented China-Southeast Asian direct business transactions from below. The private trade was deemed "illegal" as private contacts between China and the outside world, either in terms of trade or migration were forbidden by the Chinese government for centuries. Moreover, following the Zheng He voyages and the decline of the tributary system, maritime private trade became more dominant and prosperous as it featured China's expansion of commerce and population, and was more substantial. This in turn paralyzed the tributary trade. Coinciding with the private maritime trade was the emergence of sizeable Chinese communities in Southeast Asia in the late Ming period. Internationally, it ran in conjunction with "the Age of Commerce" and the Western commercial and colonial expansion. All these structured elements demonstrated the active, if not the best, commercial and social interactions in history in the age of Asia. In other words, private maritime trade was institutionalized in the Chinese junk trade, and in turn their combination for the first time gave rise to various sizeable Chinese communities in Southeast Asia. Substantial Chinese migration to Southeast Asia hence became a twin-brother of the maritime private trade. As it is best summarized by Wakeman:

> During the later years of the fifteenth century, Chinese began to colonize the Malay Archipelago, Java, Sumatra, Borneo, the Sulu Archipelago, and the Philippines. In the sixteenth century, another stream of Chinese settlers began to arrive in Siam, and by the end of the 1600s there were thousands in the capital of Ayuthhaya. The Qing (1644–1912) government continued the Ming policy of forbidding emigration.... Individual emperors issued pardons to overseas merchants, who returned home, but not until 1727 was the interdiction removed; by then, hundreds of thousands of Chinese were living abroad. A century later, virtually half the 400,000 residents of Bangkok were Chinese immigrants.(Wakeman, Jr. 1993, pp. 15–16)

Evidence suggests that Chinese private trade with traders in Southeast Asia first appeared during the Song period, became further developed during the Yuan dynasty and finally replaced the tributary trade system as the dominant economic relationship during the late Ming period. By this period, China began to emerge as a powerful sea power underpinned by the sophisticated shipping manufacturing technology since the Song dynasty (Jung-pang Lo 1955, pp. 489–503; Finlay 1992, pp. 225–41; Manguin 1993, pp. 253–80; Wakeman 1993, pp. 8–13; Sun Laichen 2003, pp. 495–517). There is reason to believe that this should have taken place at an even earlier period of the Tang dynasty. These private merchants took with them Chinese silks, tea, porcelain, metal implements and groceries and returned with Southeast Asian goods of spice, medicine and sappanwood. Because of the monsoon, Chinese merchants had to sojourn in Southeast Asia for some time; and because of the regular interactions, some Chinese merchant sojourners eventually settled down (Guo Liang 1982, pp. 83–84; Fang Fuqi 1993, pp. 48–49, 51; Zhuang Guotu 1994, pp. 55–57). The maritime trade was so prosperous during the Yuan dynasty that Quanzhou of Fujian province became the most important trading port in China, so much so that some Chinese settlements emerged in Southeast Asian port-cities, resulting in some Chinese merchant sojourners marrying local Southeast Asian women to facilitate their trade; Chinese Muslim communities were even established in places such as Mandalay by land route from Yunnan and northern Java from Quanzhou (Ptak 1993, p. 11; Maung Maung Lay 2007, pp. 50–52).

Anthony Reid contextualized long-term Chinese interaction with Southeast Asia from the turn of the sixteenth up to the mid-nineteenth century by dividing the process into five stages consisting of three transitions and two main phases. From 1500 to 1567 was the transitional period. China-Southeast Asian trade was primarily conducted through intermediate ports: the mainland Southeast Asian traditional major entrepôts of Champa and Ayutthaya on the one hand, and the maritime Southeast Asian ports of Melaka, Johor and Patani on the other. The shipping between China and the Malay world was mainly Southeast Asian junks owned by Melaka merchants, rather than China-based, and Melaka was the most important port. From 1567 to 1640 was not only the first flourishing era of the Chinese junk trade, but also the booming years of the age of commerce in Southeast Asia. Manila became the most striking case in point. But then, China-Southeast Asian trade entered into another period of transition, 1680–1740. This period witnessed one contrast: on the one hand, the overall China-Southeast Asian commercial relationship was not highly profitable; on the other, China-Dutch Indies trade was so prosperous that it was identified as "the heyday of the junk trade" by Blusse. Manila was taken over by Batavia as the major commercial centre. From 1740 to 1850 was the second flourishing era of the Chinese junk trade and a watershed period in shaping the triangular relationship of Chinese, Southeast Asians and Europeans. However, it witnessed another contrast: a sharp decline in the junk trade to Batavia and Manila on the one hand, and tremendous prosperity elsewhere as never before on the other. Bangkok hence replaced Batavia as the leading Southeast Asian port. However, in the late stage there was another transition in 1820–55, in which Singapore replaced Bangkok as the major Southeast entrepôt (Reid 1996, pp. 33–49).

There were two ancient routes linking China with Southeast Asia as previously mentioned: by land via Yunnan to Burma and by sea via Guangdong to South China Sea states. The former land trading route featured an active long-distance Chinese merchant community between Yunnan and Northern Southeast Asia, who were predominantly Muslims and specifically dealt in commodities of horse, mule and cattle from China (Maung Maung Lay 2007). The latter direction, the maritime route, could be further broken down into the western route and the eastern route. The western route connected continental Southeast Asia and western Indonesia to Hainan, Guangzhou and Yunnan. It was most likely a combination of sea and overland routes with central Vietnam at its crossroads, in which Champa was an important entrepot. From there, supplementary routes ran to Mindoro and northern Borneo that finally converged in the Sulu zone. The western route was a more ancient route used by merchants from the Indian Ocean and the main trade route under the Song period (Ptak 1998; Li Tana 2006; Whitmore 2006). The eastern sea route became an important link between insular Southeast Asia and China. It developed initially from Quanzhou Harbour, subsequently from Yuegang (Moon Harbour), both in Fujian, via Taiwan to the Sulu zone, northern Borneo, with a branch to the Celebes Sea and the Moluccas. The western route had as many as 125 possible stop-overs, while the eastern route contained some 46 branches mainly situated in the Philippines and the Sulu Archipelago. The eastern route prospered during the Yuan period when the western route was no longer as important. Owing to the Hongwu Emperor's ban on private trade, however, the eastern route declined, while piracy and smuggling were widespread and the official contacts were restricted to the western routes. After 1567 when the ban was lifted, the eastern route began to flourish again. But, Yuegang at the lower reaches of the Nine Dragon River then took over Quanzhou as the most important port to serve all the main ports of the South China Seas. Every year, some 200 trading junks were sent out to the South China Seas from Yuegang (Blusse 1996, pp. 56–59; Reid 1996, p. 16; Ptak 1998, pp. 269–94).

Records concerning the commodity flows and trading volumes have been fragmentary, yet a picture can be reconstructed.

1. *Porcelain*: Porcelain was among one of the most established exported items and the second most important trading commodity between China and Southeast Asia. The immense high-quality Chinese glazed ceramics trade reached a peak between the late thirteenth and early sixteenth centuries.

Southeast Asian trading cities, such as Banten, Gresik, Patani and Tonkin, were early entrepôts for the porcelain trade. An underwater wreck discovered in the South China Sea in 2002 yielded 6,000 archaeological findings of mostly porcelain items of the Song period; 90 per cent of them were made in Fujian (Sun Jian 2007, p. 42). In South Sulawesi in the early 1970s, archaeological findings classified 26 per cent porcelain as Ming, 28 per cent "Swatow", and less than 1 per cent Yuan (Reid 1988, pp. 104–105). In Sulu, a junk from Amoy dated January 1776 carried one million items of Chinese porcelains (Qian Jiang 1988, p. 89). In the period 1602–95, about 20 million items of Chinese porcelain were brought to Europe by the VOC. In the Dutch Indies, during 1734–56, every year about ten Chinese junks went to Batavia and a few VOC ships travelled to Canton for trade. The VOC ships purchased 406,759 items of porcelain in 1737, and 580,323 in 1743. The porcelain was mainly imported from Fujian before late Ming and from Canton during the Qing dynasty (Qian Jiang 1989, pp. 80–91; Feng Xianming and Feng Xiaoqi 1990, pp. 101–104).

2. *Tea*: Tea was the most important trading commodity in Sino-Western trade, in which Southeast Asia played an important role. However, Chinese tea was not important in the Chinese junk trade until the 1690s. Tea immediately became the largest trading item in the Chinese junk trade, which comprised 70–80 per cent of the total imports from China during the 1720s–1790s. Until the 1740s, the Dutch tea imports were mainly conducted through Batavia via the Chinese junks, one-third was sold to the Company, one-third to the Company servants and the rest for local consumption. The VOC annually purchased 400 piculs (one picul = 60.5 kg) in 1700–10, 745 piculs in 1710–20, 3,439 piculs in 1721–30, 6,048 piculs in 1731–40. But even these could not meet the demands in the Netherlands at all. So, while the Chinese junk tea trade continued in Batavia, in 1728–34 the VOC sent out eleven ships directly from the Netherlands to Canton to collect tea. After 1734, it sent two VOC ships from Batavia to Canton to purchase tea while encouraging Chinese junk tea trade (Zhuang Guotu 1993, pp. 93–121; Zhuang Guotu 1995, pp. 54–55; Zhang Yinglong 1998, pp. 93–99).

3. *Textiles*: Southeast Asia had long traded the region's pepper, spices and jungle reserves in exchange for cotton textiles from India and silks from China. China's imports of rare cotton textiles from India were indeed made via Southeast Asia. For a long time, Southeast Asian cultivated cotton had been exported to China. From the thirteenth to the seventeenth century Chinese traders collected cotton yarn and cloth at various Southeast Asian

ports, especially in Vietnam, Luzon and Java. Although silk was a luxury item, Chinese traders based in Southeast Asian ports had gained a marked advantage over the Europeans in the silk trade by the seventeenth century (Reid 1988, p. 91; K. Hall 1996, pp. 87, 105; Wang Yuanlin and Lin Xingrong, 2005, pp. 86–91).

4. *Pepper*: Pepper was ranked as the most important export of Southeast Asia in the sixteenth and seventeenth centuries. Until 1530, most Southeast Asian pepper, which was estimated at nearly 2,500 tonnes, either remained "below the winds" [i.e. Southeast Asia] or was taken north to supply the vast Chinese market (Reid 1990, p. 17; 1993, pp. 7–8). China also imported Moluccan cloves via a direct route through the Sulu zone or the longer route through the Java Sea in 960–1435. The Moluccan cloves were also re-exported to China through the ports in West Indonesia and mainland Southeast Asia. Chinese merchants also purchased cloves "wholesale" in the Moluccas, thereby bringing travel to a sizeable level. However the volume sold was rather small (Ptak 1993, pp. 1–13).

5. *Trepang*: Trepang is especially meaningful for China-Southeast Asian trade, dating back to the seventeenth century. Trepang was a premier export commodity from Southeast Asia and of interest only to the Chinese for culinary and medical uses. The major areas of Southeast Asian trepang production were in the Philippines, eastern Indonesian archipelago and Malay Peninsular. During this period, Amoy and Shanghai were the major importing centres for trepang trade, while Manila, Makassar and later Singapore were the premier entrepôts. Southeast Asian trepang comprised 80–85 per cent of China's total trepang imports. In the early eighteenth century, China-Philippines annual trepang trade ranged between 200 and 300 piculs. However, from the mid-nineteenth century on, Amoy's annual imports from Manila were between 2,000 and 3,000 piculs, while Shanghai's annual imports from Manila amounted to 3,000–4,000 piculs. Amoy's annual imports of trepang from Makassa were 3,000–4,000 piculs in 1730s and 6,000–7,000 piculs at the end of the eighteenth century. Later, China-Southeast Asian trepang increased significantly. China's total annual trepang imports from Southeast Asia amounted to 15,000 piculs in the 1860s, 20,000 piculs in the 1870s, 30,000 piculs in the 1880s, and 40,000 piculs in the 1890s (Dai Yifeng 1998, pp. 71–81; Dai Yifeng 2003, pp. 86, 91; Knaap and Sutherland 2204, pp. 98–102, 146–48; Sutherland 2004, pp. 133–57).

6. *Other Commodities*: In the Gulf of Tonkin trading zone stretching to Hainan Island and Northern Champa by sea and to Yunnan, Guanxi and

Laos by land, in the Song period, there was lucrative major trade of the slaves, horses and salt, involving both Chinese and overseas merchants (Li Tana 2006, pp. 83–102). In Burma, by land route, horse trade had also been a cross-border tradition from Yunnan, which was dominated by the Chinese Muslim community called "Panthay"; by river route the trading commodities were mainly cotton and salt from Burma and silk and tin from Yunnan (Sun Laichen 1989, pp. 18–19; Maung Maung Lay 2007, pp. 50–55). In Siam and Luzon, from the early eighteenth century, because of food storage in China due to population expansion and a decrease in arable land, rice export was especially significant for China and very much encouraged by the Qing government with reduction or exemption of tax and award of entitlements. For instance, in 1722, 300,000 shi rice (literally sacks, 1 shi = 59.2 kg) was imported from Siam to three China coastal ports of Amoy, Canton and Linbo. Moreover, under the Qing government it was compulsory for the Chinese junks to take rice on their way back to China. In Fujian, among sixteen junks returned from Southeast Asia in 1748, each junk took about 200–300 sacks of rice (Li Jinming 1990, pp. 96–104; Tang Kaijian and Tian Yu 2004, pp. 81–88). In the Straits of Malacca, as a trading commodity and as a mean of exchange, Chinese copper coins played a significant role especially in the development of Java, Kota Cina and Temasik during the tenth to fourteenth centuries. For instance, in 1078, Srivijaya received 64,000 strings of copper coins as well as 10,500 taels of silver. Shipped by Chinese traders, such massive flows of Chinese copper coins was linked to the presence of sizeable Chinese communities in these areas (Thiam Soon Heng 2006, pp. 179–203). In early Dai Viet, large amounts of copper cash from the Song flowed in as a major part of the trading commodities, which became the main source for the local economy too (Whitmore 2006). Massive amounts of Chinese copper was exported to Japan first and then shipped to Southeast Asia for trade. For instance, among the total amount of 3,345,000 jin copper (1 jin = 0.5 kg) exported to Japan in 1687, more than two-thirds were transshipped to various Southeast Asian places such as Cochin-China, Cambodia, Siam, Patani and Batavia (Li Jinming 1990, p. 53).

III. WESTERN EXPANSION AND CHINESE MIGRATION, FROM THE MID-NINETEENTH CENTURY TO MID-TWENTIETH CENTURY

If China has exerted any "transforming influence" over Southeast Asia in the social, economic or cultural spheres throughout the last fifteen hundred years of intermittent commercial and maritime contacts, it has had little or nothing to do with Chinese "hegemony" there, nor with any kind of "historic relationship" between rulers. It is to the large-scale migration flows of the period 1870–1940 that we must look for the most substantial evidence of Chinese impact on the region, not to the earlier centuries of spasmodic contact. And insofar as China's main "transforming influence" in the region has been through its contribution to the development of capitalism and colonialism by the Overseas Chinese ... I cannot imagine that many Southeast Asians would regard this as a beneficial influence. (Mackie 1983, p. 77)

Up till the mid-nineteenth century, the world situation was characterized by the changing structured circumstances, namely, the Western Powers rose to dominate the world order and replaced China's influence in the Southeast Asia. Likewise, China itself experienced one "century of humiliation" precisely imposed by the Western powers on the other. The tributary system came to be replaced by the treaty system, and Southeast Asian countries became political entities under Western suzerainties and excluded from directly dealing with China. The China-Southeast Asian relations were almost equal to those between China and Western colonial powers. China was forced to open five coastal port cities for overseas trade, and Chinese emigration was no longer forbidden. Politically however, Chinese influence in the Southeast Asia region had reached its nadir. Ironically, this period bore witness to the transformation of Chinese influence in the region through large-scale Chinese migration whereby Chinese immigrants were the pioneering forces for Southeast Asian transformation. Western expansion and Chinese migration became the most dynamic forces shaping China-Southeast Asian relations (Mackie 1983, pp. 75–80; Stuart-Fox 2004, pp. 116–28).

Because of Western colonialism and imperialism at an inter-government level, China-Southeast Asia relations came to a standstill, even the sole Southeast Asian independent state Thailand had been trying to minimize its official contacts with China. Chinese migration indeed became the most significant subject in bilateral relations between the two regions. Overseas Chinese not only formed the very substantial manifestation of the Chinese transforming influence in Southeast Asia, but also became an important foreign policy target for China-Southeast Asian relations and were incorporated into Chinese nationalism. The Qing government shifted its attitude towards Overseas Chinese from a negligent indifference or even hostility to an enthusiastic courtship in order to serve China's modern nation-building agenda. The courtship included the establishment of consular services in various Southeast Asian cities, the automatic claims of the Overseas Chinese as Chinese subjects, the sale of privileged ranks and titles, and the encouragement of Overseas

Chinese investments in the homeland (Godley 1975, pp. 361–85; Duara 1997, pp. 1043–47; Kuhn 1997).

While the Nanjing Treaty of 1842 ceded Hong Kong as an important entrepôt linking China and Southeast Asia and opened up trading ports such as Canton and Amoy, the Peking Treaty of 1860 made it possible for contract labourers to work overseas thereby repealing the Qing government's ban on emigration and finally removing any legal barrier for prohibiting free movement of immigrants. Compared to the first wave of Chinese migration in the sixteenth century, Chinese migration of this period mainly consisted of coolies labour rather than merchants. The size and scale of emigration flows were much larger and more frequent, so much so that an unprecedented number of Chinese people went overseas during this period. Chinese migrant labour was the most dynamic transforming force in Southeast Asia following colonial capitalist developments. The following demographic sketches show the growth of Chinese communities in various Southeast Asian countries.

In the Philippines, between 1850 and the mid-1880s, Chinese immigrant numbers grew from 8,000 to 100,000 or more. In 1850, 92 per cent of the Chinese were in the Manila area, while in the 1890s only 60 per cent remained in the area as the rest were scattered all over the Philippines (Wickberg 1962, pp. 278–79). In British Malaya, following the Forward Movement in the mid-1870s, Chinese immigrants increased impressively, averaging about 150,000 immigrants annually in the 1880s and 1890s, and more than 300,000 annually in the 1920s. In 1871–1947, the Chinese population ranged from 33.7 per cent to 49.3 per cent of its total population. In 1881–1940, the total number of arriving Chinese immigrants was estimated to be 10 million. In 1916–40, the total number of Chinese arrivals was 4,181,858, total departure was 2,628,811, with net immigrants of around 1.5 million (Sharon Lee 1989, pp. 310, 312, 318). In British Borneo, the first wave of large-scale Chinese immigration began in the 1850s driven by the gold mines; the second wave of the 1880s was driven by the tobacco production (Y.L. Lee 1962, p. 228). In the Dutch Indies, the so-called "liberal period" led to large numbers of contract labourers from China who started arriving in earnest in 1873 and peaked in 1928. By the mid-nineteenth century, there were nearly 150,000 Chinese in Java and Madura alone, and by 1900, the Chinese numbered 277,000 in Java and Madura and some 250,000 in the Outer Provinces. In 1930, the new immigrants from China numbered 450,000 of a total Chinese population of 1.25 million (Kahin 1946, p. 327; Lasker 1946, p. 166; Purcell, 1980, pp. 429–30). In Siam, the annual Chinese immigrant surplus increased from 3,000 in the 1820s to 7,000 around 1870, and in 1890 the Chinese formed about a third of the total population and were nearly as numerous as the Siamese. The average annual arrivals of Chinese immigrants were 16,100 in 1882–92, 35,000 in 1893–1905, and 68,000 in 1906–17, with the annual surplus 7,100, 14,900 and 15,000 respectively (Landon 1941, p. 21; Skinner 1957, pp. 58–61). In Cochin-china, there were 57,000 Chinese immigrants in 1889, 120,000 in 1906 and 156,000 in 1921. In the whole of French Indo-China in 1921–31, Chinese immigrants increased from 293,000 (156,000 in Cochin-china and 91,000 in Cambodia) to 418,000 (Purcell 1980, pp. 177–78).

Prior to World War II, Chinese comprised 42.4 per cent of the total population in British Malaya, 60 per cent in Straits Settlements, 75 per cent in Singapore, 49 per cent in Penang, 35 per cent in Malacca, 45 per cent in Bangka and Billiton, 36 per cent in Medan, 20 per cent in Manado, 18 per cent in Makassar, 16 per cent in Batavia, 14 per cent in Palembang, as high as 27 per cent in certain districts of western Borneo, 25 per cent in Saigon, and 75 per cent in Cholon (Barnett 1943, p. 33; Unger 1944, pp. 210–11; Vandenbosch 1947, pp. 80–85). Prior to 1950, the Southeast Asian Chinese population was estimated to approach about 10 million, among which nearly 3 million were in Thailand and Malaya respectively, 2 million in Indonesia, 1 million in Vietnam, Cambodia and Laos, 750,000 in the Philippines and 250,000 in Burma (Unger 1944, pp. 199, 216; Purcell 1950, pp. 194–96; Rose H. Lee 1956, p. 263; Skinner 1959, p. 137).

In contrast to the Chinese government's shifting attitude and strategy towards Chinese immigrants, the massive presence of Chinese communities had been long resented by the colonial administrations as a physical and economic form of "Chinese imperialism" in Southeast Asia. "Chinese imperialism" used to refer to the Chinese cultural prestige and recognition in general and to the Chinese principle of bureaucratic organizations established in Vietnam in particular; in modern times, it is used to denote anti-Chinese ideology and movements because of various sizable Chinese communities and strong economic forces (Vandenbosch 1930; Landon 1940; Lasker 1946, p. 169; Winzeler et al. 1976, p. 636; Finlay 1992, pp. 235–36).

IV. NATION-BUILDING AND COLD WAR, FROM MID-TWENTIETH CENTURY TO EARLY 1990s

No interstate relationships in the world — or the controversies they breed in the states that sustain them — seem more unpredictable and paradoxical to Western eyes than the relationships which exist between China and her Southwest [Southeast] Asian neighbors…. Obviously there is a deeply impacted ambivalence about contemporary China among Southeast Asians.

On the intellectual plane, it can be seen in the Southeast Asian tendency
to pendulate between sympathy for an "Asian" China" and suspicion of a
Marxist-Leninist China. (Woodside 1978, pp. 215–16)

The post-War China-Southeast Asian relations were shaped by the ideology
of anti-colonialism and anti-imperialism and Cold War on the one hand and
by the nation-building processes on the other. For the former aspect, China
had good relationships with Vietnam, Burma and Indonesia, while maintaining
a distance with other countries. For the latter aspect, Southeast Asian Chinese
identity was challenged and looked upon with suspicion by the new nation-
states, so much so that it was deemed "problematic" and became the focus of
the political controversy for their blood connection with communist China,
their association with the communist activities in the region, and their dominant
economic positions over other ethnic communities. Also, the Southeast Asian
communist guerrillas, especially in Indonesia, Malaya/Singapore, Thailand and
the Philippines, were said to have support from China and therefore posed a
serious threat for the nation-building. Therefore, after one century of forced
distance, China and Southeast Asia renewed direct inter-government relations,
while Chinese emigrants to Southeast Asia came to a halt thereafter. However,
China and Southeast Asia had little knowledge of each other and lacked
mutual understanding. As new regimes, both parties were indeed vulnerable.
Yet bilateral relations were obviously asymmetric in terms of geography,
demography and civilization. Under the radical changing circumstances, the
traditional image of peaceful China in the region was imagined and even
exaggerated with fears and anxieties into a hegemonic one. Such asymmetric
China-Southeast Asia inter-government relations were further complicated by
another set of relations between Overseas Chinese and China. This was because
of Southeast Asian governments' suspicions of their political allegiances to the
native regimes. Whether close or distant, post-War China-Southeast Asian
relationships were characterized more by political, ideological and security
considerations, and less by economic and trade cooperation. This was so much
so that the socio-cultural exchange was at its lowest ebb. Overall, Southeast
Asia regarded China as a dangerous adversary and was apprehensive of the
threat China posed (Banlaoi 2003, pp. 99–100). As Mackie argues:

> The apprehensions of most Southeast Asians about China derive less from
> any sense of an "historic relationship" or "traditional hegemonic position"
> than from other sources. These include vague fears concerning the degree of
> economic power wielded by the Overseas Chinese and the ideological threat
> China has posed since 1949 (by far their most pressing concerns); a sense
> of concern about China's vast population, which seems to constitute some

sort of potential threat in the long term; and an awareness of China's much more ancient history, high levels of civilization and social dynamics. On the whole, Southeast Asia's leaders seem not very frightened about China in the short term, but they are a good deal less confident about their ability to match China's potential strength in the long run. (Mackie, 1983, p. 76)

China-Southeast Asian relations during this period were divided into three phases. The first phase was from 1949 to the mid-1960s. China's Southeast Asian policy was subjected to its overall anti-colonialism, anti-imperialism and revisionism and mutual coexistence principles as illustrated at the Bandung Conference in 1955. Soon after the declaration of independence in 1950, China recognized the communist Northern Vietnam (in January), had diplomatic relations with Indonesia (in April) and Burma (in June). Thus, China had an ally with Northern Vietnam, a comfortable harmonious relationship with Indonesia, and a good party-to-party but a conflicting state-to-state relation with Burma (Woodside 1978, pp. 217–19; Haacke 2005, p. 112). Although China settled the dual nationality problem and encouraged Overseas Chinese to settle down in Southeast Asia, this phase still saw anti-Overseas Chinese sentiments and the repatriation of hundreds of thousands of Overseas Chinese, especially from Indonesia and Malaysia.

During this time, China-Southeast Asian trade relations were insignificant. Although in the First Five-Year Plan, China emphasized expanding trade with Southeast Asian countries, the trading volume was rather moderate. For two decades before 1972, China's overall trade volume fluctuated between US$2–4 billion and the Southeast Asian share was rather small and insignificant. Between 1952–57, Southeast Asian exports to China showed a considerable decline, falling from US$207.3 million to US$134.8 million, a drop of 34 per cent. However, China's trade with Southeast Asia constituted an important part (two-thirds) of her trade with non-communist countries (20 per cent of foreign trade). Southeast Asian exports consisted mainly of primary products and raw materials such as rubber, cotton, petroleum, jute, rice, coconut oil, non-ferrous metals, etc., while Chinese exports not only included traditional exports like agricultural and handicraft products, but also manufactured goods of light and heavy industries. China not only developed trade with Burma, Indonesia and Malaya, but also opened trade relations with Cambodia and Thailand while conducting indirect trade with South Vietnam and the Philippines via Hong Kong. The most important trading devices were trade fairs. For a few years following the establishment of the PRC in 1949, China actively participated in trade fairs and industrial exhibitions in Indonesia, Burma, Cambodia and Malaya. At the Indonesian International Trade Fair of

1955, the largest exhibitor was China. On a barter basis, China also signed various bilateral commercial agreements with Burma, Indonesia, Cambodia and Malaya, of which the most noticeable barter accord was the Sino-Burmese agreement on the exchange of Chinese goods for Burmese rice (Shao Chuan Leng 1959, pp. 3–11). With the sensitive political situation, China-Southeast Asian trade relations again reached a low level. In 1958, Thailand officially banned direct trade with China; in late 1958, as a reprisal for Malayan bans of certain Chinese publications, China suspended trade with Singapore and Malaya; in 1965, the Indonesian 30 September event brought direct trade with China to an abrupt end. However, indirect trade via Hong Kong remained.

The second phase was from the mid-1960s to the mid-1970s. This was a period of so-called Chinese intervention and export of the people's war in the case of support for Southeast Asian communist revolts and witnessed China-Southeast Asian relations at the lowest ebb politically as well as economically. The growth of China's foreign trade had been slow and unstable. In 1964, among ASEAN countries, only Singapore/Malaya and Indonesia maintained somewhat tenuous and precarious trade relations with a turnover of US$210 million, while in 1974, total ASEAN trade with the socialist countries as a whole (including China) jumped to US$1,500 million. Despite that, it consisted of 3.3 per cent of ASEAN total foreign trade. Among China's trade with non-socialist countries, Southeast Asia ranged between 5–6 per cent for the 1960s and 7–8 per cent for the 1970s (Wong 1977, pp. 330, 334–36).

The third phase was from the mid-1970s to the whole of the 1980s. In the context of Sino-United States rapprochement, this period saw the normalization of relationships between China and the ASEAN countries of Malaysia (May 1974), Thailand (June 1975) and the Philippines (July 1975) before the mid-1970s on the one hand, and the worsening of Sino-Vietnamese relations after the mid-1970s on the other. The Sino-Vietnamese tension and Vietnamese occupation of Cambodia formed the major events in shaping China-ASEAN political cooperation (Ba 2003, pp. 623–26). Yet the ASEAN fear of China's expansion and subversion remained unchanged in the long run and Sino-ASEAN trade remained quantitatively small and changed little. Data showed that between 1975 and 1984, imports from China into ASEAN averaged about 2.6 per cent of total imports per year, and exports only 0.9 per cent of total exports per year and from 1985–89 there were just 2 per cent. This was in sharp contrast with ASEAN trade relations with the industrialized countries, mainly Japan, the United States and Europe. From 1975 to 1989, the share of imports from the industrialized countries to ASEAN averaged 54 per cent, exports from ASEAN to the industrialized countries averaged 57 per cent (Herschede 1991, pp. 180–82).

V. GLOBALIZATION AND STRATEGIC PARTNERSHIP, FROM THE EARLY 1990S TO THE PRESENT

Many Southeast Asians now regard China as a benign presence to be emulated — a sharp contrast with current regional views of the United States. (Kurlantzick 2006, p. 270)

The end of the Cold War and the start of the era of globalization came simultaneously and launched a "new international era" (Neher 2002). In China, it coincided with Deng Xiaopeng's Southern Tour and the further openness and reform policy. After twenty-five years of hostility diplomatic relations were restored between China and Indonesia in August 1990. Two months later, Singapore established formal diplomatic relations with China. In 1991, Sino-Vietnamese relations began to normalize and the Cambodian issue was eventually settled. The previous ideology and security threat between China and Southeast Asia now gave way to trade promotion and political cooperation. Although Southeast Asia was still concerned with the security issue, China-Southeast Asian relations were back to normalcy and improvement and are now at a historical best. China-Southeast Asian relations were characterized by the disappearance of ideological barriers, the importance of economic links, the salience of the Spratly territorial disputes and the emergence of multilateralism as a mode of diplomatic interaction (Zagoria 1991, pp. 3–5; Kuik Cheng-Chwee 2005, p. 103). Unlike the Cold War period, this period concentrates on a strategic partnership towards peace and prosperity in the twenty-first century, which is a win-win situation both politically and economically. Unlike in previous periods, the so-called "Overseas Chinese Problem" was no longer a fundamental concern in shaping bilateral or multilateral relations.

The post-Cold War era was structurally characteristic of China's rapid rise and Sino-Japanese tension, and Southeast Asia became the key region for each side to win over. Southeast Asia now treats China's rapid rise as an economic opportunity as well as competition. Competition between China and Southeast Asia is centred on labour-intensive industries and FDI, while opportunity has provided a huge Chinese market and created enormous trading volume for Southeast Asia. China and ASEAN are not only more economically interdependent; ASEAN has now also recognized China's important role in the regional security order. While ASEAN member countries are wary of China's ongoing military modernization, the short-term tension in the Taiwanese Strait and long-term conflict in the South China Sea centring on the Spratly Islands, these nations are not as alarmed as they once would have been. ASEAN apprehensions about China's rise vary from very low in

Thailand, to mixed cautious interchange in Malaysia, deeply sceptical in the Philippines, Indonesia and Vietnam, and very high in Singapore. However, ASEAN's assessment of China's strategy within the region is more political than military. ASEAN employs two general strategies, namely hedging and engagement in dealing with China. The hedging included establishing a modest level of defence links with other large outside powers, such as the United States, Japan, Russia and India, to counterbalance Chinese influence. The engagement involved encouraging Chinese participation in multilateral organizations and international dialogue and agreements, including ARF, APEC, ASEAN+3, the ASEAN-China Dialogue, and the China-ASEAN Free Trade Area, etc. (Lee Lai To 1993, pp. 1095–104; Denoon and Frieman 1996, p. 433; Whiting 1997, pp. 299–322; Roy 2005, pp. 305–22). In the context of Sino-Japanese tension and new international situations, bilateralism remained the principal thrust of China's foreign policy towards Southeast Asia. However, since 1997, China has taken steps to forge institutional linkages with ASEAN and develop a new policy initiative of a New Concept of Security and a Peaceful Rise/Development. China argued that the use of force or threat to use force cannot fundamentally solve the problems and emphasized "four core elements: mutual trust, mutual benefit, equality, and cooperation/coordination", or "no hegemonism, no power politics, no arms races and no military alliances" (Haacke 2005, p. 115).

China's participation in the ASEAN-driven multilateral institutions experienced significant changes from caution and suspicion to optimism and enthusiasm and could be divided into three major phases: The first phase of the early 1990s to 1995, encompassed China's passive involvement with caution and suspicion towards ASEAN's proposal of multilateral security arrangements. This was seen in China's decision to attend the annual ASEAN Foreign Ministers' Meeting in 1991 and join the ASEAN Regional Forum in 1994. The second phase (1996–99) saw China's active participation in ASEAN. In July 1996, China became the Full Dialogue Partner of the ASEAN Ministerial Meeting and ASEAN+3 and ASEAN+1 in 1997. Phase three (2000 to the present) bore witness to China's proactive proposition. This phase witnessed the signing of momentous documents such as the China-ASEAN Free Trade Area and the Declaration on the Conduct of Parties in the South China Sea in November 2002. In October 2003, China became the first major power to join ASEAN's Treaty of Amity and Cooperation and signed the Joint Declaration on Strategic Partnership with ASEAN.

China-Southeast Asian close relations are best manifested in bilateral trade. Compared to the insignificant volume over the past four decades, the post-Cold War period saw the unprecedented rapid development of bilateral trading relations in terms of growth rate, trading value and trading structure. Since 1991, the average annual China-ASEAN trade growth has been more than 20 per cent. China-ASEAN total import-export which was valued at nearly US$8 billion in 1991, rose to US$41.615 billion in 2001 and ASEAN was China's fifth largest trading partner. With the prospect of the free trade area, China-ASEAN trade has grown even faster with an average annual growth rate of more than 30 per cent since 2001. It rose to US$54.768 billion in 2002, an increase of 31.7 per cent over the previous year, US$78.3 billion in 2003, an increase of 42.9 per cent, and jumped to US$105.9 billion in 2004 and reached the level of US$100 billion for the first time. Within three years, China-ASEAN trade has multiplied two and half times. The bilateral foreign trade continued to rise to US$130.4 billion in 2005 at a growth rate of 23.1 per cent over the previous year, US$160.8 billion in 2006 at a growth rate of 23.4 per cent, and US$202.55 billion in 2007, which reached the level of US$200 billion for the first time and achieved the projected target three years early (Wong and Chan 2003, pp. 512–16; Womack 2003–04, pp. 534–35; Sheng Lijun 2006, pp. 2–5). There is reason to believe that the prospect of China-ASEAN trade relations will be more promising in the future.

CONCLUDING REMARKS

Having contextualized China-Southeast Asian interactions up to the present, the chapter discovers that historical, geographical, demographical, ideological, ethnical, economic, political and territorial, social and cultural elements play roles in shaping dynamics of bilateral and multilateral relations. Historically, China-Southeast Asian relations have been abnormal and overshadowed either by their own internal developments or by external forces, such as colonialism and imperialism. However, both sides have as part of their respective historical legacies, social structures and political cultures. The short and unprecedented development of post-Cold War China-ASEAN close relation suggests that normal statehood and cooperative strategies are beneficial and important to both sides. Yet, because of the in-built structural asymmetry of bilateral relations, ASEAN long-term political and security concerns over China's domination remain unchanged. Also, because of this, the social and cultural exchanges at people-to-people level differ from the political and economic interactions at the inter-state level, therefore remaining a real challenge ahead for China and Southeast Asia.

Note

The author would like to thank Heather Sutherland for her constructive comments on this chapter.

References

English Sources

Ba, Alice D. "China and ASEAN: Renavigating Relations for a 21st-Century Asia". *Asian Survey* 43, no. 4 (July–Aug 2003): 622–47.

Banlaoi, Rommel C. "Southeast Asian Perspectives on the Rise of China: Regional Security after 9/11". *Parameters* (Summer 2003): 98–107.

Blusse, Leonard. "No Boats to China. The Dutch East India Company and the Changing Pattern of the China Sea Trade, 1635–1690". *Modern Asian Studies* 30, no. 1 (Feb 1996): 51–76.

Barnett, Patricia G. "The Chinese in Southeastern Asia and the Philippines". *Annals of the American Academy of Political and Social Science* 226 (Mar 1943): 32–49.

Chan Hok-lam. "The 'Chinese Barbarian Officials' in the Foreign Tributary Missions to China during the Ming Dynasty". *Journal of the American Oriental Society* 88, no. 3 (July–Sept 1968): 411–18.

Duara, Prasenjit. "Transnationalism and the Predicament of Sovereignty: China, 1900–1945". *The American Historical Review* 102, no. 4 (Oct 1997): 1030–51.

Fairbank, J.K. and S.Y. Teng. "On the Ch'ing Tributary System". *Harvard Journal of Asiatic Studies* 6, no. 2 (June 1941): 135–246.

Fairbank, J.K. "Tributary Trade and China's Relations with the West". *The Far Eastern Quarterly* 1, no. 2 (Feb 1942): 129–49.

Finlay, Robert. "Portuguese and Chinese Maritime Imperialism: Camoes's Lusiads and Luo Maodeng's Voyage of the San Bao Eunuch". *Comparative Studies in Society and History* 34, no. 2 (Apr 1992): 225–41.

Godley, Michael R. "The Late Ch'ing Courtship of the Chinese in Southeast Asia". *The Journal of Asian Studies* 34, no. 2 (Feb 1975): 361–85.

Haacke, Jürgen. "The Significance of Beijing's Bilateral Relations: Looking 'Below' the Regional Level in China-ASEAN Ties". In *China and Southeast Asia: Economic Statecraft and Strategic Engagement*, edited by Ho Khai Leong and Samuel C.Y. Ku. Singapore: ISEAS, 2005, pp. 111–45.

Hall, Kenneth R. "Small Asian Nations in the Shadow of the Large: Early Asian History through the Eyes of Southeast Asia". *Journal of the Economic and Social History of the Orient* 27, no. 1 (1984): 56–88.

———. "The Textile Industry in Southeast Asia, 1400–1800". *Journal of the Economic and Social History of the Orient* 39, no. 2 (1996): 87–135.

Herschede, Fred. "Trade between China and ASEAN: The Impact of the Pacific Rim Era". *Pacific Affairs* 64, no. 2 (Summer 1991): 179–93.

Ho Khai Leong and Samuel C.Y. Ku. *China and Southeast Asia: Global Changes and Regional Challenges*. Singapore: ISEAS, 2005.

Kahin, George McT. "The Chinese in Indonesia". *Far Eastern Survey* 15, no. 21 (23 Oct 1946): 326–29.

Knaap, Gerrit and Heather Sutherland. *Monsoon Traders: Ships, Skippers and Commodities in Eighteenth-century Makassar*. Leiden: KITLV Press, 2004.

Kuhn, Philip A. "The Homeland: Thinking about the History of Chinese Overseas".

The fifty-eighth George Ernest Marrison Lecture in Ethnology, 1997, Australian National University, pp. 1–11.

Kuik Cheng-Chwee. "Multilateralism in China's ASEAN Policy: Its Evolution, Characteristics, and Aspiration". *Contemporary Southeast Asia* 27, no. 1 (2005): 102–22.

Kurlantzick, Joshua. "China's Charm Offensive in Southeast Asia". *Current History* 105, no. 692 (Sept 2006): 270–76.

Landon, Kenneth Perry. "The Problem of the Chinese in Thailand". *Pacific Affairs* 13, no. 2 (Jun. 1940): 149–61.

————. *The Chinese in Thailand*. New York: Institute of Pacific Relations, 1941.

Lasker, Bruno. "The Role of the Chinese in the Netherlands Indies". *The Far Eastern Quarterly* 5, no. 2 (Feb 1946): 162–71.

Lee Lai To. "ASEAN-PRC Political and Security Cooperation: Problems, Proposals, and Prospects". *Asian Survey* 33, no. 11 (Nov 1993): 1095–104.

Lee Kuan Yew. "ASEAN Must Balance China in Asia". *New Perspective Quarterly* 18, no. 3 (Summer 2001): 20–23.

Lee, Rose Hum. "The Chinese Abroad". *Phylon* (1940–1956) 17, no. 3 (Third Quarter 1956): 257–70.

Lee, Sharon M. "Female Immigrants and Labor in Colonial Malaya: 1860–1947". *International Migration Review* 23, no. 2 (Summer 1989): 309–11.

Lee, Y.L. "The Population of British Borneo". *Population Studies* 15, no. 3 (Mar 1962): 226–43.

Li Tana. "A View from the Sea: Perspectives on the Northern and Central Vietnamese Coast". *Journal of Southeast Asian Studies* 37, no. 1 (Fall 2006): 83–102.

Lo, Jung-pang. "The Emergence of China as a Sea Power during the Late Sung and Early Yuan Periods". *The Far Eastern Quarterly* 14, no. 4 (Aug 1955): 489–503.

Mackie, J.A.C. "ASEAN Perspectives on China: A Rejoinder to Peter Polomka". *The Australian Journal of Chinese Affairs* no. 9 (Jan 1983): 75–80.

Manguin, Pierre-Yves. "Trading Ships of the South China Sea. Shipbuilding Techniques and Their Role in the History of the Development of Asian Trade Networks". *Journal of the Economic and Social History of the Orient* 36, no. 3 (1993): 253–80.

Neher, Clark D. *Southeast Asia in the New International Era*. Boulder: Westview Press, 2002.

Polomka, Peter. "ASEAN Perspectives on China: Implications for Western Interests". *The Australian Journal of Chinese Affairs* no. 8 (Jul 1982): 85–99.

Ptak, Roderich. "China and the Trade in Cloves, Circa 960–1435". *Journal of the American Oriental Society* 113, no. 1 (Jan–Mar 1993): 1–13.

————. "From Quanzhou to the Sulu Zone and Beyond: Questions Related to the Early Fourteenth Century". *Journal of Southeast Asian Studies* 29, no. 2 (Summer 1998): 269–94.

Purcell, Victor. "Overseas Chinese and People's Republic". *Far Eastern Survey* 19, no. 18 (25 Oct 1950): 194–96.

————. *The Chinese in Southeast Asia*. Kuala Lumpur: Oxford University Press, 1980.

Reid, Anthony. *Southeast Asia in the Age of Commerce 1450–1680, Volume One: The Lands below the Winds; Volume Two: Expansion and Crisis*. New Haven: Yale University Press 1993.

————. "An 'Age of Commerce' in Southeast Asian History". *Modern Asian Studies* 24, no. 1 (Feb 1990): 1–30.

————. "Flows and Seepages in the Long-term Chinese Interaction with Southeast Asia". In *Sojourners and Settlers: Histories of Southeast Asia and the Chinese*, edited by Anthony Reid, pp. 15–50. St Leonards, NSW: Allen & Unwin, 1996.

Roy, Denny. "Southeast Asia and China: Balancing or Bandwagoning?". *Contemporary Southeast Asia* 27, no. 2 (2005): 305–22.

Shao Chuan Leng. "Communist China's Economic Relations with Southeast Asia". *Far Eastern Survey* 28, no. 1 (Jan 1959): 1–11.

Sheng Lijun. "China's Influence in Southeast Asia". *Trends in Southeast Asia Series*, 4 (Apr 2006): 1–11.

Skinner, G. William. *Chinese Society in Thailand: An Analytical History*. Ithaca: Cornell University Press, 1957.

————. "Overseas Chinese in Southeast Asia". *Annals of the American Academy of Political and Social Science* 321, "Contemporary China and the Chinese" (Jan 1959): 136–47.

So Kee-Long, "Dissolving Hegemony or Changing Trade Pattern? Images of Srivijaya in the Chinese Sources of the Twelfth and Thirteenth Centuries". *Journal of Southeast Asian Studies* 29, no. 2 (Summer 1998): 295–308.

Stuart-Fox, Martin. "Southeast Asia and China: The Role of History and Culture in Shaping Future Relations". *Contemporary Southeast Asia* 26, no. 1 (2004): 116–39.

Sutherland, Heather. "Trepang and wangkang. The China trade of eighteenth century Makassar". In *Authority and Enterprise among the Peoples of South Sulawesi*, edited by Roger Tol et al., pp. 73–94. Leiden: KITLV Press, 2000.

————. "The Sulu Zone Revisited". *Journal of Southeast Asian Studies* 35, no. 1 (Fall 2004): 133–57.

Sun Laichen. "Military Technology Transfers from Ming China and the Emergence of Northern Mainland Southeast Asia (c. 1390–1527)". *Journal of Southeast Asian Studies* 34, no. 3 (Oct 2003): 495–517.

Thiam Soon Heng, Derek. "Export Commodity and Regional Currency: The Role of Chinese Copper Coins in the Melaka Straits, Tenth to Fourteenth Centuries". *Journal of Southeast Asian Studies* 37, no. 2 (Jun 2006): 179–203.

Unger, Leonard. "The Chinese in Southeast Asia". *Geographical Review* 34, no. 2 (Apr 1944): 196–217.

Vandenbosch, Amry. "A Problem in Java: The Chinese in the Dutch East Indies". *Pacific Affairs* 3, no. 11 (Nov 1930): 1001–17.

————. "The Chinese in Southeast Asia". *The Journal of Politics* 9, no. 1 (Feb 1947): 80–95.

Vatikiotis, Michael R.J. "Catching the Dragon's Tail: China and Southeast Asia in the 21st Century". *Contemporary Southeast Asia* 25, no. 1 (Apr 2003): 65–78.

Wakeman, Frederic, Jr. "Voyages". *The American Historical Review* 98, no. 1 (Feb 1993): 1–17.

Wickberg, Edgar. "Early Chinese Economic Influence in the Philippines, 1850–1898". *Pacific Affairs* 35, no. 3 (Autumn 1962): 275–85.

Winzeler, Robert L. et al. "Ecology, Culture, Social Organization, and State Formation in Southeast Asia?". *Current Anthropology* 17, no. 4 (Dec 1976): 623–40.

Whitmore, John K. "The Rise of the Coast: Trade, State and Culture in Early Đai Viet". *Journal of Southeast Asian Studies* 37, no. 1 (Fall 2006): 103–22.

Wolters, O.W. "Restudying Some Chinese Writings on Sriwijaya". *Indonesia* 42 (Oct 1986): 1–41.

Womack, Brantly. "China and Southeast Asia: Asymmetry, Leadership and Normalcy". *Pacific Affairs* 76, no. 4 (Winter 2003–2004): 529–48.

Wong, John. "Southeast Asia's Growing Trade Relations with Socialist Economies". *Asian Survey* 17, no. 4 (Apr 1977): 330–44.

Wong, John and Sarah Chan. "China-Asean Free Trade Agreement: Shaping Future Economic Relations". *Asian Survey* 43, no. 3 (May–Jun 2003): 507–26.

Woodside, Alexander. "Review Essay: History, Ideology, and Foreign Policy: A Review of Some Recent Western Works on Chinese Relations with Southeast Asia". *Modern China* 4, no. 2 (Apr 1978): 215–46.

Zagria, Donald S. "The End of the Cold War in Asia: Its Impact on China". *Proceedings of the Academy of Political Science* 38, no. 2, "The China Challenge: American Policies in East Asia" (1991): 1–11.

Zhuang Guotu. *Tea, Silver, Opium and War: The International Tea Trade and Western Commercial Expansion into China in 1740–1840.* Xiamen: Xiamen University Press, 1993.

Chinese Sources

戴一峰：《十八～十九世纪中国与东南亚的海参贸易》，《中国社会经济史》，1998年第4期，页71–81。

戴一峰：《饮食文化与海外市场：清代中国与南洋的海参贸易》，《中国社会经济史》，2003年第1期，页83–91。(English version: "Food culture and overseas trade: The trepang trade between China and Southeast Asia during the Qing dynasty", in *The Globalization of Chinese Food*, Wu, D.Y.H. & S.C. H Cheung ed. Honolulu: University of Hawaii Press, 2002.

方福祺：《古代的海上贸易与南海诸国的中国移民》，《云南教育学院学报》，1993年8月，第4期，页47–52。

冯先铭、冯小琦：《荷兰东印度公司与中国明清瓷器》，《江西文物》，1990年第2期，页101–104。

郭梁：《鸦片战争前华侨历史的发展阶段》，《南洋问题研究》，1982年第4期，页78–93。

和洪勇：《明前期中国与东南亚国家的朝贡贸易》，《云南社会科学》，2003年第1期，页85-90。

李金明：《明代海外朝贡贸易中的华籍使者》，《南洋问题研究》，1986年第4期，页107-118。

李金明：《清康熙时期中国与东南亚的海上贸易》，《南洋问题研究》，1990年第2期，页48-58。

李金明：《清代前期中国与东南亚的大米贸易》，《南洋问题研究》，1990年第4期，页96-104。

李庆新：《郑和下西洋与朝贡体系》，载《郑和远航与世界文明》，王天有徐凯万明编，北京：北京大学出版社，2005年，页228-252。

李云泉：《明清朝贡制度研究》，暨南大学历史系博士论文，2003年。

李云泉：《略论宋代中外朝贡关系与朝贡制度》，《山东师范大学学报》（人文社会科学版），2003年第48卷第2期，页101-104。

貌貌李：《缅甸华人穆斯林研究蜓曼德勒"潘泰"社区的形成》，《南洋问题研究》，2007年第1期，页50-55。

彭蕙：《明代洪武年间出使南洋使节研究》，《东南亚研究》，2004年第1期，页80-86。

钱江：《清代中国与苏禄的贸易》，《南洋问题研究》，1988年第1期，页85-92。

钱江：《十七至18世纪中国与荷兰的瓷器贸易》，《南洋问题研究》，1989年第1期，页80-91。

孙健：《南海沉船与宋代瓷器外销》，《中国文化遗产》，2007年第4期，页32-45。

孙来臣：《明清时期中缅贸易关系及其特点》，《东南亚研究》，1989年第4期，页17-26。

汤开建、彭蕙：《爪哇与中国明朝贸易关系考述》，载《东南亚纵横》，2003年第6期，页53-59。

汤开建、田渝：《乾隆时期中国与暹罗的大米贸易》，《中国经济史研究》，2004年第1期，页81-88。

王冬青：《明朝朝贡体系与十八世纪西人入华策略》，复旦大学历史系博士论文，2005年。

王天有、徐凯、万明编：《郑和远航与世界文明》，北京：北京大学出版社，2005年。

王元林、林杏容：《十四至十八世纪欧亚的西洋布贸易》，《东南亚研究》，2005年第4期，页86-91。

喻常森：《试论朝贡制度的演变》，《南洋问题研究》，200年第1期，页55-65。

张应龙：《鸦片战争前中荷茶叶贸易初探》，《暨南学报》，1998年第3期，页93-99。

周伟洲：《唐代与南海诸国通贡关系研究》，《中国史研究》，2002年第3期，页59-73。

周伟洲：《西汉长安与南海诸国的交通及往来》，《中国历史地理论丛》，2003年12月，第18卷，第4辑，页38-44。

庄国土：《海外贸易南洋开发与闽南华侨出国的关系》，《华侨华人历史研究》，1994年第2期，页55-59。

庄国土：《茶叶、白银与鸦片：1750-1840年中西贸易结构》，《中国经济史研究》，1995年第3期，页64-76。

庄国土：《略论朝贡制度的虚幻：以古代中国与东南亚的朝贡关系为例》，《南洋问题研究》，2005年第3期，页1-8。

卓建明：《试论义净在唐朝和南海诸国关系史上的作用》，《世界历史》，1992年第6期，页74-79。

2

PHILIPPINE-CHINA CONNECTION FROM PRE-COLONIAL PERIOD TO POST-COLD WAR ERA
An Assessment

Edgardo E. Dagdag

INTRODUCTION

This chapter examines the Philippines-China connection from the pre-colonial period to the post-Cold War era. It shows how the people of the two countries interacted with one another before the Philippines was colonized by Spain, how this interaction evolved during the time it was under Spanish and American colonial rule, and how this was further transformed or reconfigured after World War II and until the end of the Cold War. It also identifies the outcome of this interaction especially to the Philippines.

This chapter made use of available data in discussing and analysing the experience of the Philippines in "connecting, distancing and positioning" herself with China through time — in response to new and emerging challenges and opportunities. These three overlapping processes, especially the positioning phase, are expected to continue without let-up in the years ahead, especially now that China has emerged as a major player and strategic rival of the United States — the long-time ally of the Philippines with whom it has close and special relations. The Philippines was under the colonial rule of the United States from 1898 to 1946.

The people of the islands now known as the Philippines were "connected" with China many centuries before they were colonized by the Spaniards in 1565. Chinese records disclose that the Filipino traders from Luzon were the ones who travelled first to China long before the Chinese ever stepped foot in the Philippines.

Initial contact between the Filipinos and the Chinese took place when traders from Mai-i (now Mindoro, a major island in Luzon) went to Canton (Guangdong) in the tenth century through the Champa (Vietnam) coast. In 982, the Mai-i traders went directly to Canton for the first time. They were treated as state guests and feudatory princes by the Chinese emperor. The annals of the Sung Dynasty made mention of Mai-i for the first time in AD 998.[1] It was also reported that during the Sung dynasty, "Chinese goods began to flow in a continuous stream into the Philippines" and that "Chinese colonies were founded in the coastal towns of the (Philippine) archipelago".[2]

On 17 March 1001, the first tributary mission to China from the Philippines was organized. King Kiling of Butuan (presently a province in Mindanao) led the tributary mission. Kiling requested the Chinese emperor that his kingdom be granted equal status with Champa. Unfortunately, his request was denied. In 1011, or ten years later, the second tributary mission to China was organized by the new ruler of Butuan. He reiterated the request of Kiling and this time, the Chinese emperor was more accommodating — his request was granted. This gave rise to more contacts between the Mai-I traders and the Chinese.

By 1206, Chinese traders had already linked up with the Filipino traders not only in Butuan but also in Mindoro and Palawan (presently provinces in Luzon). About nineteen years later or by 1225, the Philippines-China trade expanded to include areas like Babuyan and Lingayen (in Northern Luzon) and Manila. Products traded by the Filipinos through barter included gold, yellow wax, hemp, betel nut, cotton, edible bird's nest, tortoise shells and pears. Chinese products included silk and brocade textiles, porcelain wares, iron, tin and umbrellas.[3]

The link between the Filipinos in Sulu (in Southern Philippines) and the Chinese started in 1417 and these were clearly depicted in the Ming annals. In that year, Paduka Batara (the eastern king of Sulu), Ma-hala-chih (the western king), and Paduka Prabu (King of the Mountain Kalabating) went to China on a one-month tributary mission together with their wives, relatives and ministers. On their way home, King Batara died. The Ming emperor Yung Lo, who reigned from 1402 to 1424, showed his respect to the late king by giving pension and accommodation to Tumahan (King Batara's son and successor) and his brothers during their three year residence in Techow as they observed the mourning rites. When the mourning period ended in 1420, Chinese Commissioner Chang escorted Tumahan and his group back to Sulu and stayed there for more than two years.

This friendly gesture of China led to a series of exchange missions between China and Sulu from 1420 to 1424 during the reign of Ming Emperor Yung Lo and the direct migration of some Chinese traders from Fujian to Sulu and other nearby areas. This explains why there are Filipinos with Chinese blood in Mindanao. The most well-received tributary mission from the Philippines (in particular, from Mindanao) was the one led by Paduka Suli in 1421.[4] He gifted the Chinese emperor with a seven-ounce pearl and stayed in Techow for two years with his nephews.[5]

It should be mentioned that even before the arrival of the tributary missions from Sulu, Ming Emperor Yung Lo had already shown his interest in the Philippines. Records show that he

> sent a large fleet consisting of more than sixty vessels to the Philippines under the command of Admiral Cheng Ho. The fleet visited Lingayen in Pangasinan, Manila Bay, Mindoro and Sulu. These visits took place in 1405–06, 1408–10, and 1417. For a short period, the Chinese emperor even tried to maintain a kind of sovereignty over Luzon and sent Ko-ch'a-lao to the island as "governor". With the death of Yung Lo, however, his pretensions to sovereignty over Luzon came to an end.[6]

These tributary missions from Sulu contributed to its rise as an international trade hub in Southeast Asia, almost a potential rival of Malacca. These missions from Mindanao, in addition to those organized by the kings from Mai-i, Pangasinan and other areas of Luzon, may be viewed as the beginning of the official relationship between China and the Philippines. This Philippine-China connection, which was formally started by the 1001 Mai-i tributary mission, antedated by more than 500 years the links of the Philippines with the West, particularly with Spain. This historical fact is one of the reasons why many Filipinos today, especially those with an awareness of history, object to the claim of some foreign and even Filipino historians that the Philippines was discovered in 1521 by Ferdinand Magellan, a Portuguese navigator working for Spain.

The introduction of Islam in the Philippines (particularly in Sulu in 1380 by the Arab scholar Makdum) and its rapid spread to other parts of the country starting in the fourteenth and fifteenth centuries through the efforts of religious leaders coming from Indonesia and Malaya like Raja Baginda, Abu Bakr and Serif Kabungsuan, adversely affected its growing trade links with China. At the start, the Chinese had difficulty plying their trade in areas that were under Islamic influence, especially Sulu and the areas comprising the Sulu Sultanate. Eventually, however, the sultans and datus tolerated their presence. In fact, some Chinese traders "connected" with these Moro rulers by marrying their daughters[7] — and this undoubtedly protected and even enhanced their economic activities in the Islam-influenced areas.

At the time the Spaniards arrived in Manila in 1570, the place was ruled by Muslim chieftains who were linked with the ruling family in Brunei. There were already some Chinese in Manila at that time. It was reported that the Spaniards, when they arrived, "... found a small settlement of forty Chinese and twenty Japanese in the Manila area who were living peacefully with the natives".[8]

"DISTANCING" FROM CHINA: SURVEY OF PHILIPPINE-CHINA RELATIONS FROM 1565 TO 1975

It is unfortunate that the early links that connected China to some islands in the Philippines were almost ruptured when the Western colonizers (the Spaniards and later on the Americans) landed on Philippine shores and after the Philippine government expressed almost unqualified support to the East Asia policies of the United States during the Cold War period (which were anti-communist and, therefore, anti-China).

From 1565 until June 1975, or for more than 400 years, the colonial authorities in the Philippines and the Philippine government officials after World War II adopted policies and pursued initiatives that had the effect of creating a cleavage or a distance between the Philippines and the Filipino people on one hand and China and the Chinese people on the other.

For more than 400 years, Philippine authorities displayed an ambivalent and often suspicious attitude towards China and the Chinese. While the Chinese in the Philippines were tolerated because their businesses generated revenues for the government and provided employment to the local people, they were viewed with suspicion because of their rebellious nature, their continued allegiance to China, the "close" and "exclusive" nature of their families and organizations, and their tendency to become more affluent than the locals. From 1949 to 1975, the perception of the Philippine government was similar to the perception of the early Spanish governor generals in the Philippines — that China, because it is a communist state, is a threat to the security of the Philippines and its people and, therefore, needs to be contained. To achieve this objective, the Philippines concluded a Mutual Defence Treaty with the United States in 1951 and allowed the latter to establish military bases in its territory.

1. During Spanish Colonial Rule

The Philippines was under Spanish colonial rule from 1565 to 1898. During this time, the Chinese in the Philippines were often viewed by the Spanish colonial authorities with suspicion, exploited and harassed, and always closely monitored. This came about because of some unfortunate developments during the early years of the Spanish occupation such as: (a) the clash between a Spanish reconnaissance fleet and a Chinese trading fleet off Mindoro on 8 May 1570; (b) the attack in Manila by Limahong, a Chinese pirate barely four years after the founding of the city in 1574 — he almost succeeded if not for the timely arrival of Spanish reinforcements; (c) the misunderstanding between Omocon, an emissary of the Viceroy of Fujian and Spanish Governor General Francisco de Sande in 1575 — this prompted Sande to plan an armed invasion of China; (d) the mutiny staged by the Chinese rowers of Spanish Governor Gomez Dasmarinas' galley which resulted in his death and that of his men; and (e) the arrival of several Chinese war junks demanding the handover to China of Chinese pirates who were still in the Philippines.[9] The latter development exacerbated the suspicion of the Spanish authorities:

> The Spaniards did not believe them. Instead, they fortified the city and brought all the Spanish forces in the Philippines to Manila. Chinese attempts to capture and punish the Chinese pirates and renegades were misinterpreted by the Spaniards as a Chinese invasion or of an impending uprising by the Chinese in the city.[10]

There are no available records or documents that show that China ever thought of occupying or invading the Philippines when it was under Spanish colonial rule. However, there are a lot of data that show that some Spanish colonial authorities in Manila wanted to conquer China using the Philippines as a staging ground. It was reported that

> in 1573, Diego de Artera wrote the Spanish crown for permission to survey China preparatory to trade and future conquest. Governor Aguilar told the Spanish Council that a well-trained battallon could defeat the Chinese armies. In 1586, Governor Santiago de Vera proposed to the King the annexation of China to the Spanish empire.[11]

Fortunately, the King of Spain in 1586 disapproved of any invasion or annexation of China and instead favoured the establishment of friendly relations with the Chinese. In response to this royal policy, the Spanish authorities in Manila thought of pursuing direct trade with China. But they were not able to carry this out since China had already established direct trade arrangements at that time with other European countries like Portugal, France and the Netherlands. Eventually, the Spanish authorities made use of the Chinese traders as middlemen. These Chinese traders contributed to the success of the Manila-Acapulco galleon trade — the only form of direct foreign trade allowed by the Spanish colonial authorities between the Philippines and the outside world from 1565 to 1815. The big profits expected from the galleon trade made the

> Chinese immigrants converged at the Parian or Alcaiceria of Manila in Binondo as early as 1637. By 1687, a community of Christian Chinese and mestizos was already formally based in Binondo. Retail and small credit business came under the control of Chinese mestizos.[12]

As mentioned earlier, the Chinese in Manila were the subject of harassment, extortion, arbitrary taxes and other forms of exactions. As a result, the Chinese revolted several times against the Spanish colonial authorities: first in 1603, and then in 1639. The Spaniards retaliated against the Chinese by pursuing policies that resulted in their segregation, expulsion and restriction of their immigration. So that they could be easily monitored, the Chinese were restricted to a place in Manila called Parian — their de facto detention area without bars. During the entire Spanish colonial occupation, the Chinese in the Philippines staged fourteen revolts. Since Spain colonized the Philippines from 1565 to 1898, or for 333 years, this means that there was one Chinese revolt every twenty-four years.

The anti-Chinese policies of the Spanish colonial authorities became more pronounced after the British military forces invaded and occupied Manila and its environs from 1762 to 1764. The Chinese supported the British forces because they had a common enemy — the Spaniards. However, when the British forces withdrew from the Philppines,

> the Chinese — whether they collaborated or not with the British — were massacred and the survivors were ordered expelled. Only Christian Chinese were allowed to remain.[13]

But the Spanish colonial authorities were not able to strictly implement their anti-Chinese policies for several reasons: (a) the willingness of the Chinese to pay the authorities (or bribe their way) to secure their person, family and businesses; (b) the end of the galleon trade in 1821 — which resulted in a dramatic drop in the income of the Spanish colonial government from foreign trade; and (c) the urgent need of the colonial government for funds (and the Chinese served as their veritable "milking cows").

The Spanish colonial authorities in Manila thought of promoting the Manila-China junk trade as an alternative to the galleon trade that ended when Mexico gained its independence from Spain in 1821. Thus, they unveiled a number of pro-Chinese policies: (a) Chinese immigration to the Philippines was encouraged; (b) decrees were issued to eliminate the petty taxes imposed on the Chinese traders; (c) a decree was issued giving the Chinese the right to choose their occupation; (d) Chinese traders coming to the Philippines were granted the most favoured nation treatment; and (e) the Chinese were granted permission to organize regional and trade associations, in addition to guild, religious and musical organizations.

Because of these pro-Chinese policies, China emerged as the principal export market of the Philippines in 1899 and ranked first as the source of Philippine imports.[14] Table 2.1 shows the distribution of Philippine imports and exports in 1899 (by country). The breakdown of Philippine-China trade from 1855 to 1895 is shown in Table 2.2.

These pro-Chinese policies of the colonial authorities gave rise to anti-Chinese sentiments. It was reported that

> the unprecedented Chinese immigration in the 1830s led to the spread of Chinese all over the Philippines. The Chinese not only moved into new fields of commerce, but competed in all kinds of commercial, trade and craft activities, dislodging the mestizos, Spanish traders and laborers in urban and rural areas. Their success led to the rise of anti-Chinese sentiments even among the native population. This time, anti-Chinese conviction was not

TABLE 2.1
Philippine Foreign Trade, 1899
(by country)

Country	Exports (in pesos)	Exports (percentage of total)	Imports (in pesos)	Imports (percentage of total)
China	8,027,012	27.0	16,666,886	43.00
Great Britain	7,603,990	23.8	6,488,218	17.00
United States	7,870,510	26.0	2,706,172	7.00
Spain	1,954,212	6.5	5,404,316	14.00
Japan	2,044,040	6.9	368,796	0.96

Source: Eufronio Alip, *Ten Centuries of Philippine-China Relations* (Manila: Alip and Sons Incorporated, 1959).

TABLE 2.2
Philippine-China Trade during the Spanish Occupation, 1855 to 1895
(in pesos)

Year	Imports from China	Exports to China	Total	Balance
1855	not indicated	not indicated	2,198,187	not indicated
1865	not indicated	not indicated	14,017,486	not indicated
1875	456,965	41,856	498,821	415,106
1880	768,005	39,563	807,568	828,442
1885	485,189	66,339	551,528	418,850
1890	4,749,054	9,143,994	13,893,048	4,394,940
1895	4,601,555	6,764,621	11,366,176	2,163,086

Source: Eufronio Alip, *Ten Centuries of Philippine-China Relations* (Manila: Alip and Sons Incorporated, 1959).

related to the Filipino identification with Spanish culture and religion but to economic competition.[15]

In 1868, China signed the Burlingame Treaty with the United States. Under the treaty, China was obliged "to establish consulates to protect the lives and properties of the Chinese in foreign countries".[16] China started to do this beginning in 1878.

In 1880, the Chinese in the Philippines requested China to negotiate with Spain for the establishment of a Chinese consulate in Manila. However, the Spanish colonial authorities initially rejected the request for several reasons — one of them being their fear "that a consulate would give the Chinese opportunity to intervene in the colonial governance of the Chinese in the Philippines".[17]

The Chinese in the Philippines appealed for the establishment of a Chinese consulate in Manila because it was apparent the pro-Chinese posture of the Spanish colonial authorities after 1821 was just an expedient and "damage control" reaction to the abrupt end of the Manila-Acapulco galleon trade. The Chinese wanted a consulate to protect themselves from the "excessive and inequitable taxation, insecurity of property against theft and the extortionate practices of Spanish officials".[18]

When the Philippine Revolution against Spain broke out in 1896, the Chinese had mixed reactions. Many rich Chinese refused to support the Filipino revolutionaries and the Spanish colonial forces. Nonetheless, there were some Chinese mestizos (like General Ignacio Paua from Bicol) who joined the revolutionary forces led by General Emilio Aguinaldo. It should be mentioned that Dr Jose Rizal, the foremost national hero of the Philippines, had Chinese blood. Rizal was executed by the Spanish authorities in 1896 even though he did not support the revolution and his advocacy was only for peaceful reforms.

The Chinese suffered much during the revolution period. Many of them were killed and arrested indiscriminately by the Spaniards and their economic enterprises damaged and looted by soldiers from both sides. At that time, the Chinese felt the urgent need for a consulate in Manila that could protect their lives and property. Since they were not sure whether Spain would allow the establishment of a Chinese consulate, nearly half of them from Manila abandoned their homes and left for Hong Kong while the revolution was going on.

The Spaniards only consented to the establishment of a Chinese consulate in Manila in July 1898 — more than two months after U.S. Commodore George Dewey defeated the Spanish naval forces in the Philippines that signalled the start of the second phase of the Philippine revolution against Spain, the impending end of Spanish colonial rule in the Philippines, the start of the American occupation of the islands, and the beginning of the Philippine revolution against the Americans.

2. During American Rule

The Philippines was under American colonial rule from 1898 to 1946, a period of forty-eight years.

Unlike the Spaniards during the initial years of their rule, the Americans did not initiate violent actions against the Chinese when they took over the Philippines from Spain in 1898. In fact, they even allowed China to establish a consulate in Manila and the first Chinese consul arrived in Manila in January 1899.

However, the Americans adopted and implemented policies that continued Spain's discriminatory treatment of the Chinese. These laws or policies: (a) prohibited Chinese immigration to the Philippines; (b) abolished the Gremio de Chinos; (c) disallowed the Chinese from acquiring lands except by hereditary succession; and (d) required all merchants (like the Chinese) to keep an account of their business in English, Spanish or any Philippine dialect.

The Philippine Commonwealth government established during the later part of the American rule also had its share of perceived anti-Chinese policies. It adopted policies that (a) prevented the Chinese (and other foreigners except the Americans) from practising their profession in the Philippines; and (b) fixed the annual immigration quota of any foreign nationality to not more than 500 — this means that not more than 500 Chinese can enter the Philippines in one year.

It was obvious that the American authorities and later on the Philippine Commonwealth officials were limiting the entry of the Chinese immigrants — because of fear that their unregulated entry could result in their control of the Philippine economy, a situation that could be prejudicial to the Philippines upon the restoration of its independence by the United States in 1946 and to the vested interests of American businessmen.

But the exclusion policies against the Chinese were not successful. It should be recalled that there were only about 50,000 Chinese in the Philippines when the Americans came. In 1904, many of the Chinese who fled to Hong Kong as a result of the 1896 Philippine Revolution returned (by now, the Chinese population swelled to more or less 100,000). Between 1903 and 1909, the number of Chinese in the Philippines increased three times for at least two reasons: (a) the need of the colonial government for skilled labour which the Chinese immigrants could provide; and (b) the illegal entry of Chinese who represented themselves as relatives of legitimate Chinese residents in the Philippines.

While there was an increase in the Chinese population, there was also an increase in their investments. "By 1939, total Chinese investments in the Philippines reached US$100 million, second to U.S. investment of US$3,315 million".[19] It was reported that

> the Chinese controlled 75–82 per cent of retail trade and operated credit facilities, directed and financed the production of rice and other staples, as well as tobacco, hemp and copra. They also invested in the logging and timber industry, manufacturing, banking and real estate.[20]

There was also an increase in Philippine-China trade. But like in the past, the trade balance remained in favour of China. This meant that Philippine imports from China exceeded the value of its exports (see Table 2.3).

During World War II, many of the Chinese in the Philippines who were Kuomintang (KMT) or communist sympathizers supported the Filipinos in their war against the Japanese because the latter was a common enemy. The reaction of the Chinese in the Philippines was expected after Japan invaded and plundered China during World War II. It was disclosed that

> both KMT and communist sympathizers established a training base for guerrilla warfare in the Philippines. The communist sympathizers later

TABLE 2.3
Philippine-China Trade during the American Occupation, 1900–45
(in pesos)

Year	Imports from China	Exports to China	Total	Balance
1900	15,476,964	8,219,642	23,696,606	7,257,322
1905	8,721,822	1,847,012	10,568,834	3,874,810
1910	5,153,152	1,481,462	6,634,614	3,671,690
1915	4,662,162	3,243,493	7,905,655	1,418,669
1920	21,487,364	4,428,117	25,915,481	18,059,247
1925	13,927,998	6,939,840	20,867,838	6,988,158
1930	11,277,190	4,215,440	15,492.630	7,061,750
1935	5,603,237	1,892,106	7,495,343	3,811,131
1940	6,211,560	3,687,494	9,899,054	2,524,066
1945	25,272	18,370	43,642	6,902

Source: Eufronio Alip, *Ten Centuries of Philippine-China Relations* (Manila: Alip and Sons, 1959).

organized the Hwa Chi combat units, joined the Hukbalahaps in carrying out guerrilla warfare against the Japanese and subsequently linking up with the U.S. armed forces in liberating the Philippines. The Hwa Chi combat units operated in Central and Southern Luzon as well as in the Visayas, while the KMT's Hsueh Kan Tuan operated in Northern Luzon and Baguio.[21]

Thus, it could be seen that the war gave the Filipinos and the Chinese in the Philippines the opportunity to relate and cooperate with one another because they were fighting a common enemy — the Japanese. However, it should be mentioned that even before the war, there was already increasing interaction between the locals and the Chinese. It was common at that time (and this has continued until today in some areas) to see in most Philippine villages Chinese retail stores where the locals buy their food and other day-to-day necessities — many times on credit and without interest. The Chinese store owner usually employed Filipino assistants, at times had a Filipina as a wife, and many times was taken as godfather in the wedding of daughters and sons of Filipino customer-friends (and in the christening of their children). In many community activities, the Chinese store owner became a participant since he was usually requested to contribute funds to finance these activities. When there is a wedding, death, or an emergency that required immediate and large cash outlay, the affected parties usually go to the Chinese store owner to negotiate a loan. If the person is a friend or endorsed by friends, the Chinese store owner usually obliged.

Thus, it could be seen that while the national authorities based in Manila were adopting and applying exclusion policies against the Chinese, the Chinese retail store owners and traders had already managed to establish rapport and build alliances with most Filipinos served by their stores and credit support. Undoubtedly, there was already a partial but steady assimilation of the Chinese going on in the communities where they transacted their business.

3. During the Post-World War II Period (1946 to 1975)

The Philippines regained its independence in 1946. However, because of its vulnerabilities that were worsened by the effects of World War II and its close relations with the United States, it had difficulty adopting realistic, independent and non-ideological domestic and foreign policies. The end of the war made the Philippines too dependent on the United States for its national security and economic growth. This dependence on the United States became more pronounced because of domestic issues (like the threat posed by communist insurgents and widening poverty), regional issues (like the establishment of Communist China in 1949 and the spread of communism in East Asia), and the advent of the Cold War (which served the strategic interests of the United States as a superpower and polarized the world, especially East Asia).

These developments had a marked impact on Philippine-China relations and Filipino-Chinese relations. The Chinese became the convenient scapegoat for the country's economic problems, and this was more or less formalized when the Philippine Congress adopted a law nationalizing Philippine retail trade — to wrest control of retail trade from foreigners, especially the Chinese.

During the Cold War era, Philippine authorities retained the anti-Chinese content of the policies adopted during the Spanish period and American occupation for several reasons: (a) the victory of communist forces in China and the rise of China as a communist state in 1949 was regarded as a threat to the national security of the Philippines; (b) continuing the status quo whereby the Chinese retained control of the Philippine economy, especially its retail trade and other businesses, was prejudicial to Philippine independence; and (c) assisting the United States in containing communist China and other communist states and the spread of communism in East Asia and other parts of the world would be in its national interests since this would result not only in winning the goodwill of the United States (and its allies) but also in enhancing regional and global peace and stability. In fact, there was one Philippine President (Elpidio Quirino) who incurred the ire of the United

States (and therefore was dumped by it in the next presidential election) when he gave passive support to the establishment of Communist China while on a trip to the United States in 1950.

The Cold War and its special relations with the United States made the Philippines adopt anti-communist policies that were invariably anti-China. It allowed the United States to keep its military bases in its territory as the Philippine way of supporting its anti-communist posture in East Asia and Asia Pacific; it signed a Mutual Defence Treaty with the United States to defend itself from external communist attack; it supported the U.S. military operations in the Korean War, in the process fighting the communist North Koreans who were supported by China; it supported the formation of the SEATO, a United States-initiated collective defence arrangement aimed at helping the United States in its anti-communist war in Indo-China; and it supported the United States-led military operations in South Vietnam during the Vietnam War to prevent communist North Vietnam from gaining control of the south (the North Vietnamese forces were supported by China).

But what was most anti-China of the initiatives taken by the Philippines after 1949 was its support for the Taiwan policy of the United States and its establishment of diplomatic relations with Taiwan — because of U.S. pressures. This meant that the Philippines considered the Republic of China (ROC) led by General Chiang Kai-shek as the one with legitimate authority over all of China; and that it would not issue travel documents to Filipinos who wanted to visit the China mainland either as students, businessmen, artists, tourists, etc. Because the Huks and the CPP-NPA are communist organizations that threatened the national security of the Philippines and because China is a communist state, Philippine authorities invariably suspected China of providing support to the local communists. As a result, the Philippine authorities considered China as a major external security threat. Of course, during the Cold War period, other communist states such as the Soviet Union and those from Eastern Europe were also in this threat category — because these countries were defined by the United States as security threats to the "Free World".

Locally, Philippine authorities adopted laws that criminalized mere membership of a communist organization and banned Filipinos from travelling to communist and socialist states like China, the Soviet Union, North Vietnam and North Korea. At that time, Filipinos suspected of having links or interacting with mainland China (and other communist states) were monitored and questioned by security and police agencies and were labelled as communists or communist sympathizers. Even Filipinos who were just critical of the anomalies and scandals in the government and who wanted reforms in a peaceful manner were also labelled as communist sympathizers. This sweeping and almost fanatical anti-communist orientation of the Philippine authorities divided the country, became an excuse for silencing legitimate dissent, and contributed to the radicalization of the nationalist and moderate forces as well as some religious groups.

Because of its anti-communist policies, Philippine trade with China suffered a dramatic decline while its trade with Taiwan posted a dramatic increase. These are presented in Tables 2.4 and 2.5. It can be seen that Philippine trade with China between 1950 and 1972 was minimal — mostly imports (see Table 2.4). The figures in Table 2.5 show that with respect to Philippine trade with Taiwan, the trade balance was in favour of the Philippines from 1952 to 1970. In 1975, however, the trade balance started to favour Taiwan.

"RECONNECTING" WITH CHINA: SURVEY OF PHILIPPINE-CHINA RELATIONS FROM 1975 TO 1990

In 1975, a dramatic foreign policy shift took place in the Philippines. Under Cold War conditions, the Philippine government headed by President Marcos decided to establish diplomatic relations with China and adopt the one-China policy which states that

> the Philippines recognizes the government of the P.R.C. as the sole legal government and respects the position of the Chinese government that

TABLE 2.4
Philippine Trade with China, 1950–75
(*in pesos; all others in US$)

Year	Exports	Imports	Total Foreign Trade
1950	*2,581,303	*7,201,956	*9,783,259
1955		817,072	817,072
1971	401,805	1,006,390	1,408,195
1972	782,550	5,530,309	6,312,859
1973	6,571,480	21,924,670	27,889,132
1974	13,306,657	23,924,670	37,231,327
1975	25,215,777	47,036,027	72,251,804

Source: Data for 1950 and 1955 came from Eufronio Alip, *Ten Centuries of Philippine-China Relations* (Manila: Alip and Sons, Incorporated, 1959). All others came from Benito Lim, *The Political Economy of Philippine-China Relations* (Philippines-APEC Study Center Network, 1999). There are no available data from 1956 to 1970.

TABLE 2.5
Taiwan Trade with the Philippines 1952–75
(in US$)

Year	Exports to RP	Imports from RP	Total
1952	76,000	740,000	816,000
1955	203,000	1,615,000	1,818,000
1960	1,848,000	3,049,000	4,897,000
1965	6,188,000	13,217,000	19,405,000
1970	16,251,000	20,659,000	36,910,000
1975	82,024,000	33,296,000	115,320,000

Note: Taiwan exports to RP are RP's imports from Taiwan while Taiwan imports from RP are RP's exports to Taiwan.
Source: Taiwan Statistical Databook, 2006.

there is but one China and that Taiwan is an integral part of the Chinese territory.[22]

The shift reversed an earlier policy expressed by the Philippines in the twenty-sixth Regular Session of the UN General Assembly which expressed support to the "two-China" proposal of the United States. In that U.N. General Assembly session, then Foreign Affairs Secretary Carlos P. Romulo said:

The Philippine position is based on the recognition of the fact that the two Governments — the Government of the People's Republic of China and the Government of the Republic of China — claim the right to represent the Chinese people or the Chinese state in the UN.

The reality of this situation has two aspects. It is an undeniable fact that since the founding of the UN, the Republic of China has continuously represented China in this Organization. Year after year, the General Assembly has upheld this continuous representation of China by the Republic of China in all bodies of the UN including the Security Council.

But it is also a fact that since 1949, the Government of the People's Republic of China has had effective control and authority over mainland China, while the Government of the Republic of China has had effective control and authority over other parts of the Chinese State, particularly Taiwan. Each has been accorded diplomatic recognition by an overwhelming number of nations.

The Philippine delegation, in a spirit of frankness and objectivity with respect to the existing situation, believes that the fair, just and realistic solution would be for both the Republic of China and the People's Republic of China to be seated in the General Assembly and be eligible to become members of other bodies of the UN.[23]

The Philippines reconnected with China in 1975 for a number of reasons: (a) its urgent need for an alternative export market and as source of capital goods in view of the end of the Laurel-Langley Agreement in 1974 (this agreement gave Philippine exports preferential access in the U.S. market provided these do not exceed the specified quotas); (b) its need to cut off the rumoured China's support to the communist insurgents that aimed to overthrow the Philippine government; (c) its need for an independent and more balanced foreign policy that will support peace, cooperation and amity with all nations; (d) its need to address promptly the problems concerning the overstaying Chinese in the Philippines; (e) its need to coexist with China given its steady rise as a major power in East Asia; (f) the steady normalization of relations between China, the ASEAN member-states and most countries composing the international community; (g) the improved relations between China and the United States; and (h) the consistent reiteration by China that it wants to have peaceful and mutually beneficial relations with all countries in the world and it does not have hegemonic ambitions as claimed by its critics.

This "reconnection" with China resulted in increased trade and state-to-state and people-to-people interaction between the two countries and the entry of more and more Chinese investments in the Philippines (see Tables 2.6 to 2.11). These occurred despite the continued existence of the Cold War, the close economic relations of the Philippines with the United States, Japan and Taiwan, and the anti-communist orientation of some influential sectors in Philippine society like the military and defence establishment.

It should be mentioned that prior to formally establishing diplomatic relations with China, the Philippines went through a long process of review and soul searching. Its efforts in this direction started in 1966, when President Marcos thought of the possibility of establishing trade relations with communist states because of the decreasing trade of the Philippines with the United States (its principal export market) and the impending end of the Laurel-Langley Agreement which gave Philippine products preferential access in the U.S. market, provided these do not exceed the stated quotas Diplomatic relations with China (and the Soviet Union) became possible only eight years later after the National Security Council and the Foreign Policy Council of the Philippines approved the position of Marcos on 4 October 1974. It took the Philippines another eight months to carry this out.

TABLE 2.6
Philippine Trade with China, 1976–90
(in US$)

Year	Philippine Exports	Philippine Imports	Total
1976	39,551,895	53,792,649	93,344,544
1977	108,020,339	78,351,890	186,372,229
1978	47,458,012	111,627,098	159,085,110
1979	51,464,459	120,953,005	172,417,464
1980	44,986,428	205,705,312	250,691,740
1981	78,225,492	194,516,918	272,742,410
1982	105,204,859	206,327,132	311,531,991
1983	29,391,507	122,150,595	151,542,102
1984	60,185,818	220,255,977	280,441,795
1985	79,792,768	276,084,896	355,877,664
1986	104,690,000	110,690,000	215,380,000
1987	87,950,000	205,960,000	293,510,000
1988	66,800,000	242,280,000	309,080,000
1989	50,230,000	221,100,000	271,330,000
1990	61,760,000	162,100,000	223,860,000

Source: Benito Lim, *The Political Economy of Philippine-China Relations* (Philippine-APEC Study Center Network, 1999).

DEEPENING THE "CONNECTIONS": SURVEY OF PHILIPPINE-CHINA RELATIONS AFTER 1991

There were several developments that took place after 1991 that contributed to the deepening of the "reconnected relations" between the Philippines and China. These developments included the following: (a) the end of the Cold War and the ideology-based polarizations that it engendered; (b) the closure of the U.S. military facilities in the Philippines (its mission included containing China and the spread of communism in the Asia Pacific) following the refusal of the Philippine Senate to ratify the 1991 Philippine-U.S. Treaty of Friendship, Cooperation and Security; (c) improved relations between China and the United States — the long-time closest ally of the Philippines; (d) improved relations between China and the international community; (e) improved relations and deepening engagement between China and ASEAN (through the ASEAN Regional Forum, ASEAN+3 mechanism, China-ASEAN Free Trade Area, China-ASEAN Strategic Partnership Agreement, etc.); and (f) the steady rise of China as a regional power and engine of economic growth in East Asia, as a potential global power that could rival the United States, and as a major source of official development assistance to its less developed neighbours like the Philippines.

TABLE 2.7
Chinese Investments in the Philippines 1976–90
(in pesos)

Year	Amount
1976	27,515,000
1977	25,935,000
1978	9,178,000
1979	41,191,000
1980	37,995,000
1981	41,677,000
1982	36,033,000
1983	17,879,000
1984	43,255,000
1985	111,895,000
1986	38,236,000
1987	169,425,000
1988	556,665,000
1989	740,485,000
1990	441,497,000

Source: Florencio Mallare, "Unification Process of China and its Implications for the Philippines", in *China, Taiwan and the Ethnic Chinese in the Philippine Economy*, edited by Ellen Palanca (Quezon City: Philippine Association of Chinese Studies, 1995).

TABLE 2.8
Filipino Investments in China 1984–90

Year	No. of Projects	Amount
1984	4	2,100,000
1985	22	40,560,000
1986	9	3,810,000
1987	10	30,500,000
1988	22	15,530,000
1989	12	4,710,000
1990	18	10,780,000

Source: Aileen Baviera, *Comprehensive Engagement: Strategic Issues in Philippine-China Relations* (Manila: Philippine-China Development Resource Center, 2000).

TABLE 2.9
Major Philippine-China Bilateral Agreements, 1976–90

No.	Year	Bilateral Agreement Memorandum of Agreement
1	1975	Trade Agreement
2	1976	Memorandum of Agreement for the exhibition of Chinese products in Manila
3	1978	Agreement on cooperation in the field of agriculture and other related areas; Agreement on scientific and technical cooperation
4	1979	Memorandum of Understanding on Scientific and Technical Cooperation in agriculture
5	1989	Agreement to expand bilateral trade over a five-year period to US$800 million
6	1990	Agreement on tourism

Source: Edgardo Dagdag, *Instructional Materials on Philippine-China Relations* (Asian Center, 2005).

TABLE 2.10
Selected Initiatives of the Philippine Government
Towards China and the Filipino-Chinese, 1975–90

Year	Philippine Initiative
1975	President Marcos issued Letter of Instruction (LOI) 270 creating a special committee on naturalization and providing for mass naturalization of aliens by presidential decree. (11 April)
1975	President Marcos issued LOI 292 authorizing Chinese nationals applying for Philippine citizenship to apply for a change of name. (9 July)
1975	President Marcos issued Presidential Decree (PD) 275 authorizing the Special Committee on Naturalization to screen applications for repatriation of Filipino women who lost their citizenship through marriage to aliens, and natural born Filipinos who lost their citizenship in some other way. (1 August)
1976	President Marcos issued PD 885 amending the 1957 anti-subversion law. Under the 1957 law, mere membership in a communist organization like the CPP-NPA is already a crime. This provision was repealed by PD 885.
1984	Imelda Marcos, wife of President Marcos, visited China.
1986	President Aquino extended the Executive Programme of the RP-China Cultural Agreement.
1987	President Aquino extended again the Executive Programme of the RP-China Cultural Agreement.
1988	President Aquino made a personal and state visit to China.
1989	President Aquino visited China for the second time.

Source: Edgardo Dagdag, *Instructional Materials on Philippine-China Relations* (Asian Center, UP Diliman, 2005).

TABLE 2.11
Selected Initiatives of the Chinese Government
Towards the Philippines, 1976–90

Year	China Initiatives
1976	China held archeological and trade exhibits in Manila.
1978	China's Vice Prime Minister and Vice Chairman of the Chinese Communist Party, Li Hsien-nien and Foreign Minister Huang Hua visited the Philipines. During their visit, the Philippine-China Agreement on scientific and technical cooperation was signed.
1980	China extended a US$30 million loan to the Philippines for the purchase of 500 min-hydropower plants.
1981	Chinese Prime Minister Zhao Ziyang made a state visit to the Philippines. He was accompanied by other high-ranking Chinese officials. During Zhao's visit, China agreed to supply the Philippines crude oil at concessional rates, increase its importation of Philippine coconut oil and facilitate Philippine purchase of high-grade coal from China. Zhao pledged that China would not intervene in Philippine internal affairs.
1984	During the visit of Mrs Marcos, China agreed to increase its trade volume with the Philippines, buy more Philippine products, and supply the Philippines US$60 million worth of oil on deferred payment basis.
1989	During the visit of President Aquino, Chinese officials reiterated their policy of non-interference in Philippine domestic affairs and their support of President Aquino's government; donated 10,000 metric tons of rice to the Philippines; and agreed to increase bilateral trade with the Philippines to US$800 million over a five-year period.

Source: Edgardo Dagdag, *Instructional Materials on Philippine-China Relations* (Asian Center, UP Diliman, 2005).

Many Filipino leaders today from the public and private sectors tend to worry less about China, despite its being a communist state. Now, they talk more about the opportunities and benefits that may be derived by the Philippines if it pursues an independent and development-oriented foreign policy that allows close relations and long-term partnership not only with its traditional allies (like the United States and Japan), but also with emerging powers like China.

These post-1991 developments resulted in (a) more bilateral agreements between the Philippines and China and more multilateral agreements between ASEAN and China that promote and sustain bilateral and multilateral cooperation in various fields; (b) more trade between the Philippines and China; (c) more Chinese investment in the Philippines and more Filipino investment in China; (d) more development assistance from China to the

Philippines; and (e) more comprehensive and sustained cooperation between the two countries and their nationals in various fields of endeavour. The results of these deepening connections or interaction between China and the Philippines after 1991 are best shown in their trade and investment relations — see Table 2.12 (Philippine Trade with China, 1992–2006), Table 2.13 (Major Trading Partners of the Philippines, 2006), Table 2.14 (Chinese Investments in the Philippines after 1991), and Table 2.15 (Filipino Investments in China after 1991).

Table 2.12 shows that from 1991 to 1999, the trade balance was in favour of China. But there was a turnaround starting in 2001 when the trade balance started to be in favour of the Philippines. This means that presently, Philippine exports exceed Philippine imports and its trade with China is working to its advantage.

In 2006, China was the third largest trading partner of the Philippines, accounting for 8.3 per cent of its total foreign trade. (However, if one includes the Philippine exports going to Hong Kong, the overall China total will be 17.6 per cent — good for Number Two spot.) The Top Two were the United States (17.3 per cent) and Japan (15.3 per cent). Trade balance was in favour of the Philippines, insofar as its three major trade partners are concerned.[24] The data concerning the major trade partners of the Philippines in 2006 are presented in Table 2.13.

TABLE 2.12
Philippine Trade with China, 1992–2006*
(in US$)

Year	Philippines' Exports	Philippines' Imports	Trade Volume
1991	127,769,000	223,499,000	351,268,000
1993	173,874,000	180,663,000	354,537,000
1995	213,966,000	578,619,000	792,585,000
1997	244,412,000	871,594,000	1,116,008,000
1999	574,808,000	1,038,420,000	1,613,228,000
2001	1,950,000,000	1,620,000,000	3,570,000,000
2003	6,300,000,000	3,100,000,000	9,400,000,000
2004	9,060,000,000	4,270,000,000	13,330,000,000
2005	4,080,000,000	2,970,000,000	7,050,000,000
2006	4,627,660,000	3,647,350,000	8,275,010,000

Note: *This does not include the foreign trade figures between the Philippines and Hong Kong.
Source: National Statistics Office, Philippines.

TABLE 2.13
Major Trading Partners of the Philippines, 2006
(percentage of total Philippine foreign trade)

Country	Export	Import
United States	18.3	16.3
Japan	16.7	14.0
Netherlands	10.1	
China	9.8	7.0
Hong Kong	7.8	
Singapore		8.5
Taiwan		8.0
Others	37.3	46.2

Source: National Statistics Office (Philippines).

The data on Chinese investments in the Philipppines after 1991 are shown in Table 2.14.

Chinese investments in the Philippines, as a percentage of the total foreign investments in the Philippines, are increasing although still low. The Chinese investments in 2000 and 2001 were only 0.2 per cent of the total foreign investments received by the Philippines during those years. This went up to

TABLE 2.14
Chinese Investments in the Philippines after 1991
(in US$)

Year	Amount
1995	13,700,000
1996	3,100,000
1997	1,970,000
1998	884,000,000
1999	111,400,000
2000	48,480,000
2001	146,400,000*
2002	892,800,000*
2003	39,600,000
2004	684,000,000
2005	3,800,000
2006	340,000,000

Note: * Investment amount in Philippine pesos.
Source: National Statistics Office (Philippines).

2 per cent in 2002. Approved Chinese investments in 2006, which amounted to P17 billion, is 11.7 per cent of the total approved foreign investments for the year — more than seven times higher than the Chinese investments in 2000. This means that China is fast becoming a major investor in the Philippines.

Ambassador Li, Chinese Ambassador to the Philippines, was reported in the Philippine media as saying that

> many Chinese investors have eyed investments in Mindanao, particularly in tourism, agriculture, fisheries, mining and infrastructure. However, Chinese businessmen are just waiting for developments because they are worried about the little and incorrect information they know about Mindanao.[25]

It should be mentioned that the Filipinos, particularly the Filipino Chinese, are also investors in China, especially in Guangdong, Fujian and Shanghai. This makes investments between the two countries a two-way activity. The amount of Filipino investments in China after 1991 is shown in Table 2.15.

TABLE 2.15
Filipino Investments in China after 1991
(in US$)

Year	Amount
1992	16,300,000
1993	122,500,000
1994	140,400,000
1996	55,500,000
1998	144,400,000
2000	111,100,000
2001	209,400,000
2002	186,000,000
2006	542,690,000

Source: Data for years 1992 to 2002 are from the *Yearbook of China's Foreign Economic Relations and Trade, 1993, 1994, 1995, 1997, 1999, 2001 and 2002*. These were cited in the paper of Liao Shaolian entitled "Sino-Philippine Economic Relations: Features and Prospects for the Future". Data for 2006 are from the study of the Institute of National Security Studies of the National Defense College of the Philippines entitled "Overview of Philippine-China Relations".

The close relations and interactions between the Philippines and China after 1991 also came about because of the following: (a) the designation of China as one of the dialogue partners of ASEAN (and as such, as one of the regular participants in the ASEAN Regional Forum (ARF); (b) the establishment of the ASEAN+3 mechanism in 1997 to enhance economic and other forms of cooperation between the ASEAN countries and China (and two other Northeast Asian states); (c) the establishment of the China-ASEAN Free Trade Area (CAFTA); and (d) the establishment of a strategic partnership for peace and prosperity between China and the ASEAN countries in 2003.

But the most important document that manifests the growing friendship and cooperation between the Philippines and China is the Framework of Bilateral Cooperation in the Twenty-first Century which they adopted on 16 May 2000. The two sides, according to the document, are committed to "establish a long-term and stable relationship on the basis of good neighborliness, cooperation, and mutual trust and benefit" and to "elevate Philippines-China relations to greater heights in the twenty-first century".[26]

To attain these two objectives, both China and the Philippines agreed to: (a) respect the independence, sovereignty and territorial integrity of each other; (b) maintain close and frequent high-level contacts and exchange of visits at all levels; (c) have annual meetings between their foreign ministers and senior officials for consultations on bilateral, regional and international issues; (d) make further exchanges and cooperation in the military and defence field; (e) develop bilateral tourism cooperation; (f) explore new areas of cooperation among their law enforcement, judicial, security and defence agencies to address transnational crimes; (g) optimize the use of existing frameworks for cooperation in the fields of trade, investment, science and technology, agriculture, education and culture, tourism, civil aviation and taxation; (h) enhance their exchanges and cooperation in the fields of culture, arts, education, film, sports, healthcare, religion, social sciences and book publication; and (i) continue their coordination and cooperation at the ASEAN, ARF, AOEC, ASEM, WTO, UN and other multilateral fora.[27]

DEEPENING PHILIPPINE-CHINA LINKS SOCIO-CULTURALLY

What further deepens the Philippine-China connection which was officially restored in 1975 were socio-cultural factors like the continued presence and expansion of Chinese communities in the Philippines and their gradual assimilation; the adoption by Filipinos of some aspects of the Chinese culture brought by the earlier Chinese immigrants; and the rise to key positions in the public and private sector of Filipinos with Chinese blood.

It is estimated that there are 1,146,250 ethnic Chinese and 9,757,693 Filipino-Chinese (or Filipinos with Chinese blood) in the Philippines (or about 1.5 per cent and 10 per cent of the Philippine population respectively).[28] About 90 per cent of the ethnic Chinese are born in the Philippines and belong to either the second, third or fourth generation.[29] It is reported that "as many as 98.5 per cent of the Chinese in the Philippines trace their ancestry to the southern part of Fujian province" while the others are "descendants of migrants from Guangdong, Hong Kong or Taiwan".[30]

The Chinese in the Philippines

> may be classified into three types, based on when their ancestors first immigrated. Most of the Chinese mestizos, especially the landed gentry trace their ancestry to the Spanish era. They are the "First Chinese", whose descendants nowadays are mostly either the Chinese mestizos or have integrated into the local population. The largest group of Chinese Filipinos in the Philippines are the "Second Chinese", who are descendants of migrants in the first half of the twentieth century, between the Manchu revolution in China and the Chinese civil war. The group accounts for most of the full-blooded Chinese. The "Third Chinese" are the recent immigrants from mainland China after the Chinese economic reform of the 1980s. Generally, the "Third Chinese" are the most entrepreneurial and had not totally lost their Chinese cultural heritage in its purest form and therefore are paradoxically misunderstood or feared by the "Second Chinese" and "First Chinese," most of whom have lost their entrepreneurial drive and have adopted much of the laid-back Spanish cultural values of Philippine society.[31]

The ethnic Chinese and the Filipino Chinese (or Tsinoys) use the Lannang variant of Min-Nan (also known as Hokkienese or Fukien) as their lingua franca. However, because of their exposure to Filipino culture and their trading activities, most of them are also fluent in English, Tagalog and in the dialect of the region where they reside (like Ilocano, Cebuano, and Chabacano).[32] Most Filipino Chinese continue to use Chinese surnames and the most common are "Tan, Ong, Lim, Go/Ngo, Ng/Uy, Chua and Lee/Dy and Chinese surnames that have hispanized spellings such as Lacson, Biazon, Tuazon, Ongpin, Yuchengco, Quebengco, Cojuangco, Yupangco and Tanbengco".[33]

The Filipino Chinese are unique in Southeast Asia since they are overwhelmingly Christians — like most native Filipinos.

Almost all Chinese Filipinos, including the Chinese mestizos but excluding the recent immigrants, had or will have their marriage in a Christian church. This proves that the majority of Chinese Filipinos have been baptized in a Christian church with Catholics forming the largest group.

However, many Chinese Filipino Catholics still tend to practise the traditional Chinese religions side by side with Catholicism, although a small number of people practicing sole traditional Chinese religions do exist as well. Mahayana Buddhism, Taoism and ancestor worship (including Confucianism) are the traditional Chinese beliefs that continue to have adherents among the Chinese Filipinos. Some may even have Jesus Christ as well as Buddha statues or Taoist gods in their altars. It is not unheard of to venerate the blessed Virgin Mary using joss sticks and Buddhist offerings, much as one would have done for Mazu.

A comparatively large number of Chinese Filipinos are also Protestants. One of the largest evangelical churches in the Philippines, the United Evangelical Church of the Philippines, was founded by Chinese Filipinos, and they form the majority of the worshippers.[34]

While the Chinese in the Philippines and their descendants have undergone gradual acculturation, the native Filipinos also learned a lot from them. Their food, language, clothing and even cultural practices and beliefs carry traces of the Chinese influence (see Table 2.16).

Also contributing to the deepening of connections between the Filipinos and the Chinese in the Philippines are the Filipino Chinese who became heroes, public servants, successful entrepreneurs and outstanding professionals in their respective fields (see Table 2.17).

Also facilitating the cultural assimilation and integration of the Chinese in the Philippines was the growing intermarriage between the children of native Filipinos and Chinese mestizo families and the Filipinization policy adopted by the Philippine government that ultimately influenced those born in the Philippines to Chinese mestizo parents to acquire Philippine citizenship so that they could acquire lands, exercise their professions, engage in retail trade and hold public office — privileges that only Filipino citizens can enjoy.

"POSITIONING" WITH CHINA

After 1991, the trend shows continued improved relations between the Philippines and China (and the Filipinos and Chinese) in many fields. In fact, it may be said that Philippine-China relations today are quite close and could be already a source of concern to the United States, Japan and

TABLE 2.16
Some Chinese Influences on Philippine Culture
(Examples only)

Item	Chinese Influence
Food*	am-pau (ampaw); bi-hun (bihon); bi-koe (biko); di-kiam (dikyam); lun-pia (lumpia); ma-mi (mami); mi-ki (miki); mi-soa (miswa); pian-e-sit or pan-sit (pansit); ho to tay (a soup dish)
Language*	a-chi (ate or sister); bi-wo (bilao); hok-bu (hukbo or army); ko-a (kuya or brother)
Clothing	Camisa de chino (undershirt for Barong Tagalog)
Architecture**	Chinese stone lions in the entrance of Catholic Cathedral in Vigan (Ilocos Sur), Manila's San Agustin Church and other churches where the Chinese mestizos live
Cultural beliefs and practices*	Arranging marriage of children by parents; wearing white dress while in mourning; use of go-between to negotiate marriage; use of fireworks to mark the start of the New Year and important celebrations

Source: * Teodoro Agoncillo, *A Short History of the Filipino People*.
** <http:www.chinahistoryforum.com/index.php?showtopic=9779&st=30>.

of course Taiwan. If one considers the number of visits done by Philippine Presidents and high government officials to China (and vice versa), and the number of concessional development assistance and loans extended by China to the Philippines as indicators of close relations, then it may be said that Philippines-China relations today is very close indeed. This is expected to continue to grow in the future — as in the case of ASEAN-China relations in general.

While the United States, Japan and Taiwan will not publicly oppose Philippine initiatives that could bring her closer to China, it is likely that they may pressure the Philippines not to do so at their expense. These three countries have leverages in dealing with the Philippines because they are the latter's major trade partners. Moreover, the United States is its principal source of defence aid, and together with Japan, they are its principal sources of official development assistance. Indeed, having balanced relations with China and its long-time allies is not easy for the Philippines to do — not only because of their competing strategic interests in East Asia that are not easy to reconcile, but also because of its own vulnerabilities with respect to these countries.

TABLE 2.17
Outstanding Filipino Chinese and Filipinos with Chinese Blood
(Partial list only)

NAME	POSITION/ACHIEVEMENTS
Jose Rizal	National hero of the Philippines
General Ignacio Paua	One of the generals of the Philippine Revolutionary Army who led Filipino forces during the Philippine revolution against Spain
Corazon Aquino	President of the Philippines, 1986–92
Antonio Chan	Sugar tycoon
Claudio Teehankee	Retired Chief Justice of the Philippine Supreme Court
Jose Mari Chan	Popular singer and songwriter
Albino Sycip	Dean of Philippine Banking
Washington Sycip	Founder of Sycip, Gorres and Velayo (SGV), one of the largest accounting firms in Asia
Alexander Sycip	Founder of the largest and leading law firm in the Philippines
Eduardo Cojuangco	Business tycoon and politician; leader of the Nationalist People's Coalition, member of the ruling political coalition in the Philippines
John Gokongwei	Business tycoon
Andrew Gotianun	Real estate tycoon
Ferdinand Marcos	President of the Philippines, 1966–86
St. Lorenzo Ruiz	First Filipino saint
Jaime Cardinal Sin	The most influential leader of the Catholic Church during his time; one of those who caused the downfall of former President Marcos and the rise to power of President Aquino in 1986
Sergio Osmena, Sr	President of the Philippines, 1944–46; prominent Filipino nationalist
Henry Sy	Shopping mall tycoon
Lucio Tan	Business tycoon; patron of Chinese language and education
Jose Yao Campos	Founder of United Laboratories, a leading pharmaceutical company in the Philippines
Bobby Ongpin	Trade and Industry Minister of President Marcos
Tony Tan Caktiong	Fast food chain tycoon
George Ty	Banking tycoon
Alfonso Yuchengo	Insurance tycoon
Howard Dee	Former Philippine ambassador to the Vatican and Malta; business tycoon
General Vicente Lim	First Filipino graduate of West Point; Filipino World War II hero
Alfredo Lim	Incumbent Mayor of Manila, former Senator and outstanding police officer
Arthur Yap	Incumbent Secretary of Agriculture
Emilio Yap	Owner of Manila Hotel, Manila Bulletin (a nationwide newspaper), etc. and an influential business tycoon
Enrique Yuchengco	Insurance tycoon

Source: Wikipedia, the free encyclopedia <http://en.wikipedia.org/wiki/Chinese_Filipino>.

For the Philippines, it must position itself well so that it can enhance its strength and minimize its weaknesses when it deals with China (and other major powers). It can do this by pursuing the following courses of action: (a) strengthen its national power attributes; (b) avail of the negotiating strength of the ASEAN community and work through it; (c) maximize the use of the ASEAN+3 mechanism; (d) fast-track the formation of the East Asia community with ASEAN as the driving force and work through it in dealing with China; (e) contribute to the improvement of relations between China and Japan and China and the United States since improved and friendly relations among the major powers will make it easy for the Philippine to make strategic and hard decisions.

It is likely that the Philippines will have a better positioning with respect to China if it relies not only on the strength of their bilateral relations but also on the multilateral agreements that ASEAN has with China. How the Philippines will position itself with respect to a rising China in the twenty-first century is indeed a big challenge especially in the light of its close and vulnerable relations with the United States. But this task will become less difficult and formidable once ASEAN becomes a more united, credible and responsive regional organization — and a true driving force in achieving peace and prosperity in East Asia.

Notes

1. See Eufronio Alip, *Ten Centuries of Philippine-China Relations* (Manila: Alip and Sons, Incorporated, 1959).
2. Teodoro Agoncillo, *History of the Filipino People*, 8th ed. (Quezon City: Garotech Publishing, 1990), p. 24.
3. Esteban de Ocampo, "A Brief Survey of Sino-Philippine Relations", in *Philippine-Republic of China Scholars' Conference on Economic Development* (Manila: Jose Rizal-Sun Yat Sen Society, Inc., 1982). Cited in Analyn de Leon, "Assessment of Philippine-China Economic Relations (1975–91)", p. 5.
4. See Benito Lim, "A History of Philippine-China Relations", in *Philippine External Relations: A Centennial Vista*, edited by Aileen Baviera and Lydia Yu-Jose (Manila: Foreign Service Institute, 1998). The article of Lim is a valuable source of information on the history of Philippine-China relations. He is a Filipino Chinese and a retired professor of the Asian Center, UP Diliman.
5. Ibid.
6. See Teodoro Agoncillo, *History of the Filipino People*, p. 25.
7. See Cesar Adib Majul, *Muslims in the Philippines* (Quezon City: University of the Philippines, Asian Center, 1974).
8. Lim, "A History of Philippine-China Relations", in *Philippine External Relations: A Centennial Vista*, edited by Baviera and Jose, p. 205.

9. Ibid., p. 205.
10. Ibid., p. 206.
11. Ibid.
12. Agoncillo, *History of the Filipino People*, pp. 85–86.
13. See Lim, "A History of Philippine-China Relations", in *Philippine External Relations: A Centennial Vista*, edited by Baviera and Jose, p. 207.
14. See Alip, *Ten Centuries of Philippine-China Relations*.
15. See Lim, "A History of Philippine-China Relations", in *Philippine External Relations: A Centennial Vista*, edited by Baviera and Jose, p. 211.
16. Ibid.
17. Ibid., p. 212.
18. Ibid.
19. Ibid, p. 219.
20. Agoncillo, *History of the Filipino People*, p. 366.
21. See Lim, "A History of Philippine-China Relations", in *Philippine External Relations: A Centennial Vista*, edited by Baviera and Jose, p. 220.
22. See Article III of the Joint Communiqué establishing diplomatic relations between Philippines and China, 1975.
23. See Lim, "A History of Philippine-China Relations", in *Philippine External Relations: A Centennial Vista*, edited by Baviera and Yu-Jose, p. 238.
24. Data came from the National Statistics Office, 2006.
25. Walter Balane, "China Eyes Multibillion Dollar Investments in Mindanao", *Minda News*, 26 July 2006.
26. See "Joint Statement Between the Government of the Republic of the Philippine and the Government of the People's Republic of China in the Framework of Bilateral Cooperation in the Twenty-First Century".
27. Ibid.
28. See <http://en.wikipedia.org/wiki/Chinese_Filipino>. According to KAISA-Angelo King Heritage Center (a major and very active Tsinoy NGO in the Philippines), the ethnic Chinese in the Philippines "number from 750,000 to one million, or roughly between 1.2 per cent and 1.5 per cent of the Philippine population; that about 52 per cent of the ethnic Chinese in the Philippines are in Metro Manila; and that native Filipinos with Chinese blood comprise about 10% of the Philippine population — this means that one out of every ten Filipinos have Chinese blood." See <http://www.philonline.com.ph/com.ph/~kaisa/kaisa_fact.html>.
29. See <http://www.philonline.com.ph/~kaisa/kaisa_fact.html>.
30. See <http://en.wikipedia.org/wiki/Chinese_Filipino>.
31. Ibid.
32. Ibid.
33. Ibid.
34. Ibid.

References

Alip, Eufronio. *Ten Centuries of Philippine-Chinese Relations*. Manila: Alip and Sons Incorporated, 1959.

Baviera, Aileen. *Comprehensive Engagement: Strategic Issues in Philippine-China Relations*. Manila: Philippine-China Development Resource Center, 2000.

Baviera, Aileen and Yu-Jose, eds. *Philippine External Relations: A Centennial Vista*. Pasay City: Foreign Service Institute, 1998. See in particular Benito Lim, "A History of Philippine-China Relations".

Churchill, Bernardita, ed. *An Assessment: Philippine-China Relations, 1975–1988*. Manila: De La Salle University Press, 1990. See in particular Benito Lim, "China under Deng Xiaoping and its Commercial Relations with the Philippines".

Dagdag, Edgardo E. *Instructional Materials on Philippine-China Relations*. Asian Center, University of the Philippines, 2005

Gaa, Willy. *Philippines-China Agreements (1975–2005): Bridges Towards the Golden Age of Partnership*. Beijing: Philippine Embassy, Department of Foreign Affairs, 2005.

Ho Khai Leong and Hou Kok Chung, eds. *Dynamics of China-Taiwan Relations and Southeast Asia*. Kuala Lumpur: Institute of China Studies, University of Malaya, 2006. See in particular Edgardo E. Dagdag, "China-Taiwan (Cross-Strait) Relations and the Philippines".

Lim, Benito. *The Political Economy of Philippine-China Relations*. Philippine-APEC Study Center Network, 1999.

Palanca, Ellen, ed. *China, Taiwan and the Ethnic Chinese in the Philippine Economy*. Quezon City: Philippine Association for Chinese Studies, 1995. See in particular Theresa Carino, "China, Taiwan and The Ethnic Chinese in the Philippine Economy: An Overview"; Florencio Mallare, "Unification Process of China and its Implications for the Philippines", and Wily Laohoo, "Filipino Reactions to Philippine-Chinese Investments: An Exploratory Survey".

———. *China-ASEAN Relations: Political, Economic and Ethnic Dimensions*. Manila: China Studies Program, De La Salle University, 1991.

Philippines-Republic of China Scholars' Conference on Economic Development. Manila: Jose Rizal-Sun Yat Sen Society, Inc., 1982. See in particular Esteban de Ocampo, "A Brief Survey of Philippine-China Relations".

Chinese Filipino. See <http://en.wikipedia.org/wiki/Chinese_Filipino>,

Chinatown-Philippines. See <http://www.huayinet.org/chinatown/chinatown_philippines.htm>.

Chinese and Chinese Mestizos. See <http://countrystudies.us/philippines/7.htm>.

Fact Sheet on the Chinese in the Philippines. KAISA-Angelo King Heritage Center, Manila, Philippines. See <http://www.philonline.com.ph/~kaisa/kaisa_fact.html>.

Chinese in the Philippines (Forum). See <http://www.chinahistoryforum.com/index.php?showtopic=9779&st=30>.

3

DEFINING IDENTITY THROUGH REMEMBERING THE WAR
Representation of World War II in Chinese Newspapers in the Immediate Post-war Singapore

Mike Shi-chi Lan

Collective memory, as Maurice Halbwachs has argued, is not given but rather "socially constructed".[1] Based on this understanding, memory of the War as collectively recognized in a given society should be considered as purposefully constructed. In the process of constructing historical memory, *commemoration* — in which people "remember in common the deeds and accomplishments of long-departed members of the group" — is critical as it helps individuals to preserve memories and define as well as perpetuate a sense of collective identity.[2] Madelon de Keizer further argues, "the core meaning of any individual or group identity ... is sustained by remembering; and what is remembered is defined by the assumed identity".[3]

In previous studies, it has been found that in constructing an historical memory of the war, different countries have chosen different *dates* to commemorate and, furthermore, to define a collective identity. For example, scholars have found that in Japan "the dropping of the atomic bombs and the terrible casualties that Japan suffered in the War caused the Japanese to view themselves as victims of aggression", and thereby 6 August, the day on which an atomic bomb was dropped on Hiroshima, subsequently becomes the national day to commemorate the War in general.[4] Examples like this shows that the dates (chosen to be) commemorated are not innocent; rather, the dates represent and construct the particular political identity of the people who commemorate them.

In (the studies of) East Asia in general, memory and commemoration of the War has been an important scholarly topic in recent years.[5] In Singapore, specifically, this topic has also attracted significant attention from disciplines ranging from History, Geography, to Museum Studies.[6] It is found that in recent years, "an elaborate programme of commemoration" has been instituted to remember the War and to "etch the collective experience of war into public memory and to derive from this memory production a grand narrative of national beginning and destiny".[7] Historically, this "programme of commemoration" began as soon as the War ended in 1945. To further study how commemoration of World War II helped to, to quote from Lewis Coser again, "define as well as perpetuate a sense of collective identity" in post-War Singapore, this chapter aims to examine the earliest war commemoration in Singapore in the immediate post-War years of 1946 and 1947.

In order to examine the earliest commemoration of World War II in Singapore, this chapter will focus on one particular group in Singapore, the Overseas Chinese community,[8] and analyse representation of the War in Chinese-language newspapers, most notably *Nanyang Siang Pau* [Nanyang shangbao], from the immediate post-War years of 1946 and 1947. As sojourners and settlers in a colonial setting, the Overseas Chinese in Singapore played an active role in the fight against the Japanese — in both Singapore and China — and experienced tremendous hardship after the British withdrawal in 1942. After the War ended in 1945, how did the Overseas Chinese community remember the War? What did this community remember — as collective memory — about the War?

In particular, this chapter will focus on reports of war commemoration — particularly the dates being commemorated and the narrative of commemoration — in Chinese newspapers. In recent years, more and more scholars have recognized "the role of war commemoration and indeed war itself in the reproduction of national and ethnic identities".[9] So what impact did the War experience and memory of War make on the identity of the Overseas Chinese? By examining how the Chinese community represented and remembered World War II in retrospect, this chapter will try to further understand the identity-formation, and assess the impact of the War on such identity, of the Overseas Chinese in Singapore in the immediate post-War years.

I. DATES COMMEMORATED AND THEIR SIGNIFICANCE

In *Nanyang Siang Pau*, news reports related to the War were abundant between 1946 and 1947. In the month of September, news coverage was centred on commemoration of the War, particularly of the (anniversary of the) end of the War. Interestingly, the Overseas Chinese in Singapore commemorated the War on three different dates — 3, 5 and 12 September, each had its own symbolic and political meaning.

5 September

On 5 September 1945, the British forces returned to Singapore for the first time since February 1942. One year later, 5 September was commemorated by commanders of the Allied Forces and the British authorities as the day of "glorious recovery of Singapore".[10] The commemoration of 5 September unequivocally emphasized the British (and the Allied Forces in a broader sense) takeover and re-occupation of Singapore after Japan's surrender. *Nanyang Siang Pau* reported a statement made by the commander of the Allied Air Force, in which the role of the British Royal Air Force was strongly stressed to show the British "contribution to the benefit of Malaya".[11] The emphasis of the British role, particularly its contribution to the end of the War, in post-War news reports demonstrates that the commemoration of 5 September, conspicuously, was based on and subsequently reinforcing a British perspective of the War in post-War Singapore.[12]

However, as represented in *Nanyang Siang Pau*, this British perspective of the War was rather alien to the Chinese community. Based on the news reports, although 5 September — to be more specific, the Allied and the British commemoration of 5 September — was mentioned in the newspaper, no activity was organized by the Chinese community to commemorate or celebrate 5 September. This lukewarm attitude and conspicuous lack of response from the Chinese community, including the newspaper itself, showed that in the immediate post-War period, the Overseas Chinese in Singapore did not strongly endorse the British view of the War.

12 September

On 12 September 1945, Japanese military forces officially signed the agreement and surrendered in Singapore. In 1946, the colonial authority designated 12 September as a school holiday and a ceremony was held at the City Hall to commemorate the first anniversary of Japan's official surrender in Singapore.

Nanyang Siang Pau reported that "leaders from various ethnic groups" attended and gave speeches at the ceremony.[13] The report indicated that this commemoration ceremony was meant to be inclusive and the ceremony was planned for the local population. In other words, 12 September was the date that was more widely commemorated and celebrated by the local population. The Overseas Chinese community was no exception as Chinese community leaders took part in the ceremony on 12 September. It was further reported that the Chinese General Chamber of Commerce [*Zhonghua zong shanghui*] and other community organizations planned to contribute a floral float and a marching band to the ceremony and hold a "parade to celebrate the victory" after the ceremony.[14]

Obviously, the Overseas Chinese community paid more attention and made more efforts in commemorating 12 September than 5 September. The commemoration of 12 September by the Chinese community showed that the Overseas Chinese in Singapore did identify with the local view of the War. However, in comparison, the Overseas Chinese in Singapore commemorated and identified more with another marker of the War — 3 September.

3 September

On 3 September 1945, Japan officially signed the agreement and surrendered to the Allied Forces, on board *USS Missouri* in Tokyo Bay. Although the Japanese forces in China officially surrendered to the Chinese authority in Nanjing on 9 September, 3 September has since been commemorated in China as the end of the "war of resistance".[15] In Singapore — and across Malaya, as reported in *Nanyang Siang Pau* — 3 September is also the date that most Chinese commemorated and celebrated one year after the War ended.

On 3 September 1946, *Nanyang Siang Pau* carried an editorial, titled "Celebrating 3 September Victory Day" [*shengli ri*]. The article categorically presented its position by stating at the onset: "We China resisted Japan (for an) eight-year war, finally being proclaimed victorious, the central government designated 3 September as the day commemorating victory".[16] This statement clearly showed that the paper was commemorating China's War victory and China's first anniversary of victory. The subtitle of the editorial, "(we) should keep the spirit of the war of resistance and national construction" [*kangzhan jianguo jingshen*], was the focus of the editorial. The editorial advocated to its readers to support China's post-War "peaceful unification" (amidst the ongoing civil war) and "national construction" for the sake of "national consciousness" [*minzu yishi*] and "soul of the country" [*guojia linghun*].[17] According to the editorial, Overseas Chinese such as the readers of *Nanyang Siang Pau* identified/should identify with China, both the country and the nation, and made/should make efforts to help China's development and growth. Clearly, political identity of the Overseas Chinese as represented and promoted by this particular piece of editorial was Chinese nationalistic.

Nanyang Siang Pau further reported on the following day that the Chinese business and community organizations in Singapore jointly hosted a ceremony on 3 September to celebrate China's first "Victory Day" at the Chinese General Chamber of Commerce.[18] It reported, with a photograph, that a gigantic map of China's territory was made and hung predominantly at the venue. The map, which highlighted the "gloriously recovered Eastern Three provinces and Taiwan" [*dong san sheng*, or Manchuria], was said to symbolize "the fruit of victory". The map was adorned with two "gigantic plaques", stating "river and mountain of the ancestral land" [*zuguo heshan*] and "commemoration of glorious recovery" [*guangfu jinian*]. The map was accompanied by the portraits of "Chairman Jiang" (Chiang Kai-shek) and the "national father" (Sun Yat-sen) as well as the "national flag" (of China) and "party flag" (of the Nationalist Party or Guomindang).[19] The presence of this map, plaques, portraits, and flags constituted a symbolic attachment to the state of China.

Statements made by the organizers further conveyed an unequivocal Chinese nationalistic identity. Lian Yingzhou, who was the chairman of the ceremony, made it clear in his opening speech: "We Overseas Chinese [huaqiao] all love and protect the ancestral land". He then spoke of the contribution made by Overseas Chinese to China during Sun Yat-sen's revolution and during the war of resistance led by Chiang Kai-shek. Lian advocated to his audience: "We Overseas Chinese have been making our efforts, devoting human and material resources to serve the ancestral land; so we shall continue to work hard to build the new China".[20] Throughout his speech, Lian demonstrated and promoted a strong Chinese nationalistic sentiment, which was presumably shared among the Overseas Chinese participants at the ceremony.

To further strengthen the nationalistic appeal to his audience, Lian made a reference to the map of China hung at the ceremony at the end of his speech:

> we see the vast territory of our ancestral land; to become a strong and powerful country in the world, (a country) must have a huge land and a large population to obtain (its) final victory ... look at our magnificent, rich, and vast territory, together with our four hundred fifty million peace-loving hard-working compatriots, we will surely achieve the grand goal of national construction.[21]

According to Lian, seeing the strength — as represented by territory and population — of China and the pre-eminent international standing of China in the immediate post-War years, Overseas Chinese would and should reinforce an existing and/or develop a new Chinese nationalistic sentiment and identity among themselves.

In the following year, *Nanyang Siang Pau* reported that the Chinese community in Singapore continued to hold ceremonies to commemorate and celebrate China's victory in the War. The aforementioned Chinese General Chamber of Commerce in Singapore, joined by more than a hundred "Chinese overseas organizations" [*qiaotuan*], again hosted the "Nine Three [3 September] Victory Commemoration Ceremony" [*jiusan shengli jinian dahui*] on 3 September 1947.[22] And again, in commemorating 3 September, the Chinese community organizations in Singapore showed a strong attachment to China. The Chinese General Chamber of Commerce stated that in hosting its ceremony on 3 September, it celebrated the "victory day of our country" [woguo shengli ri]. The Chairman of the Chamber, Lee Kong Chian (Li Guangqian), pointed out that "our country" accepted Japan's "surrender and kneeling-down" two years ago today. Clearly, Lee's term "our country" referred to China. Statements like this showed that Overseas Chinese leaders such as Lee saw China as where their political identity, as well as allegiance, belonged to.

In a British colony such as Singapore, the presence of the British rule was certainly not hard to find in any ceremony commemorating the War. *Nanyang Siang Pau* reported in 1947 that the national flags of both China and Great Britain were raised at one such ceremony to symbolize that "victory was the result of Chinese-British comradeship in fighting". However, to the organizer and the audience, the significance of the Chinese flag — as symbol of the state of China — was much higher. It was also reported that the "bright red national flags (of China)" were found everywhere at the venue of the ceremony.[23] The ceremony began with the singing of the national anthem (of China), followed by a speech by the Chairman of the Chamber, Lee and, like the ceremony in 1946, a speech by the Chinese Consul General, Wu. The Chinese General Chamber of Commerce concluded the ceremony by adopting a resolution to pay respect to soldiers and families of the fallen soldiers of China.[24]

Elsewhere in Singapore, other Overseas Chinese organizations also commemorated the War in their own ways. For example, the Three People's Principle Youth Corp [*san qing tuan*] of Singapore hosted its own celebration ceremony on the same day in 1947.[25] Liang Houzhou, the Director of the Three People's Principle Youth Corp, spoke to the Chinese community at the Corp's own ceremony to "celebrate" [qingzhu] the "victory day" of 3 September: "We fought hard in the war of resistance for eight years to gain the victory ... to make [sic] our international standing, listed as one of the four major powers, we should be proud of this spirit".[26] Clearly, the "we" that Liang referred to was the people of China and the Overseas Chinese were an integral part of "we". Together with remarks made by Lian Yingzhou in the previous year, Liang's perception of China's strength and eminent post-War international standing provided an excellent explanation to the formation and reinforcement of Chinese nationalistic sentiment and identity among Overseas Chinese in the immediate post-War years.

Because Singapore was at the time administratively a part of Malaya, as drawn up by the British colonial authority, *Nanyang Siang Pau* also covered stories across Malaya. The paper reported that similar to their counterparts in Singapore, Overseas Chinese organizations in Kuala Lumpur, Selangor, Johor Bahru, Malacca, and elsewhere also organized their own celebration ceremonies to commemorate the victory of "Nine Three".[27] Overseas Chinese communities in various cities hosted ceremonies to celebrate the "victory of the ancestral land" [*zuguo shengli*] and commemorate "the eight-year war of resistance of our country" on 3 September. At these ceremonies, the national flag of China and the portrait of Dr Sun Yat-sen, considered as China's "national father" [*guofu*], were commonly found.[28] And similar to the speech made by Director Liang Houzhou in Singapore, ceremonies across Malaya showed a strong sense of Chinese national pride. The victory of "Nine Three" was referred to as the moment in which Overseas Chinese across Malaya could "stand tall and feel proud" [*yangmei tuqi*, literally raising the eyebrow and exhaling].[29] Similar to Singapore, the emphasis of Overseas Chinese contributing to the "national construction" of post-War China was widely found in ceremonies across Malaya, often placed in the context of "being loyal to the country, being loyal to the nation" [*jinzhong guojia, jinzhong minzu*]. Many Overseas Chinese community leaders advocated to the audience at these ceremonies in Malaya to "fulfil duty of reviving the new China as citizens" [*guomin*].[30]

The analysis above shows that Overseas Chinese continued to identify themselves as Chinese and with the Chinese nation-state through commemorating the War in 1946 and 1947. It is worth noting that this nationalistic identity was further strengthened by the Chinese government and its officials, such as Chinese diplomats dispatched to Singapore. For example, as mentioned earlier, Chinese Consul-General Wu was invited to speak at the "Victory Day" commemoration ceremonies hosted by the Chinese General Chamber of Commerce on 3 September in 1946 and again in 1947. At both occasions, Wu praised the "patriotic spirit" [*aiguo jingshen*] of his Overseas Chinese audience,[31] and repeatedly asked his audience to contribute, as their "duties" [*zhize*], to the "national construction" [*jianguo*] of the "ancestral land" [*zuguo*] of China.[32] Wu's statements at both ceremonies showed that the Chinese government continued to consider, and to advocate, Overseas Chinese in Singapore as its people. In other words, the Chinese government and its officials also played a role in shaping and reinforcing the aforementioned Chinese nationalistic identity of Overseas Chinese, who identified themselves as people of China.

It is worth pointing out that as a leading newspaper in the Overseas Chinese community, *Nanyang Siang Pau* adopted the calendar of Min Guo, side by side with the Western calendar. The Min Guo calendar was adopted and used exclusively by the Republic of China government, counting the founding of the Republic in 1912 as the first year of the Min Guo calendar. The fact that *Nanyang Siang Pau* adopted the Min Guo calendar and used it continuously throughout this immediate post-War period demonstrated an outright identification of the newspaper itself — and to a certain extent, its readers — with the state of China.

Consistently and conspicuously, the Overseas Chinese in Singapore and Malaya demonstrated a strong Chinese nationalistic identity in their post-War commemoration and celebration of the end of the War. Commemorative activities, as well as Chinese diplomats and media such as *Nanyang Siang Pau*, further reinforced such identity. However, the political allegiance of the Overseas Chinese was not exclusive to China. As other newspaper reports showed, at these War commemoration and celebration ceremonies, Overseas Chinese in Singapore and Malaya demonstrated a double identity — or rather, a dual allegiance — toward China on the one hand and the colonies where they settled on the other hand.

II. DUAL ALLEGIANCE AND ITS PREDICAMENT

It has been argued that since the 1950s, in the context of newly independent nation-states in Southeast Asia, "both Chinese and local elites needed to believe that a separate cultural identity did not conflict with the demand of political loyalty".[33] Before the nationalist independence movement rose in Southeast Asia in the 1950s, however, the Overseas Chinese were negotiating between two political allegiances. On the one hand, they were attracted to the rising nationalism in China, especially during World War II; on the other hand, Overseas Chinese were showing local loyalties, as defined by the colonial rulers.

For example, *Nanyang Siang Pau* reported in 1946 that an Overseas Chinese leader in Malaya, Zhang Yucai, spoke of the double allegiance of the Overseas Chinese at a ceremony celebrating China's victory. He spoke of the "peculiar" situation of Overseas Chinese holding dual nationality in Malaya. Zhang elaborated that on the one hand Overseas Chinese should be loyal to the local government; and on the other hand, Overseas Chinese should be loyal to their "ancestral land" and support the Chinese Consulate there. Speaking of the Overseas Chinese living in cities across Malaya, Zhang stated that they were simultaneously "people of the Chinese Consulate" and "people of the British government". Therefore he advocated that the Chinese Consul, who represented the Chinese government, should "support local government on all fronts" and "supervise and encourage the Chinese who belonged to both sides (Chinese and British governments) to work hard to obey the law".[34]

According to Zhang's argument above, allegiance of Overseas Chinese to the state of China could co-exist with allegiance to the British colonial authority. But at times, the two allegiances could come into conflict, and the conflict highlighted the relationship (and tension) with local/colonial government and the native non-Chinese population. Two incidents of such conflict of allegiance, as manifested in commemoration of World War II, took place in September 1946 and were reported in *Nanyang Siang Pau*. One conflict concerning the dates to commemorate the War in Singapore was rather subdued, while the other conflict in Malaya was more open and intense. In Singapore, the conflict over dates was related to the aforementioned "victory day" celebration ceremony hosted at the Chinese General Chamber of Commerce on 3 September.[35] The organizers reported that the local government planned to hold a "multi-ethnic" ceremony and "lantern parade" on 12 September to celebrate the anniversary of Malaya's "glorious recovery" (from Japanese occupation) and had "ordered" the Chamber to mobilize Chinese overseas organizations to participate. At its own celebration ceremony on 3 September, the Chamber discussed the request made by the local government with representatives from other Overseas Chinese organizations. But the Chamber first expressed its reservation by saying that "the date (12 September) is approaching, and (the Chamber is) afraid that it will be too late to make preparation".[36] However, during the discussion, a handful of representatives from other Overseas Chinese organizations expressed willingness to take part in the ceremony on 12 September. At the end of the discussion, it was decided to "order" all Overseas Chinese to celebrate on 12 September by hanging flag and closing down business for a day.

But more significantly, at the discussion it was further concluded that it would now be too late to prepare for the "lantern parade"; and instead of organizing the local Chinese community and various organizations as groups, the Chamber would only ask other Overseas Chinese organizations to send "representatives" to take part in the ceremony.[37] This story showed that although the Overseas Chinese community leaders decided to support the celebration on 12 September to a certain extent, the degree of commitment and enthusiasm for the 12 September ceremony commemorating Malaya's recovery was far less than that for the ceremony celebrating China's victory on 3 September. The subtle but categorically different attitude expressed by the Overseas Chinese toward two ceremonies and two different dates of commemoration showed that the identity of Overseas Chinese was tied much stronger to China than to the settlement in colonial Singapore/Malaya.

In comparison, the other conflict of double allegiance in Malaya was much more open. In one city in Malaya, the local Chinese Community Association [*zhonghua gonghui*] was planning and preparing to hold a lantern parade in the evening of 3 September. However, on 2 September, the Chinese Community Association suddenly issued a notification to the local Chinese community, stating that the local authorities did not endorse the lantern parade as planned. Therefore, the Chinese Community Association had no choice but to announce the cancellation of the parade at the last minute.[38] *Nanyang Siang Pau* further reported that hearing this notification, the local Chinese community was utterly disappointed and discouraged, and many felt a strong "sense of sorrow" [*yihan*]. The report continued to describe the response from the community: "the glorious and great Victory Day (of China) was spent amidst cool air; facing this festive date, Overseas Chinese found an unusual feeling in their heart, with unspeakable (feeling of) bitterness and sourness".[39] This report showed that the ban on a parade celebrating 3 September was regarded as a serious blow to the Chinese community. And the disappointment as expressed in and by *Nanyang Siang Pau* further attested the importance of celebrating 3 September — China's Victory Day — to the Chinese community and a strong identification with the state of China among Overseas Chinese.

The Chinese community there then turned their attention to other minor community events and insisted on commemorating the "Victory Day" of 3 September in other ways. For example, a sports competition for students was held jointly by several Chinese schools there on 3 September. *Nanyang Siang Pau* reported that the Chinese community recognized that an event like this that promoted the "physical education of Overseas Chinese children" also brought "significant meaning" to the celebration of the "great and glorious date" of 3 September.[40] Having the planned lantern parade banned by the local authority, this sports competition became an alternative way for the local Chinese community to celebrate China's "Victory Day".

Were it not for the sports competition, as *Nanyang Siang Pau* reported, the community would feel "tremendously sad" on the "Victory Day".[41] Similar to the aforementioned incident in Singapore, this story in Malaya not only illustrated the tension between the Overseas Chinese community and the local authority over the commemoration of the War, it further demonstrated the strong Chinese nationalistic sentiment and identity among Overseas Chinese in the immediate post-War years. In terms of identity and allegiance, these two incidents of conflict over the issue of war commemoration in 1946 showed that the Overseas Chinese had a very strong allegiance to China and relatively weak local loyalties. In addition, Overseas Chinese identified themselves more as a distinct group and identified more with the people of China than with the local population.

CONCLUSION

As Wang Gungwu points out, Chinese nationalist identity reached its peak in the 1930s and 1940s among Overseas Chinese in Southeast Asia.[42] Wang further finds that "[b]y the beginning of World War II, local loyalties had become suspect as identification with China had become increasingly necessary". As Overseas Chinese developed (and showed) stronger and stronger "patriotic sentiment" toward China during the War, Wang continues, "colonial powers as well as native rulers began to develop genuine fears, deep-seated fears, about the ambitions of China and Overseas Chinese".[43]

This chapter, by examining the commemoration of World War II by the Overseas Chinese community in Singapore and Malaya, finds that the suspicion and fear that the "colonial powers as well as native rulers" held against the Overseas Chinese are not unfounded. As the analysis above shows, Overseas Chinese in Singapore and Malaya did demonstrate a strong Chinese nationalistic identity in the immediate years after World War II. China's perceived strength and post-War international standing fostered and further reinforced this sense of identity. As a result, Overseas Chinese were constantly negotiating across dual political allegiance between the Chinese government and the British colonial and local governments.

Notes

1. Lewis A. Coser, "Introduction", in Maurice Halbwachs, *On Collective Memory*, edited and translated by Lewis A. Coser (Chicago and London: University of Chicago Press, 1992), p. 22.
2. Ibid., pp. 24, 27.

3. Madelon de Keizer, "Focus: History and Memory — Introduction", *European Review* 11, no. 4 (2003): 519.

4. Mark Eykholt, "Aggression, Victimization, and Chinese Historiography of the Nanjing Massacre", in *The Nanjing Massacre in History and Historiography*, edited by Joshua A. Fogel (Berkeley: University of California Press, 2000), p. 24.

5. For example, P. Lim Pui Huen and Diana Wong, eds., *War and Memory in Malaysia and Singapore* (Singapore: Institute of Southeast Asian Studies, 2000), and T. Fujitani, Geoffrey M. White, and Lisa Yoneyama, eds., *Perilous Memories: The Asia-Pacific War(s)* (Durham and London: Duke University Press, 2001).

6. Recent studies include, Hamzah Muzaini and Brenda S.S. Yeoh, "War Landscape as 'Battlefields' of Collective Memories: Reading the Reflections at Bukit Chandu, Singapore", *Cultural Geographies* 12 (2005): 345–65; Hamzah Muzaini and Brenda S.S. Yeoh, "Contesting 'Local' Commemoration of the Second World War: The Case of the Changi Chapel and Museum in Singapore", *Australian Geographer* 36, no. 1 (March 2005): 1–17; and Donna Brunero, "Archives and Heritage in Singapore: The Development of 'Reflections at Bukit Chandu', a World War II Interpretive Centre", *International Journal of Heritage Studies* 12, no. 5 (September 2006): 427–39.

7. Diana Wong, "Memory Suppression and Memory Production: The Japanese Occupation of Singapore", in *Perilous Memories: The Asia-Pacific War(s)*, edited by T. Fujitani, Geoffrey M. White, and Lisa Yoneyama (Durham and London: Duke University Press, 2001), p. 219.

8. In this article I use the term "Overseas Chinese" to refer to "anyone identifiably Chinese who is outside China", a definition given by Wang Gungwu; see his *China and the Chinese Overseas* (Singapore: Eastern Universities Press, 2003), particularly p. 284, footnote 2.

9. T.G. Ashland, Graham Dawson, and Michael Roper, "The Politics of War Memory and Commemoration", in *The Politics of War Memory and Commemoration*, edited by T.G. Ashland, Graham Dawson, and Michael Roper (London: Routledge, 2000), p. 5.

10. "Benpo guangfu yizhounian" [the first anniversary of the glorious recovery of Singapore], *Nanyang Siang Pau*, 5 September 1946, Minguo 35, p. 3.

11. Ibid.

12. Commemoration of 5 September was featured predominantly in the English newspapers such as *Straits Times*, and 5 September, the day the British forces returned to Singapore, was commemorated as "Liberation Day" in 1946. See *Straits Times*, 5 September 1946, pp. 1, 5. For an extensive analysis of war commemoration and the British colonial perspective of the War as represented in the English media, see Mike Shi-chi Lan, Kawashima Shin, Victory and 'independence' in Singapore (in Japanese), in *August 15 of the World in Historical Documents* (Tokyo: Yamakawa Publishing Co., forthcoming 2008).

13. *Nanyang Siang Pau*, 5 September 1946, Minguo 35, p. 3.

14. Ibid.

15. For example, in 2005, China commemorated the sixtieth anniversary of the end of the War and state ceremonies, attended by President Hu Jintao and Premier Wen Jiabao, were held on 3 September. It is reported that "China marked the sixtieth anniversary of the victory of the war against Japanese aggressors and the world anti-fascist war on 3 September, with a red carpet and gun salute to war veterans, a national commemoration of its war dead, and calls for national unity and peaceful development". See statement released by Embassy of the People's Republic of China in the Untied States of America, "War remembered for peace, future: Hu (09/03/05)", at <http://www.china-embassy.org/eng/gyzg/t210060.htm> (accessed 18 November 2007). *People's Daily*, the official state newspaper, also reported "the memorial ceremony held in the Great Hall of the People in Beijing, capital of China, on 3 September 2005", see "Sixtieth anniversary of Anti-Japanese War celebration", at <http://english.peopledaily.com.cn/200509/04/eng20050904_206414.html> (accessed 18 November 2007).

16. "Celebrating 3rd September Victory Day" [qingzhu jiu san shengliri], *Nanyang Siang Pau*, 3 September 1946, Minguo 35, p. 1.

17. Ibid.

18. *Nanyang Siang Pau*, 4 September 1946, Minguo 35, p. 3.

19. Ibid.

20. Ibid.

21. Ibid.

22. *Nanyang Siang Pau*, 4 September 1947, Minguo 36, p. 5.

23. Ibid.

24. Ibid.

25. Ibid.

26. Ibid.

27. *Nanyang Siang Pau*, 5 September 1946, Minguo 35, p. 4; and *Nanyang Siang Pau*, 6 September 1946, Minguo 35, p. 4.

28. *Nanyang Siang Pau*, 5 September 1946, Minguo 35, p. 4.

29. Ibid.

30. Ibid.

31. *Nanyang Siang Pau*, 4 September 1946, Minguo 35, p. 3.

32. *Nanyang Siang Pau*, 4 September 1946, Minguo 35, p. 3, and *Nanyang Siang Pau*, 4 September 1947, Minguo 36, p. 5.

33. Wang Gungwu, "The Study of Chinese Identities in Southeast Asia", in *China and the Chinese Overseas*, edited by Wang Gungwu (Singapore: Eastern Universities Press, 2003), p. 227.

34. *Nanyang Siang Pau*, 5 September 1946, Minguo 35, p. 4.

35. *Nanyang Siang Pau*, 4 September 1946, Minguo 35, p. 3.

36. Ibid.

37. Ibid.

38. *Nanyang Siang Pau*, 6 September 1946, Minguo 35, p. 4.

39. Ibid.

40. Ibid.
41. Ibid.
42. Wang Gungwu, "The Study of Chinese Identities in Southeast Asia", in *China and the Chinese Overseas*, edited by Wang Gungwu (Singapore: Eastern Universities Press, 2003), p. 224.
43. Wang Gungwu, "The Chinese as Immigrants and Settlers: Singapore", in *China and the Chinese Overseas*, edited by Wang Gungwu (Singapore: Eastern Universities Press, 2003), p. 197.

4

RE-POSITIONING "PATRIOTISM"
Various Aspects of Financial Support to China in Penang around 1911

Shinozaki Kaori

The epithet "Overseas Chinese as the mother of the revolution" (华侨为革命之母) has been attributed to Sun Yat-sen, and is widely accepted in Southeast Asia, especially Singapore and Malaysia, although recent study has cast doubt on its authenticity.[1] Museums related to Sun Yat-sen have been opened in Singapore and Penang. A love story based on Sun Yat-sen's actual stay in Penang in 1910 was filmed on location in Penang and released with the title of *Road To Dawn* [夜 • 明] in September 2007[2] in Malaysia.

It is true that Overseas Chinese including those in Malaya supported the revolutionary party by providing shelter and donating money. Some of them even sacrificed their lives. They are praised as "patriotic", contributing tremendously to the revolutionary cause which achieved Chinese nationalism against the Manchu administration (Yen 1979, 2006; Chen 1986; Jiang 1986; Zhang 2003).

However, among Chinese in Penang for example, there were those who did not support the revolutionary movement. Donations were collected right after the Wuchang uprising in October 1911, but it was not equal to supporting the revolution. The donation drive was named "Donation for the Relief and Security of Guangdong and Fujian[3] Provinces" (广福两省救济保安捐), and it was ostensibly for the maintenance of security in their hometown under the chaotic situation caused by the revolution. Donation campaigns did not always display the solidarity of patriots. There were fraudsters who collected money in the name of donations and disappeared with the money. The Chinese in Penang monitored how the donated money reached their target. They demanded administrators to secure efficient and transparent management of the money.

Though this chapter does not deny the precious devotion of Chinese people in Penang to the revolutionary cause with their lives and money, however, it seeks to highlight the different aspects of the "revolutionary" and "patriotic" donation campaign in Penang between 1911 and 1913. This chapter is divided into three parts. The first section discusses the reaction of the Chinese in Penang to revolutionary movements led by Dr Sun Yat-sen before the Wuchang uprising. It explains the structure of leadership of the Chinese community in Penang at that time which was divided into three: Penang Chinese Chamber of Commerce (槟榔屿中华总商会, hereafter PCCC), Chinese Town Hall (平章公馆) and Penang Philomathic Union (槟城阅书报社, hereafter PPU). The second part discusses the reaction of the Chinese in Penang to the Wuchang uprising. It demonstrates the process in which the whole Chinese community became gradually involved in the campaign for the "Donation for the Relief and Security of Guangdong and Fujian Provinces". The third part discusses the reaction of the Chinese in Penang to the "National Donation". This episode demonstrates that the close scrutiny with which the Chinese in Penang watched their donations by demanding the authorities in China to use the procured funds accountably and transparently.[4]

1. CHINESE COMMUNITY IN PENANG AND REVOLUTION

(1) Structure of Leadership of the Chinese Community in Penang in the Early 1910s

Though the Overseas Chinese have been dubbed the mother of the revolution, the Chinese in Penang showed various responses to the revolutionary activities led by Sun Yat-sen. Those who supported Sun Yat Sen gathered under the Tung Meng Hui Penang branch (同盟会槟城分会) and the Penang Philomathic Union. But prominent figures regarded as leaders of the Chinese community rarely participated in these organizations.

At that time, in Penang, there were two main organizations where community leaders gathered to discuss matters affecting the community and facilitate good relations with the authorities. They were the Chinese Town Hall and the Penang Chinese Chamber of Commerce.

The Chinese Town Hall was established in 1881 to resolve disputes between the Hokkien community and Cantonese community, when Guang Fu Gong (广福宫) lost its function as a mediator in the Chinese community in Penang. The establishment of the Chinese Town Hall could be seen as a reaction to the establishment of the Town Hall in July 1880 (Tan 1983), which was called "Ang Mo Gong Guan (红毛公馆)" European Town Hall in Hokkien (Lo 1900, p. 227).

The PCCC was established in June 1903 with three main functions. First, it was a framework to supervise business transactions among Chinese in Penang with the same business practices. Secondly, it helped to create consensus among the Chinese merchants and exert pressure on the Straits Settlements government. For better communication with the Straits Settlements government, the PCCC also struggled to win the right to send a representative to the Legislative Council. Third, it was intended to settle problems which occurred in China or the problems of debtors who absconded to China through its ties with the Bureau of Commerce of the Qing government and its network of chambers of commerce in China (Shinozaki 2006).

Most community leaders were involved in either organization or both. Members of these organizations overlapped each other.

The PPU was established in December 1908 and registered under the Society Ordinance in March 1909 (*SSGG* 17 May 1912]. Its main protagonists were the members of Tung Meng Hui Penang branch established in September 1905, including Goh Say Eng (吴世荣),[5] Wee Kim Kheng (黄金庆),[6] Tan Sin Cheng (陈新政),[7] Khoo Beng Cheang (邱明昶),[8] and Xiong Yu Shan

FIGURE 4.1
Members of PCCC and Trustees of Chinese Town Hall in 1911

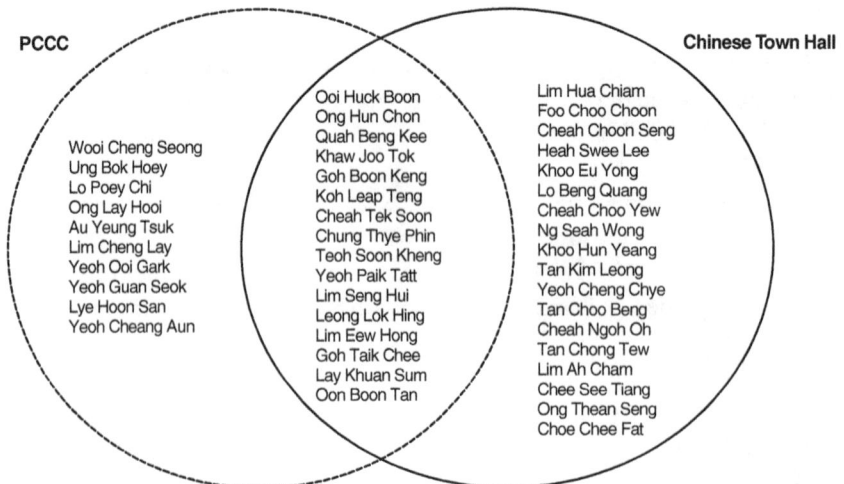

PCCC   Chinese Town Hall

PCCC	Overlap	Chinese Town Hall
Wooi Cheng Seong	Ooi Huck Boon	Lim Hua Chiam
Ung Bok Hoey	Ong Hun Chon	Foo Choo Choon
Lo Poey Chi	Quah Beng Kee	Cheah Choon Seng
Ong Lay Hooi	Khaw Joo Tok	Heah Swee Lee
Au Yeung Tsuk	Goh Boon Keng	Khoo Eu Yong
Lim Cheng Lay	Koh Leap Teng	Lo Beng Quang
Yeoh Ooi Gark	Cheah Tek Soon	Cheah Choo Yew
Yeoh Guan Seok	Chung Thye Phin	Ng Seah Wong
Lye Hoon San	Teoh Soon Kheng	Khoo Hun Yeang
Yeoh Cheang Aun	Yeoh Paik Tatt	Tan Kim Leong
	Lim Seng Hui	Yeoh Cheng Chye
	Leong Lok Hing	Tan Choo Beng
	Lim Eew Hong	Cheah Ngoh Oh
	Goh Taik Chee	Tan Chong Tew
	Lay Khuan Sum	Lim Ah Cham
	Oon Boon Tan	Chee See Tiang
		Ong Thean Seng
		Choe Chee Fat

(熊玉珊)[9] (Zhang 2004, p. 32). Penang was a base in Southeast Asia for Sun Yat-sen and his supporters or revolutionists at that time. Compared with the situation in Singapore, where the Tung Meng Hui Southeast Asia Branch (established in 1908) started to face declining support, Sun Yat-sen had a great deal of support from Penang at the time. The revolutionists' base in Southeast Asia (中国同盟会南洋总机关部) shifted to Penang from Singapore presumably in February or March 1910 (Liu 1986, pp. 48–49). Sun Yat-sen and his family even stayed in Penang in 1910. It is said that eleven people including Goh Sey Eng, Wee Kim Kheng, Tan Sin Cheng, Khoo Beng Cheang and Xiong Yu Shan provided shelter and the cost of living for the family (Zhang 2004, p. 116).

The PPU leaders and leaders from PCCC and Chinese Town Hall rarely overlapped. Among the members of PPU, only Goh Say Eng and Lim Joo Tek (林如德)[10] participated in the Chinese Town Hall or PCCC at this stage (*PS* 27 February 1911).[11]

(2) Rivalries

As often noted, there were big differences between PPU leaders and leaders from the PCCC and the Chinese Town Hall on the revolutionary movement led by Sun Yat-sen. This was most clearly seen in the election result of the Municipal Commissioner for Georgetown that took place on 6 December 1910.

During the election, leaders from the Chinese Town Hall and PCCC supported H.A. Neubronner.[12] Neubronner was elected as a candidate by the committee members of Ratepayers' Association, a multi-ethnic association[13] established in November 1910 by ratepayers of Georgetown municipality to facilitate better administration. Many leaders of the Chinese Town Hall and PCCC participated in the association and were appointed committee member as shown in Figure 4.2.

However, Neubronner lost badly to another candidate, Yeoh Guan Seok.[14] Yeoh won 638 votes, while Neubronner won only 85 votes. The number of votes for the two candidates reached 723 votes, while the average number of votes in the 1900s was between 130 and 160. It demonstrates that the voters[15] opposed strongly the choice of the candidate by the Ratepayers' Association. It is reported that Yeoh's supporters were well organized and succeeded in winning support in almost all parts in the Municipality (*SE* 5–7 December 1910).

In a letter to the *Penang Gazette and Straits Chronicle*, a reader described the election as a battle between leaders of the Chinese community who had

FIGURE 4.2
Chinese Committee Members of Ratepayers' Association

PCCC   Chinese Town Hall

Ong Hun Chon
Khaw Joo Tok
Goh Boon Keng
Koh Leap Teng
Yeoh Ooi Gark   Cheah Tek Soon
Chung Thye Phin
Teoh Soon Kheng
Lim Seng Hui
Lim Eew Hong
Goh Taik Chee

Heah Swee Lee
Khoo Eu Yong
Ng Seah Wong
Tan Kim Leong
Yeoh Cheng Chye

stakes in Penang and the Reformists of the young Chinese Party who had no stakes (*PGSC* 5 December 1910). After the election, the Ratepayers' Association dissolved. P.V. Locke,[16] president of the Ratepayers' Association, criticized the *Straits Echo*'s article about Sun Yat-sen for paralyzing and bringing about the death of the Ratepayers' Association (*SE* 28 December 1910). The *Straits Echo* was owned by Lim Seng Hooi (林成輝)[17] who was a committee member of the Ratepayers' Association as well as that of the Chinese Town Hall and PCCC. Its board members were also members of the PCCC. The paper published an editor's column titled "Dr Sun Yat-sen" on 2 November 1910 which severely criticized the speech made by Sun Yat-sen on 30 October in Georgetown.

The column admitted there was justice in what Sun Yat-sen pointed out, such as China's bad administration, inability to protect her own legitimate interests, and improper treatment of Chinese in various lands. However, the column criticized Sun Yat-sen for being "a revolutionary who didn't revolutionize". The column cited Sun's speech and inserted ironic asides after sentences as seen in the following abstract (sentences in the brackets are inserted by the *Straits Echo*):

> The Chinese Revolutionary Party came into being some twenty years ago. [Twenty years and nothing done!] Its numbers have increased. It has fought on fifteen occasions against the Manchu Government, but without success. [Then it is time it retired from business and went into liquidation.] On the last occasion it was intended to start fighting on 10 February 1910.... We had a few thousand armed soldiers. We had all kinds of weapons but were short of bullets, to procure which a sum of $10,000 was necessary to procure the bullets. Therefore the date of fighting was postponed. [Dr Sun Yat-sen is probably the world's record postponer.]

The column went on to say that Dr Sun Yat-sen constantly needed funds for the revolutionary effort without using it effectively. It added that it could not believe the Overseas Chinese were so unintelligent as to be unable to see that a revolution with "millions" of backers, failed fifteen times to organize a revolution because of a lack of ten thousand dollars' worth of bullets. The column continued by pointing out that a levy of ten cents a head on the Party, if it was as big as Dr Sun claimed it was, would have been ample. The column concluded that Sun Yat-sen "tells our local Chinese that if they would be patriotic, they must financially support him. That is rubbish. If they do, they will be not so much patriotic as fatheaded" (*SE* 2 November 1910).

As this episode shows, there was a great gap in the Chinese community in Penang between Sun Yat-sen's supporters and non-supporters. In such a milieu, the so-called Penang Conference was held on 13 November 1910, where Sun Yat-sen appealed to attendees to support him financially, saying that he could succeed in the uprising to overthrow the Qing Dynasty because he had secured support from armies. The attendees decided to support him and set a target to collect HK$130,000 as a whole, HK$50,000 from Malaya and East Indies respectively, and HK$30,000 from Siam and Indochina in total (Zhang 2004, p. 39). HK$47,659 was collected in Malaya, among which HK$11,500 was from Penang.[18] Total donations from all over the world amounted to HK$224,443. The fund in its entirety was used to support the uprising in Huang Hua Gang, Guangzhou, on 29 March 1911, which was the largest in scale and most intense of the eleven uprisings, including Wuchang uprising (Chen 1986, p. 250).

The total sum of financial support given to the eleven uprisings was HK$3,942,810 of which HK$1,019,555 came from Malaya. The Malayan contribution accounted for 25.86 per cent of the total sum. Financial support from Malaya went mostly to the third to eighth uprisings where a sum of HK$98,000 (accounting for 32.98 per cent of the total sum of HK$298,550), and the tenth and eleventh uprisings where a sum of HK$873,896 (HK$3,000 before the uprising) was deployed, amounting to 29.30 per cent of the total HK$2,982,817 (Chen 1986, pp. 246–53).

While it is still unclear how much money the Chinese in Penang contributed beyond the HK$11,500 to the Huang Hua Gang uprising, it cannot be denied that they must have contributed a large sum. There were a large number of Sun Yat-sen's supporters in Penang as shown in the election result of the Municipal Commissioner for Georgetown. The PPU could have had the ability to mobilize a large part of the Chinese community in Penang.

Nevertheless, the PPU, which led most of the donation campaigns to support the new regime in China after the Wuchang uprising, always tried

TABLE 4.1
Financial Support for Uprisings (including the Wuchang Uprising)

Region	Sum (HK$)	Percentage
Hong Kong	1,110,000	28.15
Malaya	1,019,555	25.86
French Indochina and Siam	633,434	16.07
United States	348,711	8.84
Burma	278,800	7.07
East Indies	184,050	4.67
Philippines	101,150	2.57
Canada	74,000	1.88
France	65,000	1.65
Cuba	62,000	1.58
Japan	49,000	1.24
Sun Yat-sen himself	15,000	0.38
Others	1,950	0.05
Total	3,942,810	100.00

Source: Chen 1986, p. 254.

to work with the leaders from the PCCC and the Chinese Town Hall in the campaign even though it felt that the latter was no longer "revolutionary". The PPU tried to organize the campaigns on a community level so as to mobilize a wider range of people including non-PPU sympathizers. It demonstrates that the leaders from the PCCC and the Chinese Town Hall were still influential political and social players.

2. BEYOND THE REVOLUTION — DONATION CAMPAIGN IN PENANG RIGHT AFTER WUCHANG UPRISING

A faction of new armies sympathetic with the revolutionary ideals launched the Wuchang uprising on 10 October 1911. Sun Yat-sen only heard about the uprising through the newspapers in the United States. The city of Wuchang was captured by the revolutionaries and they announced the establishment of the Military Government of Hubei of the Republic of China. The other provinces followed suit by declaring independence from the Qing Dynasty one after another. Guangdong and Fujian provinces, where most of the Chinese in Penang came from, also declared independence from the Qing Dynasty on 8 and 9 November.

The Chinese in Penang were informed of the situation through the waves of telegrams sent from China. They remitted money to China as early as 14 October 1911 as shown in the Table 4.2.

TABLE 4.2
Remittance from Penang to China right after the Wuchang Uprising

Date	Remitted to	Original value → converted value (Straits dollar) (HK$)	
14 October	Hong Kong (金利源)	$ 1,500 →	$1,170.43
18 October	Hong Kong (金利源)	$ 2,000 →	$1,556.3
Same	Shanghai (渔父)	$ 2,800 →	$2,873.37
20 October	Hong Kong (金利源)	$ 3,000 →	$2,358.9
1 November	Hong Kong (金利源)	$ 5,000 →	$4,000
4 November	Hong Kong (金利源)	$10,000 →	$7,988.85
6 November	Fujian (民心报 → Military Govt)	$ 5,000 →	$3,994.85
8 November	Hong Kong (金利源)	$10,000 →	$8,015
Total		$39,300 →	$31,957.7

Source: *PS* 12 January 1912.

This figure is based on the accounting report of "Donation for Relief and Security of Guangdong and Fujian Provinces" published in *Penang Sin Poe* on 11 March 1912 by Leong Lok Hing, Wee Kim Kheng and Khoo Ewe Bee. It reveals that the amount of money remitted to China from 14 October 1911 to 2 January 1913 amounted to $135,389.06 (*PS* 12 January 1912). This process can be divided into three stages based on the actors involved and the outcome of two general meetings held on 11 November and 11 December 1911.

(1) First Stage: Before the General Meeting on 11 November

As Table 4.2 shows, between the events of the Wuchang uprising and the meeting on 11 November 1911, the Penang Chinese remitted at least $31,957, mainly to Hong Kong (*PS* 12 January 1912). However, it is not clear who actually donated the money.

(2) Second Stage: General Meeting Organized by PPU

The second stage is marked by the general meeting at the Chinese Town Hall organized by the PPU on 11 November 1911. It was the first community-wide meeting of the Chinese community in Penang in response to the post-Wuchang uprising situation. It was reported that there were more than a thousand attendees.[19] However, most of the attendees were actually members of PPU. There were only four representatives from the Chinese Town Hall

and PCCC, namely, Leong Lok Hing (梁乐卿),[20] Ooi Huck Boon (黄学文),
Teo Soon Kheng (张舜卿) and Lim Joo Tek (*SE* 13 January 1911).

During the meeting, attendees stressed the importance of restoring
peace to China. Wee Kim Kheng stressed that everyone should fulfil his/her
obligation to support their fellowmen, families and country. Tan Sin Cheng
stated that the attendees should be proud that the Wuchang uprising led to
the "recovery of the lost territory" (光复) as it foretold much happiness to
Chinese people everywhere. He proposed to carry out fund-raising campaigns
for the continued maintenance of China's independence. Tan's proposal was
accepted unanimously, and donation promoters were appointed. Though the
members of PCCC or Chinese Town Hall were also appointed promoters
(*PS* 14 November 1911), it is unlikely that they were involved in the campaign.
During this campaign, they collected $36,000.

TABLE 4.3
Donation for Relief and Security of Guangdong and Fujian Provinces, at the Second Stage

Date	Remitted to	Original value → converted value (Straits dollar) (HK$)
13 November	Fujian (民心报 → Military Govt.)	$ 5,000 → $ 4,044.85
20 November	Amoy (Zhuang Yin An)[21]	$ 5,000 → $ 4,000
1 December	Shanghai (Military Governor Chen)	$20,000 → $21,361.82
9 December	Amoy (Zhuan Yin An)	$ 6,000 → $ 4,815
Total		$36,000 → $34,221.67

Source: (*PS* 12 January 1912).

(3) Third Stage: Involvement of PCCC and the Chinese Town Hall

The third stage is marked by the general meeting on 11 December 1911 with
1,000 attendees as well as many leaders from the Chinese Town Hall and the
PCCC. At this meeting, a large-scale fund-raising campaign was discussed.

The Chinese in Penang, most notably Tan Sin Cheng and Wee Kim
Kheng received telegrams from the new leaders of Fujian and Guangdong
provinces such as Sun Dao Ren (孙道仁), new Military Governor of Fujian
Province, and Wong Nai Siong (黄乃裳), Director of Transportation (交通
司长) and Fund-Raising (筹饷局总办). These telegrams called for Tan and
Wee to help the new provincial government financially (*PS* 20 November
1911). Leong Lok Hing also received telegrams from the new governors of
Fujian and Guangdong provinces, stating that they needed financial support
to assist the refugees displaced in the revolution (*PS* 12 December 1911).

In order to respond to these requests, a general meeting was held on 11 December 1911, in which leaders of PPU, PCCC and the Chinese Town Hall attended. The full list of the notable attendees may be seen in Figure 4.3.

The meeting was chaired by Khoo Cheow Teong (邱昭忠).[22] Leong Lok Hing, who represented the Cantonese community in the Chinese Town Hall and assumed the Presidency of the PCCC, urged the Chinese in Penang to demonstrate their commitment to the cause by not falling behind the billions of dollars collected in the other major cities in Southeast Asia. Qiu Jin Jing (邱金经)[23] pointed out that the previous campaign was unable to collect much funds because prominent Chinese leaders did not band together to appeal to the Chinese organizations in Penang for donations.

Fifty donation promoters were elected from the Trustees of Guangfu Gong and from the Hokkien and Cantonese business communities respectively. It included leaders from the Chinese Town Hall, PCCC and PPU (*PS* 12 December 1911).

To this end, a meeting of donation promoters was held on 13 December at Chinese Town Hall. However, Leong Lok Hing lamented that the response was poor and only half the designated number of promoters turned up.

FIGURE 4.3
Leaders of Each Organization who Attended Meeting on 11 December 1911

Chinese Town Hall

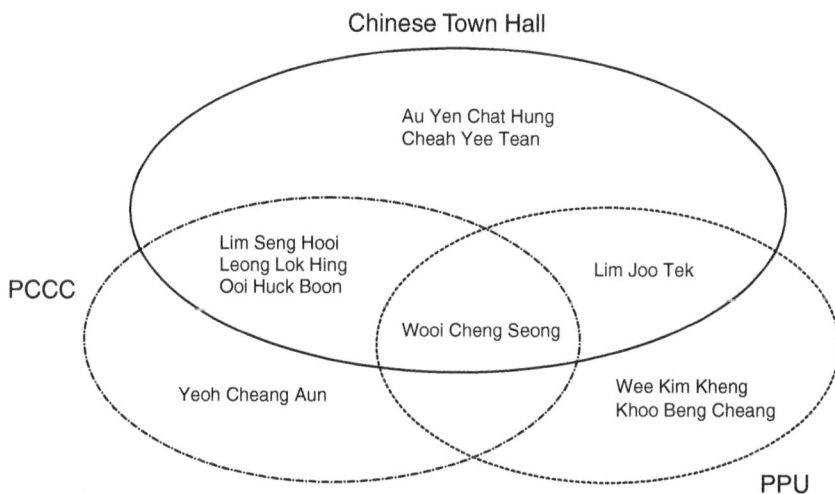

Au Yen Chat Hung
Cheah Yee Tean

Lim Seng Hooi
Leong Lok Hing
Ooi Huck Boon

Lim Joo Tek

PCCC

Wooi Cheng Seong

Yeoh Cheang Aun

Wee Kim Kheng
Khoo Beng Cheang

PPU

Source: Affiliations of individuals are based on Zhang 2004, p. 196; *PS* 1 October 1906; *PS* 27 February 1911; *SE* 6 January 1911.

FIGURE 4.4
Donation Promoters Elected (Main Figures)

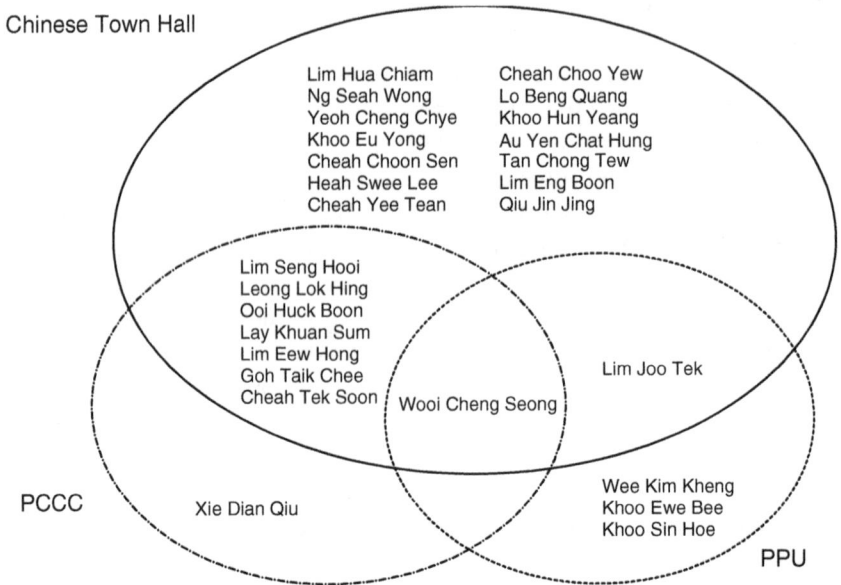

Chinese Town Hall

Lim Hua Chiam	Cheah Choo Yew
Ng Seah Wong	Lo Beng Quang
Yeoh Cheng Chye	Khoo Hun Yeang
Khoo Eu Yong	Au Yen Chat Hung
Cheah Choon Sen	Tan Chong Tew
Heah Swee Lee	Lim Eng Boon
Cheah Yee Tean	Qiu Jin Jing

Lim Seng Hooi
Leong Lok Hing
Ooi Huck Boon
Lay Khuan Sum
Lim Eew Hong
Goh Taik Chee
Cheah Tek Soon   Wooi Cheng Seong   Lim Joo Tek

PCCC   Xie Dian Qiu

Wee Kim Kheng
Khoo Ewe Bee
Khoo Sin Hoe

PPU

FIGURE 4.5
Attendees of the Meeting of Donation Promoters on 13 December 1911 (Main Figures)

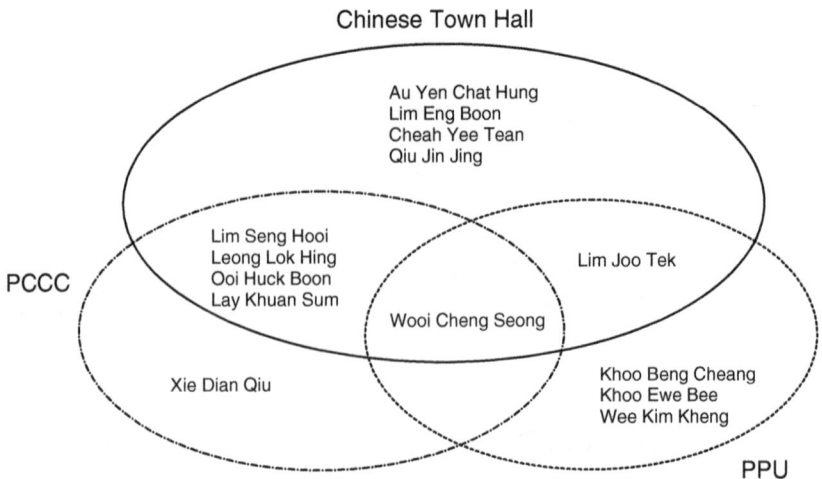

Chinese Town Hall

Au Yen Chat Hung
Lim Eng Boon
Cheah Yee Tean
Qiu Jin Jing

Lim Seng Hooi
Leong Lok Hing
Ooi Huck Boon   Lim Joo Tek
PCCC   Lay Khuan Sum

Wooi Cheng Seong

Xie Dian Qiu

Khoo Beng Cheang
Khoo Ewe Bee
Wee Kim Kheng

PPU

During the meeting, it was decided that the campaign was to be named the "Donation for Relief and Security of Guangdong and Fujian Provinces". Accordingly, committee members were elected to oversee the campaign. In the ensuing discussion, Leong Lok Hing was elected president of the Cantonese community, Wee Kim Kheng as president of the Hokkien community, Khoo Ewe Bee as treasurer, Tao Le Fu (陶乐甫) as auditor, Qiu Zhe Qing (邱哲卿) as secretary, and Teo Soon Kheng, Lin Wen Qin (林文琴), Cheah Yee Tean, and Ou Yang Ri Kui (欧阳日葵) as chief promoters. As most of the appointees were from the PPU, it demonstrates that this campaign was led by the PPU in conjunction with leaders from the PCCC and the Chinese Town Hall. The campaign was carried out from 15 to 22 December, with the exception of 16 and 17 December. The promoters appealed to each household, shop, and guide for donations (*PS* 14 December 1911). During the campaign, they collected $70,000, which was then remitted to China.

TABLE 4.4
Donation for the Relief and Security of Guangdong and Fujian Provinces, at the Third Stage

Date	Remitted to	Original value → converted value (Straits dollar) (HK$)	
28 December 1911	Foo Chou, Military Governor Sun	$20,000 →	$16,000
2 January 1912	Shanghai, Military Government	$50,000 →	$53,195.69
Total		$70,000 →	$69,195.69

Source: (*PS* 12 January 1912).

Fund-raising campaigns after the Wuchang uprising were mainly organized by PPU members and came to gradually involve leaders of the Chinese Town Hall and the PCCC. Their aim was to support their fellowmen in China who were put in a chaotic situation caused by revolution. The name of the campaign, "Donation for the Relief and Security of Guangdong and Fujian Provinces" demonstrates their aspiration. It should be noted that the community-wide donation campaign of the Chinese community in Penang immediately after the Wuchang uprising was to restore peace to China rather than in support of the revolution.

3. "NATIONAL DONATION"
(1) Background to the National Donation

When the Republic of China was formally instituted on 1 January 1912, it was already almost bankrupt. Xiong Xi Ling (熊希龄), the then Minister of

Finance stated at the upper house on 13 May 1912 that the financial status of the Central Government was dire, adding that there was only expenditure and no income. As a result, the Republic of China could not help but rely on foreign loans. He lamented that the people of the Republic did not have the ability to cover all the expenditure and their future was very harsh (*EM* 1912d, 21600).

To remedy this situation, many proposals were made to restore state finances without relying on foreign loans. One of the proposals was the National Donation (国民捐) proposed on 29 April 1912 by Huang Xing (黄兴), one of the members of Tung Meng Hui since its foundation in 1905 in Tokyo and closely allied to the Chinese in Penang since his attendance of the Penang Conference in 1910 (*EM* 1912c, 21427). The proposal opposed the contract of loans between the Ministry of Finance of the Republic of China and four countries, namely, the United Kingdom, the United States, Germany and France on 17 May. Huang Xing urged the institution of National Donations as a means of rebuilding state finances without foreign loans. He proposed to set twenty categories of rates ranging from 0.02 per cent to 14 per cent the value of property and/or income for those whose property and/or income was more than $500 and less than $10 million; likewise, those with property and/or income worth more than $10 million would be imposed a 16 per cent tax of their property and/or income (*EM* 1912d, 21625).

Although National Donations was not an official project organized by the government, it gained official recognition. A Presidential Decision Directive issued on 30 June 1912 recognized National Donations as a voluntary campaign proposed by philanthropists and forbade coercive donation collection methods (*EM* 1912e, 21822). The Ministry of Finance announced in March 1913 that it would confer awards on those who contributed greatly to the National Donation (*PS* 12 March 1913).

(2) Response in Penang

Penang Sin Poe reported that there were active responses in Nanjing, Shanghai, Hong Kong, Singapore and Perak to the donation drive and urged the Chinese in Penang to follow suit. Gu Mei Dun Gen Sheng (古梅钝根生), a leading writer of the *Penang Sin Poe*, wrote that people in the United Kingdom, France, Germany and Russia were burdened with tax to support their army and navy and urged the Chinese in Penang to fulfil their obligations by donating as people in European countries did (*PS* 24 May 1912). The writer on the other hand demanded government transparency in the administration of the finances. He stressed that the state be held accountable by laying bare its income and expenditure in both the upper and lower houses so as to allow people to participate in the budget-making process (*PS* 28 May 1912).

In Penang, the PPU members initiated the campaign for National Donations at the community level. They held a meeting on 25 June and decided to encourage PPU members to donate within their means. They also decided to invite various Chinese organizations, especially the Chinese Town Hall, and elected eight committee members, including Wee Kim Kheng, Tan Sin Cheng, Khoo Beng Cheang, Xiong Yu Shan, Lim Joo Tek to liaise with the Chinese Town Hall to co-organize the campaign (*PS* 26 June 1912).

However, such cooperation did not materialize. It remains uncertain whether the PPU failed in its attempt at coordinating the campaign with the Chinese Town Hall or if they decided not to invite the Chinese Town Hall after all. When PPU members held a general meeting on 8 July at Nam Wah hospital to discuss the campaign, a few members of the Chinese Town Hall and the PCCC attended the meeting. Despite the apparent failure of the scheme, the PPU members remained committed to involving the non-PPU prominent members of the Chinese community in the campaign. They appointed Chang Pi Shi (張弼士)[24] President of the National Donation committee, Lim Ewe Hong Vice President, and Tye Kee Yoon (Chinese Consul in Penang) Financial Secretary. This was despite the fact that none of them attended the meeting. Twenty-four committee members were also elected, twelve members from Hokkien and Cantonese communities respectively, including those involved in the Chinese Town Hall and PCCC (*PS* 6 July 1912). However, Chang and Tye did not work with the PPU, instead, they held a gathering on National Donation whereby they collected $28,600 on their own (*PS* 28 June 1912).

(3) Negative Reaction

All in all, the campaign was largely inactive. Between 7 September 1912 and 2 January 1913, the Hokkien community collected $7,000 (*PS* 7 January 1913; 24 October 1913) and the Cantonese community collected $15,000 (*PS* 14 April 1913). The National Donation drive only amounted to $22,200 in Penang, which was a significantly lower sum than the $135,389 collected between October 1911 and January 1912 in the aftermath of the Wuchang uprising.

The Chinese Town Hall and the PCCC did not have any marked reaction to the campaign. Even the donation promoters elected at the 8 July meeting were relatively inactive. Three promoters sent a joint letter to *Penang Sin*

Poe lamenting that save themselves, they had never encountered any other promoters in town. They demanded that other promoters should actively solicit for funds too if Penang was to keep up with the successful donation drives in the other cities (*PS* 12 August 1912). An article published in *Penang Sin Poe* on 28 September reported that the Chinese in Penang were not active in the campaign; in contrast, Chinese communities in other cities were responding to the same campaign in full force (*PS* 28 September 1912).

The passiveness of the Chinese in Penang is especially puzzling. This is more so given that there were hardly any Straits Settlements government restrictions on the Chinese community there. While there was no real episode demonstrating the Straits Settlements government curtailment of Chinese activities, there was a notable incident in Perak whereby the attitude of British officials are most clearly seen. Foo Choo Choon (胡子春),[25] the then president of Perak Chinese Chamber of Commerce, reported to the Chinese Protector in Perak that the Chinese community in Perak had held a meeting and was resolved to carry out a National Donation campaign to save the financial crisis of the Republic of China. Foo Choo Choon asked the Chinese Protector for permission to launch the campaign. While the Chinese Protector approved the campaign, he requested that Foo Choo Choon establish a committee to supervise the campaign and submit its rules and regulations to the government. Foo Choo Choon accepted this compromise. The Chinese in Penang regarded it as a rather necessary intervention. An article in the *Penang Sin Poe* explained that the Chinese Protector in Perak aimed to prevent the misuse of donations, for there were pseudo collectors of donations right after the Wuchang uprising who disappeared with the money (*PS* 26 June 1912).

One of the reasons for the passivity of the Chinese in Penang lay in their uncertainty as to how the donation funds were managed and spent in China. When the Hokkien community in Penang held a meeting on 2 July 1912 to discuss the matter, Xu Ji Jun (徐季钧), a leading writer of *Penang Sin Poe*, suggested that it was better to pool the donated money at the local bank in Penang for the time being as officials in China might misappropriate the money. Xu recommended that they should wait until the parliament passed regulations and set down guidelines as to how the money would be spent (*PS* 3 July 1912). In actuality, the Chinese in Penang did not send the bulk of the collected funds. The Hokkien community kept $5,793 on hand in October 1913 (*PS* 24 October 1913), while the Cantonese community had $13,000 dollars in September 1913 (*PS* 20 September 1913).

Donated money sometimes disappeared. The *Penang Sin Poe* introduced an episode, reproduced in various newspapers in Hong Kong and Guangdong involving the donation funds collected by the Cantonese community in the United States and Canada and sent to Guangdong when the province declared independence in 1911. $30,000 was remitted to Guangdong province, but they received a receipt showing that Guangdong only received $10,000 (*PS* 11 March 1913).

The donors needed help in tracing their donations until they reached their target destination. In July 1912, the Le Le Association (乐乐公社), a charity organization affiliated with the Guang Fu Gong and the Chinese Town Hall, organized a fund-raising campaign to help victims of a flood in Dong Bei Jiang, Guangdong Province. They collected $5,173 and remitted it to the Relief Operation Centre in Guangdong through the Military Governor of Guangdong (*PS* 21 February 1913). It was very common for the recipients of donation to put articles in newspapers to introduce the names of donors and amount of donation in acknowledgement of their support. The donors read these articles to check whether their money had arrived at their target destinations. The Le Le Association found their members' names missing from the report published by the operation centre (*PS* 16 April 1913), and launched an investigation to trace their missing money. They contacted the operation centre and the Military Governor of Guangdong, before finally receiving confirmation that the operation centre had received their money in May 1913 (*PS* 23 May 1913).

(4) End of Campaign

As a result of the changing political situation in China, most of the money collected in Penang was not sent to China. This was because the contract of loans between the Republic of China and Western powers was concluded in April 1913. The National Donation campaign that aimed to restore the state treasury without borrowing foreign loans now lost its purpose. Huang Xing, the protagonist of the National Donation campaign, left China in September 1913 with other Kuomintang leaders including Sun Yat-sen after they had failed in their so-called Second Revolution.

In light of this, the Chinese in Penang recognized that the National Donation campaign was over. They held a meeting to decide what to do with the money collected. The Cantonese community held a meeting on 17 September 1913 and decided to donate 20–30 per cent of the money to the victims of the flood in Dong Xi Jiang, Guangdong Province, and refund 70 per cent of the money to the original donors (*PS* 18 September 1913). The Hainanese community reached the same decision (*PS* 19 September 1913). The Hokkien community held a meeting on 24 October and decided to refund all the money to the representatives of neighbourhood communities along streets, for they carried out the campaign by neighbourhood communities (*PS* 24 October 1913). Each neighbourhood community decided what to do with the money. Most of them chose to donate a part of the collected funds towards the refurbishment of the common facilities and refunded the rest to the original donators (*PS* 30 September 1913).

The National Donation campaign in Penang was initiated by PPU members. They tried to mobilize the whole Chinese community in Penang as well as the various Chinese organizations such as the Chinese Town Hall. The PPU members were relatively inactive in the campaign. One of the main reasons for their negative response was their uncertainty of the efficacy of the campaign in China. The Chinese in Penang feared that the money they collected would be lost due to poor management and misappropriation in China.

While they may be regarded as unpatriotic, it was their right to negotiate with the state. They observed the situation and decided to bide their time throughout the National Donation campaign. They demanded authorities' accountability and transparency in the management of the collected funds. Civil society today is encouraged to monitor governments and demand efficient and transparent administration. This was exactly what the Penang Chinese did during the National Donation campaign.

CONCLUSION

The contribution of the Overseas Chinese to China has often been measured based on the money and lives they devoted to the revolution in 1911. However, as this chapter has shown, it is also fair to highlight other aspects of financial support to China in Penang around 1911.

The donation remitted to China right after the Wuchang uprising sought to alleviate the chaotic situation in China rather than forward the revolution. The Penang Chinese sometimes took a wait-and-see attitude to the appeal for donations from China when it was uncertain as to how the donated money would be managed. They checked to ensure their donations reached their target destination. They also demanded the authorities' accountability and transparency in the management of the donated money.

Donation campaigns in 1911 Penang demonstrate that the Penang Chinese were more concerned with social security and order, good governance, as well as government transparency and accountability. As early as a hundred years ago, the Chinese in Penang already had values necessary to the development of modern civil society. It is fair to evaluate these aspects when discussing the contribution of the Overseas Chinese to the revolution in China.

Notes

1. Huang Jianli points out that there is no evidence of this exact phrase in Sun's speeches and writings. He concludes that the only traceable direct reference to the epithet can be found in Teo Eng Hock's memoir (Huang 2006).
2. This is a movie directed by Derek Chiu, costing RM8 million, invested by Malaysia's Rimbunan Hijau Group and China's Pearl River Film Company and Shenzhen Film Production Company (*Star*, 24 June 2007). It was distributed by Wawasan Open University <http://www.cinemaonline.com.my/movie/movie. asp?search=roaddawn>.
3. This paper use "Guangdong" and "Fujian", instead of "Canton" and "Hokkien", for the name of the provinces in China, while it uses "Cantonese" and "Hokkien" for the dialect groups in Penang who came from the provinces, as well as for their language and culture.
4. Though this paper focuses on donations to China, various donation campaigns were organized by the Chinese in Penang on occasions of British royal ceremonies. One such example is the Diamond Jubilee of Queen Victoria in June 1897 (CO273/226/17842), the coronation ceremony of Edward in June 1902 (*PS* 1902.6.19; 20; 21; 24; 25), and so forth. They tried to show their commitment to the ceremonies so as to win recognition from the Straits Settlements' authorities. The Chinese Town Hall was one of the main driving forces of those campaigns.
5. Goh Say Eng was born in 1875 in Penang. He received informal education in Chinese and English. He took over Chop See Hock (瑞福号), a company established by his father Goh Yu Chai (吴有才) that manufactured flour, meehoon and safety matches. Say Eng became a strong supporter of the Chinese revolutionary movement in Malaya. He was founding chairman of the Penang Tung Meng Hui established in 1906, and founder and director of *Kwong Wah Yit Poh* (光华日报) in 1910. He mobilized financial and manpower support for Sun Yat-sen in 1910–12. He was elected the Southeast Asian Chinese representative to the National Convention of Tung Meng Hui in China (Lee and Chow 1997, p. 48).
6. Wee Kim Kheng was born in Penang. His ancestors originated from Dong An prefecture, Quan Zhou Fu, Fujian province and resided in Siam for generations. Kim Kheng's father, a tin trader, moved from Siam to Penang. Kim Kheng succeeded to his father's business and made a fortune. He married the daughter of Koh Sim Kong, Assistant Governor of Ranon in southern Siam. His business slowed down in later years. He went to Singapore in 1915 was appointed manager of 中华国货公司, but died from sickness in 1916 (Zhang 2004, pp. 121–25).

7. Tan Sin Cheng was born in 1881 in Dong An prefecture, Quan Zhou Fu, Fujian province. He came to Penang at the age of eighteen to help his father. His original name was Tan Lan or Tan Wen Tu, but he changed his name to Sin Cheng (新政) when he joined Dong Meng Hui. He established trading companies and a rubber factory. He soon expanded his business to encompass shipping and made a fortune. He was Bureau Chief of Guo Ming Dang Penang Branch in 1914, and Vice President of the PCCC between 1916 and 1917. He established Chung Ling Secondary School. As he opposed the Education Ordinance of 1920, he was banished from the Straits Settlements to Fujian province in October 1921. He returned to southern Siam and founded a mill factory there. He made a speech in January 1921 to commemorate the thirteenth anniversary of PPU. This speech was published as the *History of Overseas Chinese Revolution* (华侨革命史). He died in 1924 (Lee and Chow 1997, p. 163).

8. Khoo Beng Cheang was born in Sandou Xinan She, Hai Cheng prefecture, Zhang Zhou Fu, Fujian province. He came to Penang when he was young. After working as a clerk, he founded Ji Chang Hao (吉昌号), a company that traded in oil and rope. He established a branch in Singapore and Bayan Api. He purchased land and planted rubber. He cut his queue in 1909. He was a committee member of the Chinese Town Hall and PCCC (Zheng 1983, p. 175).

9. Xiong Yu Shan was born in Mei prefecture, Guangdong province. He came to Penang in his early youth and worked as shop clerk. After failing to successfully dredge tin in Perak, he returned to Penang and founded a hostel (恒益兴旅店), from which his business grew (Zhang 2004, p. 264).

10. Lim Joo Tek was born in Lin Dong She, Hai Cheng prefecture, Zhang Zhou Fu, Fujian province. He was the general manager for Mi Jiao Gong Si (米较公司). He was also a committee member of the Chinese Town Hall in 1928–33, as well as a board member of Chung Ling high school and Chung Hua high school (Zheng 1983, p. 179).

11. PCCC accepted a large number of PPU members in May 1912, including Wee Kim Kheng, Khoo Beng Cheang, and Tan Sin Cheng.

12. H.A. Neubronner was born in 1872 in Malacca, and returned to Penang in around 1899 after studying and working in London. He started Wilson and Neubronner, a construction and renovation firm in Penang that refurbished and built notable buildings such as Kapitan Kling Mosque, Aceh Mosque, Nagor Mosque, and so on (RAP 1909).

13. It had multi-ethnic committee members such as P.V. Locke, C.W. Barnett, H.A. Neubronner, J.Chenney, J.D. Scully, J. Martin, A.O. Merican, M.M. Noordin, K. Patchitt, Hadji Zachariach, and R.K. Nambyar. See Figure 4.2 for Chinese committee members.

14. Yeoh Guan Seok was born in 1883 in Penang. He was educated at the Penang Free School where he was awarded a Queen's Scholarship in 1901. He proceeded to England where he studied history and law at St John's College, Cambridge,

as a Foundation Scholar. He was called to the Bar at Gray's Inn, London. He returned to Penang as the first Chinese lawyer in the state. He was a Municipal Commissioner for Georgetown in 1911–22 and was appointed a member of the Legislative Council of the Straits Settlements in 1923. He was the first Penang Chinese appointed to that position. He was also a committee member of the Chinese Town Hall (1922–26) (Zheng 1983, p. 185; Lee and Chow 1997, p. 193).

15. In the Straits Settlements, only British nationals were eligible to become Committee members of the Municipality. However, male ratepayers of the Municipality who paid rates as much as or more than the amount regulated by the ordinance were eligible to become voters regardless of nationality. Ratepayers were those who satisfied one of the following conditions: (1) owners who owned property in the Municipality paying rates as much as twenty dollars or above in half years, (2) owners whose property was evaluated at more than 480 dollars, or (3) a tenant who lived in property who paid rates more than 480 dollars a year (Ord. No. IX of 1887).

16. Dr P.V. Locke was born in 1869 in Penang. He received his education at the Penang Free School until he was nearly eighteen years old and at Raffles Institution for a few months where he won the Queen's Scholarship in 1887. He went to Edinburgh University with Dr Lim Boon Keng to study medicine, and after a brilliant career there returned to the Straits. On his return, he was attached to the General Hospital, Singapore, as House Physician. But he only remained there for a short while before going into private practice in Penang. He gradually built up the largest practice there and retired with a comfortable fortune. He was the first elected Municipal Commissioner and ever since then, with brief intervals represented the ratepayers on the Municipal Board until he passed away in July 1911 (*SE* 12 November 1903, 13 July 1911).

17. Lim Seng Hooi was born in Penang in 1872. He was educated in Chinese and English. He was a son of Lim Hua Chiam (林花簪), a prominent leader of the Chinese community in Penang, who made a fortune through dealing in Chinese medicine. Seng Hooi took over Criterion Press (点石齐印字公司) founded by Hua Chiam in 1883 and published the *Penang Sin Poe* in 1895, and *Chahayah Pulau Penang* in 1900, under the editorship of Abdul Ghani b. Mohd. Kassim who had been an editor of *Jawi Peranakan*, and *Straits Echo* in 1903 under the editorship of Chesney Duncan from Hong Kong. Criterion Press became a limited company and Seng Hooi became its managing director. He was also a board member of the Eastern Trading Company and an agent of the Great Eastern Assurance Company. He was appointed member of the Chinese Advisory Board, Justice of the Peace, and District Hospital Committee. He was also the president and vice president of the Chinese Town Hall, Kong Hock Kong, and Hokkien Kongsi (Lee and Chow 1997, pp. 114–15; Roff 1972, p. 5; PCTH 1983, p. 170).

18. The following amounts were collected: $32,550 from the East Indies, $30,434

from French Indochina and Siam, $15,000 from the United States, $74,000 from Canada, and $300 from Cuba.

19. Key attendees were Leong Lok Hing, Ooi Huck Boon, Teo Soon Kheng, Lim Joo Tek, Wee Kim Kheng, Khoo Beng Cheang, Khoo Ewe Bee, Khoo Sin Hoe, Lim Eng Ho, Khoo Cheow Teong, Cheah Cheang Lim, Khoo Tek Suan, Lim Ee Phok, Yeow Hooi Seong, Li Hong Pow, Lee Yong Kheng, Khoo Kim Keng, Shum Hin Chun, and Low Chzee Khuan.

20. Leong Lok Hing was born in 1851 in Guangdong and educated in the United States. He started his career as a merchant in California. He came to Penang in 1888 and set up Kwong On & Co. (广安号), an import firm with branches in Ipoh and Tapah under the name of Kwong Kut Cheong & Co. (广吉昌号). He owned several large tin mines in Bidor, Chenderiang, and Kuala Lumpur, and extensive rubber, coconut, and tapioca estates in Sungei Semambu. He was also a provisions supplier to tin mines and rubber estates. He sold his tin through European agency houses and traded in European provisions and merchandise. He was appointed a Justice of the Peace at the Chinese Advisory Board. He played leading roles in various Chinese organizations. He was the president of the Chinese Town Hall, Penang Chinese Chamber of Commerce, and Vice president of the Guangdong and Tingchou Association, etc. (Lee and Chow 1997, p. 97; PCTH 1983, pp. 183–84).

21. Zhuang Yin An (庄银安) was born in 1854. He moved to Burma in his youth, where he found his company (源记栈号) which managed plantations. He founded Chung Hua Yi Xue (中华义学) with his friends such as 徐赞周 in 1903 as well as a night school (益商夜校). He became the Bureau Chief of Tung Meng Hui Rangoon Branch in November 1908. He published *Guang Hua Bao* (光华报) within the same year and became its general manager, but the *Guang Hua Bao* was closed in 1910 and he moved to Penang, where he published *Kwong Wah Yit Poh*. He was appointed representative of Tung Meng Hui of Nanyang Cities (南洋各埠同盟会总代表) and returned to Amoy. He was appointed advisor of the provincial government of Fujian, Chairman of the Amoy Council, Bureau Chief of Financial Bureau. After the failure of the Second Revolution, he went back to Burma where he established Da Dong Oil Factory (大同油厂). He was elected president of the Fujian Hua Qiao Association (福建华侨公会会长). He went back to Fujian in his later years and was appointed member of the Fujian Overseas Chinese Affairs Committee (福建侨务委员会委员) and its acting president (代理主任委员) (Zhou 1995, p. 320).

22. Khoo Cheow Teong was born in 1849 in Penang. He was educated in a Chinese school, and joined a Chinese firm as an assistant. Having served his apprenticeship, he went to Perak where he traded and assisted others in trade for some time. He subsequently chose to settle in Asahan, on the east coast of Sumatra, where he conducted business as a general merchant. That venture was largely successful and he soon amassed a fortune. His business led him from one part of Malaya to another. In his sojourn to Malacca in 1874, he married

the eldest daughter of the late Mr Lim Cheoh, a popular rice merchant of that settlement. In 1878, the Dutch Government made him Kapitan China of Asahan and he was put in charge of the revenue farms of Deli, Asahan, Begkalis, Penang as well as business activities in several other places. In 1904 he resigned the post of Kapitan China on account of old age, but he still spent a considerable part of his time in Asahan. He made his home in Penang in around 1909 where he owned considerable landed property and was regarded as one of the wealthiest inhabitants (Wright and Cartwright 1908, p. 777; Zheng 1983, p. 184).

23. Qiu Jin Jing was born in Xin An She, San Dou, Hai Cheng, Zhang Zhou, Fujian (福建省漳州府海澄县三都新安社), came to Penang when he was young and had been there for 50–60 years. After working for a shop, he founded his own company dealing with rice trade (Zheng 1983, p. 174).

24. Alias Cheong Fatt Zte, Thio Thiau Siat (张兆燮), or Chang Chin Hsun (张振勋). See Godley (1981) for more on the career of Chang Pi Shi.

25. Foo Choo Choon was born in 1860 in Yong Ding District, Ting Zhou, Fujian (福建省汀州府永定县) and Hakka. His grandfather was an early immigrant to Penang and his father was born there. Choo Choon came with his father to Penang where he received a few years of traditional Chinese education. Later, he went to work for an uncle in Taiping who was engaged in tin mining, Foo struck out on his own in Lahat, Kinta district where he successfully opened up mines employing several thousand workers. He was later known as the King of Tin Mining. However ill-health forced him to return to China for a rest. On his return to the Federated Malay States, he took over the Tronoh Mines which had been abandoned. He introduced modern methods and successfully revived the mine. He owned mines in Sungei Besi, Ipoh Keladang, Lahat, Kaki Bukit as well as a mine in southern Thailand known as Tongkah. In 1906, he expanded his mining business to include China. In 1906 as a token of loyalty to the Chinese imperial government, he was rewarded for his donation of S$10,000. He also invested in Fukien Province Railway Company (福建省铁道公司). He held positions in many organizations including the Perak Chinese Chamber of Commerce, Kinta Planting Association, and served as member of Perak State Council and Perak Chinese Advisory Board. He was also a member of the Chinese Town Hall in Penang (Lee and Chow 1997, pp. 42–43).

References

Government Gazette
SSGG: *Straits Settlements Government Gazette.*
CO273: *Straits Settlements Original Correspondence, Colonial Office Record.*
CO273/226/17842: Queen's Reign Celebration, SS to CO, 21 July 1897.
RAP: Annual Administration Report, Penang.

Periodicals
PGSC: *Penang Gazette and Straits Chronicle.*

SE: *Straits Echo.*
ST: *Straits Times.*
PS: *Penang Sin Poe* (《槟城新报》)
EM: *The Eastern Miscellany* (《东方杂志》)
EM 1912c: 8(12) 民国元年六月初一日
EM 1912d: 9(1) 民国元年七月初一日
EM 1912e: 9(2) 民国元年八月初一日

English books and articles
City Council of Georgetown. *Penang: Past and Present 1786–1963*, Penang, 1966.
Goldley, Michael R. *The Mandarin-Capitalists from Nanyang: Overseas Chinese Enterprise in the Modernization of China, 1893–1911.* Cambridge: Cambridge University Press, 1981.
Huang Jingli. "Writings on Sun Yat-sen, Tongmenghui and the 1911 Revolution: Surveying the Field and Locating Southeast Asia". In *Tongmenghui, Sun Yat-sen and the Chinese in Southeast Asia: A Revisit,* edited by Leo Suryadinata. Singapore: Chinese Heritage Centre, 2006, pp. 61–107.
Lee, Kam Hing and Chow Mun Seong. *Biographical Dictionary of the Chinese in Malaysia.* Petaling Jaya: Pelanduk Publications, 1997.
Lo, Man Yuk. "Chinese Names of Streets in Penang". *Journal of the Straits Branch of the Royal Asiatic Society* 33 (January 1900): 197–246.
Shinozaki Kaori. "The Foundation of the Penang Chinese Chamber of Commerce in 1903". *Journal of the Malaysian Branch of the Royal Asiatic Society* 79, no. 1 (June 2006): 43–65.
Suryadinata, Leo, ed. *Tongmenghui, Sun Yat Sen and the Chinese in Southeast Asia: A Revisit.* Singapore: Chinese Heritage Centre, 2006.
Wright, Arnold and H.A. Cartwright, eds. *Twentieth Century Impressions of British Malaya: Its History, People, Commerce, Industries, and Resources.* London: Lloyd's Greater Britain Publishing Company Ltd., 1908.
Yen, Ching Hwang. *The Overseas Chinese and the 1911 Revolution: With Special Reference to Singapore and Malaya.* Kuala Lumpur: Oxford University Press, 1976.
———— 2006. *Tongmenghui, Sun Yat-sen and the Chinese in Singapore and Malaya: A Revisit,* edited by Leo Suryadinata. Singapore: Chinese Heritage Centre, 2006, pp. 109–146.

Chinese books and articles
PCCC 2003: 槟州中华总商会《槟州中华总商会100周年纪念特刊》。
PCTH 1983: 槟州华人大会堂特刊编辑委员会《槟州华人大会堂庆祝成立一百周年新夏落成开幕纪念特刊》槟州华人大会堂。
Chen 1986: 陈树强〈辛亥革命时期南洋华人支援起义经费之研究〉辛亥革命南洋华人研讨会论文集编辑委员会1986, 238–266。

Jiang 1986: 蒋永敬〈辛亥前南洋华人对孙中山先生革命运动之支援〉辛亥革命南洋华人研讨会论文集编辑委员会、1986、222–237。

Kua 1995: 柯木林主编《新华历史人物列传》教育出版私营有限公司，新加坡。

Liu 1986: 刘世昌〈中山先生与南洋〉《辛亥革命与南洋华人研讨会论文集》47–64。

Tan 1983: 陈剑虹〈平章会馆的历史发展轮廓 1881–1974〉 PCTH 1983、135–162。

———— 2 0 0 3〈槟州中华总商会的百年发展〉PCCC 2003, 43–46。

Zhang 1994: 张少宽〈十九世纪槟榔屿福建公冢研究〉《槟城联合福建公冢二百年》249–261。

———— 2002: 张少宽《槟榔屿华人实话》燧人氏事业公司，Kuala Lumpur。

———— 2003: 张少宽《槟榔屿华人史话续编》南洋田野研究室, Penang。

———— 2004: 张少宽《孙中山与庇能会议策动广州三、二九之役》南洋田野研究室, Penang。

Zheng 1978: 郑永美〈槟州中华总商会战前史料〉槟州中华总商会《槟州中华总商会赞禧纪念特刊 (1903–1978)》, 75–87。

———— 1983: 郑永美〈平章先贤列传〉PCTH 1983, 169–193。

辛亥革命南洋华人研讨会论文集编辑委员会 1986《辛亥革命与南洋华人研讨会论文集》国立政治大学国际关系中心，台北。

Zhou 1995: 周南京（主编）『世界华侨华人词典』，智力出版社，香港、新加坡、马来西亚柔佛新山（原由北京大学出版社出版，1991）。

5

PERCEPTIONS OF CHINA FOR THE OVERSEAS CHINESE TEA TRADERS IN COLONIAL SINGAPORE, 1928–58

Jason Lim

INTRODUCTION

Among the Overseas Chinese, research has focused on a small group of rich merchants who had invested time and money on rubber, pineapple and other products in Malaya. Few studies have been conducted on other, less wealthy, Overseas Chinese merchants in colonial Singapore. These merchants imported goods from either China or Southeast Asia for re-export or sale to local clientele.

The Overseas Chinese tea traders were one such group of merchants. Many of them left Fujian Province amidst political strife in the 1920s and established branches of their family businesses in Singapore. Over the years, these firms became part of an extensive business network stretching from Anxi and Xiamen in Fujian to Kuala Lumpur and Singapore. In September 1928, the traders came together and registered the Singapore Tea Merchants Association (星州茶商公会) — which was renamed the Singapore Chinese Tea Importers and Exporters Association (SCTIEA) in 1948 — with the British colonial authorities in Singapore to further their political and commercial interests.

From the founding of the SCTIEA to questions of nationhood in Malaya and Singapore in the late 1950s, the traders remained attached to a "China" based on their political concerns. This chapter will examine how "China" came to be perceived in the eyes of the traders through the minutes of the SCTIEA, newspaper reports and oral history interviews conducted by the Oral History Centre in Singapore.

PERCEPTIONS OF "CHINA" BEFORE WORLD WAR II, 1928–42

With the end of the Northern Expedition led by Chiang Kai-shek, the Republic of China (ROC) was finally unified under Kuomintang (KMT) control. Unfortunately for Chiang and the KMT, the unification of China came at a time when Japan began carving a new role for itself in Asia. By 1931, Japan signalled its intention to be a military and political force in Asia by invading Manchuria and setting up a puppet regime in the so-called "State of Manchukuo" in 1934.

The Overseas Chinese monitored these events in East Asia with concern. Major Chinese merchants in Southeast Asia began clamouring for action against Japanese imperialism and there were increasing calls for Overseas Chinese unity. The Overseas Chinese community leaders in Southeast Asia also appealed for participation in anti-Japanese activities and greater motivation to aid China economically. For the tea traders in Singapore, China was regarded as the "motherland" and the tea traders expressed their loyalty through various campaigns to support China in her fight against Japanese imperialism.

Promotion of Tea as a "National Product"

The SCTIEA was founded as a consequence of the Jinan Incident in 1928. The incident had sparked off a wave of patriotism among the Overseas Chinese and the tea traders in Singapore wanted to help China in the crisis. The association was formed so that the traders could participate in relief efforts.[1] China teas were also promoted by the SCTIEA as a "national product" in colonial Singapore that should be purchased and consumed by patriotic Overseas Chinese.

The tea traders in Singapore monitored developments in Chinese production techniques and organization. In May 1935, two officials from China arrived in Singapore for an inspection of the tea trade between China and Southeast Asia before travelling to India and Ceylon for a further study on tea production techniques. One of them was Wu Juenong (吴觉农), who came as a representative of the National Economic Commission of the National Government in Nanjing. Accompanying him was Ko Chung Cheng (柯仲正) who was sent by the Fujian Provincial Government.[2] Wu mentioned that China teas were not doing well overseas because of the high cost of production at home. He noted that the Chinese tea industry lacked organization, capital and reform. Lim Keng Lian, Chairman of the SCTIEA, reiterated that Wu should return to China and introduce measures to reform the industry and restore national pride.[3]

The traders were also actively boycotting Japanese and Taiwanese teas. Strong popular pressure also inhibited the Chinese tea firms from selling non-Chinese tea. Even selling China teas sometimes carried risks as poor quality Chinese tea could be regarded as "substandard" and therefore not a "national product". The SCTIEA would investigate any claims made against its members for selling "enemy products", which in the late 1930s and early 1940s included Taiwan teas, even though Singapore was not a major market in Southeast Asia.[4] Members were encouraged to make a public stand for "national products" and the association pledged to take full responsibility for ensuring that its members sold only "national products".[5]

Sometimes the sense of patriotism from the Overseas Chinese could go too far. A major case occurred in November 1939 when unnamed "patriotic organizations" accused an association member, Joo Hiang Tea Merchant, of selling "enemy products". Lim Keng Lian was asked to conduct a preliminary investigation and report his findings.[6] Five investigators were tasked by the SCTIEA to look into the matter.[7] In December, Gan Wei Hoon reported that he had gone to Joo Hiang Tea Merchant with Koh Hoon Peng and Pek Kim Aw and checked the account books and the stocks of tea, but they found no trace of "enemy products" on the premises. The other members felt that since the "patriotic organizations" also produced no evidence, the investigation should end.[8] This incident, more than anything else, highlighted the dangers of the time. Unlawful "patriotic groups", declaring their whole-hearted love and devotion to China, were also striking fear in the hearts of Singapore merchants. The experience of Joo Hiang showed that merchants accused by unscrupulous members of the community could suffer maximum damage to their businesses and be publicly shamed.

Patriotism towards China

Despite the sense of fear caused by unlawful "patriotic groups", the feeling of patriotism in the hearts of the Overseas Chinese tea traders remained strong. The SCTIEA would send representatives to any meetings organized by recognized "patriotic Chinese organizations" seeking to raise funds and political support for China's war efforts. In November 1940, when it was announced that Wu Te-chen, the Secretary-General of the Central Executive Committee of the KMT, would be visiting Singapore to boost the war against Japan, the association chose Gan Wei Hoon as its representative to welcome the Secretary-General.[9]

The years 1939 to 1941 were a period of intense "patriotic" activity among the Overseas Chinese in Singapore. Many activities were organized to raise funds or political support for China. These were mainly organized by Tan Kah Kee, a China-born merchant who had made his fortune in rubber in Malaya before most of his businesses collapsed as a result of the Great Depression. He had been immensely vocal in his calls for the Overseas Chinese in Southeast Asia to support China's war efforts. The SCTIEA picked Gan Wei Hoon and Koh Hoon Peng as its representatives to attend the welcoming party for the return of Tan from one of his missions to China.[10] Similarly, when a meeting of all the Singapore Chinese organizations was organized to galvanize support for China, the SCTIEA chose Lim Kim Thye Tea Merchant as its representative in December 1941. The Singapore Chinese Mobilization Council, chaired by Tan, aimed to energize the Overseas Chinese to assist the British and Empire forces in defending the island.[11]

However, it should be noted that their patriotism towards China was in line with the political ideals of the ruling Kuomintang (KMT). It is highly unlikely that the traders would have been supporters of the Chinese Communist Party (CCP). Some of the traders' families who owned tea gardens in Fujian province, for instance, faced constant raids from communist "bandits". Lim Keng Lian was also the only Overseas Chinese tea trader in Singapore to join the KMT.[12] He had been the representative of the Overseas Chinese of Malaya in the National People's Congress in Nanjing and was a member of the People's Political Council in Chongqing; he could have joined the KMT around 1944.[13]

PERCEPTIONS OF "CHINA" AFTER WORLD WAR II, 1945–58

Once the CCP proclaimed the founding of the People's Republic of China (PRC) on 1 October 1949, the attitude of the tea traders towards China changed. Many of the first generation of tea traders in Singapore continued to remain loyal to the ideals of the KMT. Despite the defeat of the KMT, and the retreat of the Nationalist Army to Taiwan, for the traders, the term "China" still means the ROC. Their suspicion of the communists was not helped by the seizure of their family tea gardens by the new Communist regime in Fujian, land that was redistributed to poorer tea farmers.

China as a Trading Partner

After 1949, it is clear from the SCTIEA minutes that China was just a nation for the tea trade. The traders remained concerned about the imports and prices of China teas. In January 1950, the SCTIEA contacted the Xiamen Tea Merchants Association about trade conditions and deposits imposed for exports from Xiamen. The association also enquired on how it should continue with the trade from Xiamen. It sent an appeal to the Xiamen Chamber of Commerce to reduce foreign exchange rates in order to improve trade.[14] The reply from the Chamber was read out to members in May, announcing that the export charges would be reduced from S$660 per picul to S$450 per picul.[15] The SCTIEA also enquired from the Shantou Chamber of Commerce in Guangdong Province on 11 May about prices, exports and foreign exchange rates.[16] In its reply, the Shantou Chamber of Commerce reported that each picul of tea exported from Shantou would be charged S$400 per picul.[17] Clearly the SCTIEA was either helping its Teochew members to secure tea imports, or looking for cheaper alternatives to Fujian tea. In November 1951, the SCTIEA asked the Central People's Government in Beijing to reduce export rates. It noted that export rates remained high in China, made worse by the realization that Fujian teas faced competition from Java and the Cameron Highlands.[18]

The high prices led to the traders looking for other supplies of tea. Taiwan looked like a possible alternative as it also produced oolong teas popular among the Overseas Chinese. In October 1952, a Mr Chen was introduced to members with tea samples from Taiwan. Members were urged to purchase the tea as it was also a "national produce" (国产). The sale tactic was reminiscent of pre-War days when merchants were expected to purchase tea on the basis of loyalty to country, and not the quality of the tea on sale. Members were shown statistical figures on Taiwanese exports and prices. Mr Chen also distributed several forms to traders who wished to make purchases.[19]

In March 1954, the SCTIEA received a letter from Fujian which would have sunk the hearts of members as it stated that the cost of tea had risen, *regardless of the quality*. Once again, the association urged the Central People's Government, the Bureau of International Trade of the Xiamen City Government and the Overseas Chinese Commission in Beijing to reduce the cost price of tea and the foreign exchange rate.[20] It seemed that the association never received any replies. By July there was still no news from Xiamen.[21] It was only in December 1955 that it was reported that the price of Fujian teas had stabilized, and members were urged to maintain current prices as the association awaited further developments.[22]

Trade Mission to Taiwan in 1957

In 1957, the SCTIEA was one of three trading associations in Singapore invited by the KMT Government to visit Taiwan, along with Malayan traders, to negotiate on trade between Singapore and Malaya and the ROC. When a trade mission to China was organized in mid-1956, it is noticeable that, although the mission was promoting the sale of Malayan rubber to China, other merchants had been invited to join. The SCTIEA, however, was not involved, despite the mission having more than 100 representatives from 39 trade associations and business firms.[23] The minutes of the association during this period do not even mention the trade mission to mainland China. This reflects the suspicions the tea merchants held towards any trade with the Communist regime. One can surmize that the conservative outlook of the tea merchants probably did not endear them to communism, and Lim Keng Lian — a forceful personality within the SCTIEA — remained avowedly pro-KMT and anti-communist.

The Singapore-Malaysia Trade Mission to Taiwan that June was, not surprisingly, led by Lim Keng Lian. The SCTIEA nominated four tea merchants from among its members, all of whom had to travel at their own expense. They were Lim (representing Lim Kim Thye Tea Merchant), Chan Teng Wah (representing Kim Leng Thye Tea Merchant), Ang Kwee Kee (representing Jian Chang Hang Tea Merchant) and Tjo Jak Min (representing Teo Thian Guan Tea Merchant). What is particularly interesting is that when members were asked if they would like to be involved in the preparatory work for the Trade Mission to Taiwan, representatives of 12 out of 14 firms present voted in favour.[24] Most of the traders, then, were sympathetic to the KMT.

Just as the Trade Mission was about to leave, Koh Kian Huat Tea Merchant informed the association that the price of tea from Xiamen had increased once again. This time the association merely wrote to the Xiamen Branch of the China Tea Company (CTC), urging it not to increase prices as it would be disadvantageous to both Xiamen and Singapore. The association also sought support from Chinese tea merchants in the Federation of Malaya in its appeal.[25] In the midst of preparing for the trip to Taiwan, increased tea prices from Xiamen did not receive so much attention, particularly as the traders had an impression that Taiwan teas were cheaper. After the Trade Mission returned from Taiwan, however, the issue was brought up as there had been no reply from Xiamen. It was decided then to contact the Xiamen Branch of the CTC about the quality of tea leaves harvested that autumn.[26]

The Trade Mission to Taiwan was considered a success and the four representatives were given a warm reception when they returned to the

SCTIEA in July.[27] The association was also introduced to a representative of the China-American Tea Company from Taipei. The four SCTIEA representatives reported on the Taiwanese tea trade, informing members that the Taiwan Provincial Government (TPG) had been informed about the conditions of the Singapore tea market and price hikes from mainland China. The representatives considered China and Taiwan teas as no longer in competition, implying their belief that Taiwan (being now a part of "China") teas were essentially Chinese. Members were, however, reminded that Taiwan teas were cheaper than Fujian teas. The representatives had also met a delegation from the TPG to discuss the possibility of lowering foreign exchange rates.[28]

The representative of the China-American Tea Company was grateful to the SCTIEA for promoting the purchase of Taiwan teas. He gave a sample of current tea prices in Taiwan and briefed the association that the Taiwanese tea trade was conducted completely by private enterprise. Members needed to contact individual merchants in Taiwan to conduct any purchase. There was no government intervention in the Taiwanese tea trade. He also noted, however, that Taiwanese tea prices in 1957 had risen by 20 per cent from the year before. Tea traders in Singapore could make purchases in American currency and pay later in New Taiwan Dollars. Members were also told that the exchange rate had fallen slightly; one American dollar now fetched NT$34.[29]

The SCTIEA subsequently decided to postpone any decision on the allocation of tea purchases. The minutes of a meeting held later on 20 July, however, do not record any quantity of Taiwan teas purchased by members. They reiterate that Taiwan teas were 30 per cent cheaper than Fujian teas, and that the TPG could assist with purchases wherever possible. While the Taiwanese tea industry was not a state enterprise, members were assured that the Central Trust of China (in Taiwan) would provide favourable exchange rates.[30] Members, however, maintained a wait-and-see attitude and there was no rush to purchase Taiwan teas.

Competition between Taiwan and Fujian Teas

The promotion of cheaper Taiwan teas could not have come at a better time for the traders. Barely a week after they were assured of favourable exchange rates from Taiwan came the news from the Xiamen Branch of the CTC that Fujian tea prices had gone up again. The CTC claimed that the quality of tea exports was constantly improving, resulting in higher costs of production for farmers. Therefore, the price of exports had to be increased. The prices of low-grade teas increased by as much as 30 per cent over the previous two months, while prices of high-grade teas shot up by 25 per cent. However, it seemed that prices of Taiwan teas had also increased by 25 per cent. Regardless of the increase in prices, the merchants in Singapore decided it was best to maintain stability by keeping retail prices reasonable.[31]

The SCTIEA eventually got used to recurring increases in Fujian tea prices. Three months after the Trade Mission returned from Taiwan, prices soared again. It was announced that the price of Wuyi Mountain tea, souchong tea and Tieguanyin tea in Fujian had risen by another 30 per cent. One member of the SCTIEA, Chan Tee Seng, understood the temptation by members to raise tea prices, but urged them not to do so. The association eventually voted to maintain current prices in Singapore and monitor the state of the trade before making any decision to increase prices further.[32]

The CTC, on the other hand, saw the need to maintain the Fujian tea trade and it gave the SCTIEA four free cans of Wuyi Mountain tea.[33] In thanking the CTC, however, the association also raised several points. First, standards should be set on the quality of Fujian tea. Second, tea prices needed to be re-adjusted as current prices were too high. Last, the CTC was reminded that each firm in Singapore had its own trademark, and most were retailers. In other words, the CTC would need to meet the needs of individual firms.[34] The CTC responded by informing the association that it would be exporting Fujian tea through Hong Kong. The association disagreed with this new regulation, since it would now take longer for the teas to reach Singapore, which meant the loss of valuable time and freshness of the tea. It requested the CTC to consider the difficulties faced by the merchants if they were to trade via Hong Kong, and the possibility that some merchants in Hong Kong might demand deposits before exporting the tea to Singapore.[35]

In May 1958, the *Nanyang Siang Pau* reported that cargoes of tea from China would be arriving in Singapore by mid-June. It seemed that both China and Taiwan were actively promoting their teas, resulting in increased production from both sides. Unfortunately, both sides exported more black tea. The decline in the export of semi-fermented tea would push up prices in Singapore. While supplies of spring teas were expected from China, the Taiwanese had already dispatched their spring tea. The sudden influx of Taiwanese teas depressed their prices slightly compared to China teas.[36] However, by the end of May, it was found that there would be a limited amount of tea exports from both China and Taiwan to Singapore. In addition, higher costs of production in China would increase prices in Singapore. A huge order to Taiwan from South Africa meant that larger quantities of tea had to be sent there at the expense of Singapore, and this would likewise increase Taiwanese tea prices in Singapore.[37]

Despite the competition between China and Taiwan for the Singapore market, however, China remained the main supplier of tea. It supplied seven times as much tea as Taiwan because traders in Singapore were also now importing black teas from Yunnan and Guangdong provinces, but China teas remained dearer. The best tea from Taiwan — "Biao Zhun Dui" tea — cost S$1.50 per catty, which was equivalent to the price of third-grade oolong tea from China. Tieguanyin tea from Fujian cost S$12 per catty. But the price difference increasingly came to be interpreted among traders in Singapore as evidence that the quality of China teas was superior to Taiwan teas.[38] This was more a matter of taste rather than production methods. A month later, the *Nanyang Siang Pau* reported that there was an influx of Taiwan teas the year before because of an increase in demand for China teas from Europe and Africa but the price of China teas in 1958 had fallen by 13 per cent.[39] This was the first time in a long while that the tea traders in Singapore actually heard some good news concerning tea prices.

Continued Recognition of the ROC

After 1948, the attitudes of the tea traders to China changed. In March that year, members voted to change the organization's name to the Singapore Tea Importers and Exporters Association (新加坡茶业出入口商公会).[40] But the Chairman, Gan Wei Hoon, reported a week later that the words "Overseas Chinese" should be retained since the association was an organization of Overseas Chinese.[41] This was confirmed on 15 March when members voted to adopt the name of "Singapore Overseas Chinese Tea Importers and Exporters Association" (新加坡华侨茶业出入口商公会).[42] The Chinese name retained "Overseas Chinese" (华侨) in its title, but somehow the English title was registered in the Chinese Secretariat as the "Singapore Chinese Tea Importers and Exporters Association". The latest name was adopted by the association in a meeting on 8 April.[43] The word "Overseas" may not have been used in its English title, but it was maintained in the Chinese script in order to reflect its identity as an organization of "Overseas Chinese" tea traders. As an Overseas Chinese organization, it informed the OCAC in Nanjing of the name change.[44]

The association also remained loyal to the ROC and this loyalty out-lasted the defeat of the Nationalists in 1949. This is evident from the post-War order of its swearing-in ceremonies. Typically, it would begin by members bowing three times before the ROC flag, the KMT flag and the portrait of Dr Sun Yat-sen. This would be followed by the reading of Dr Sun's last will and testament. After the document was read, there would be three minutes of silence as a sign of respect. After these formalities were carried out, the Chairman would address the meeting before members of the new Executive and Supervisory Committees were sworn in.

By the 1950s, there is a slow recognition that the old days of KMT rule on the mainland were over and that now a life in Singapore should be contemplated. The mainland was "lost" to the communists and it was highly unlikely that the traders would want to return to a communist China. Settling down in Malaya and Singapore did not seem to be a bad option. The attitude of the traders towards even the ROC can be seen in the changes in the swearing-in ceremonies of the Executive Committee. Whereas new Executive Committee members had to bow to the ROC flag, KMT flag and a portrait of Dr Sun in early 1949, before the proclamation of the PRC, later Committee members would only bow to a portrait of Dr Sun from 1951 to 1959. By 1960, new Executive Committee members sworn into office did not even bow to the portrait — Singapore had attained self-government and the merchants had begun to distance themselves from China by taking on Singapore citizenship.

At least one crisis faced by a member tea firm serves as an example of how the traders also continued to recognize the existence of the ROC. In June 1950, Wang Zeng Yuan Tea Merchant had 124 chests of tea recently purchased from Xiamen seized by the ROC military near Jinmen Island on its way to Siam. Wang Zeng Yuan Tea Merchant asked if the SCTIEA could negotiate with the "government of the motherland" (祖国政府) to secure the release of the cargo. It is evident from the minutes that the "government of the motherland" refers to the KMT Government in Taiwan, implying that the ROC is the "legitimate" China and not the PRC. In response, the SCTIEA contacted both the Ministry of Industry and the Overseas Chinese Affairs Commission (OCAC) in Taipei.[45]

The association later announced that it had received a letter from the ROC Minister of Economic Affairs. He instructed Wang Zeng Yuan Tea Merchant to send documents concerning the 124 chests including shipping documents and the bill of lading to the ROC military which would then be passed on to the Ministry of National Defence.[46] Upon further enquiry by the SCTIEA, the firm was notified that the 124 chests would be returned, provided its proprietor went to Taiwan to collect them himself.[47] In January 1951, the ROC Government confiscated all 124 chests again because the proprietor of Wang Zeng Yuan Tea Merchant had sent someone to collect the tea.[48] The chests of tea were eventually returned after another long negotiation with the ROC Government. In November 1951, more than a year after the cargo had been seized, the OCAC sent a letter to the SCTIEA, noting that the latter had proven the tea belonged to Wang Zeng Yuan Tea Merchant. The association wrote to the proprietor with the good news that the ROC Government would be returning the tea to him.[49]

CONCLUSION

When it comes to converging, distancing and positioning between Southeast Asia and China, as far as the Overseas Chinese tea traders are concerned, their lives are intertwined with the international political and economic scene in the region. The Overseas Chinese in Singapore (if not the whole of Southeast Asia) faced different challenges when it came to their thoughts on China.

The tea traders mentioned in this chapter reflects that very challenge whenever the term "China" is used. In the 1930s, China was their motherland. It represented home as the traders were in Singapore purely for trade, albeit in a commodity produced by their hometowns in Fujian province. The sense of patriotism is evident when one looks at their response to Japanese imperialism and the burning desire to do something for their home country. In this sense, there was a deep sense of "connecting" with China.

After the proclamation of the People's Republic of China, however, the traders appeared to move away from seeing "China" as the motherland because of their sympathy for the KMT. The traders continued to regard the ROC as the real "China" and seemed to regard mainland China only as a trading partner since Fujian teas continued to be imported by them. Decolonization in Malaya and the subsequent move to drop references to their status as "Overseas Chinese" meant that they now saw themselves as citizens (or at least residents) in their adopted countries. They had now "distanced" themselves from China. By the late 1950s a second generation of traders — mostly sons of the first generation — had taken over the management of the SCTIEA. This second generation had continued to "position" themselves as Singapore citizens trading in Fujian teas that remain a popular beverage among the local Chinese.

Notes

1. National Archives of Singapore (NAS), Microfilm No. NA 531, Records of the Singapore Chinese Tea Importers and Exporters Association (SCTIEA), Minutes of Annual General Meetings and Executive Committee Meetings, Swearing-in Ceremony of the New Executive Committee on 16 February 1952. The "Jinan Incident" referred to the Japanese military resistance to the attempt by the National Revolutionary Army of Chiang Kai-shek to capture Beijing during the Northern Expedition.

2. *Nanyang Siang Pau*, 14 May 1935.
3. *Nanyang Siang Pau*, 16 May 1935; 18 May 1935.
4. The main overseas market for Taiwanese pauchong tea before the Sino-Japanese War was the Dutch East Indies, especially Java. Research work on this topic is Naoto Kawarabayashi, *Kindai Ajia to Taiwan: Taiwan Chagyōno Rekishiteki Tenkai* [Modern Asia and Taiwan: Historical Development of the Tea Industry] (Kyoto: Sekaishiso, 2003). See also Hsu Hsian-yao, "Taiwan Baozhong Chazhi Shuchu Zhaowa (1894–1936)" [Taiwanese pauchong tea exports to Java, 1896–1936], *Taiwan Wenxian* 56, no. 2 (June 2005): 233–76.
5. NAS, Microfilm No. NA 531, Records of the SCTIEA, Minutes of Annual General Meetings and Executive Committee Meetings, Third Staff Meeting of eleventh term on 2 May 1939.
6. NAS, Microfilm No. NA 531, Records of the SCTIEA, Minutes of Annual General Meetings and Executive Committee Meetings, Third Emergency Meeting of eleventh term on 29 November 1939.
7. NAS, Microfilm No. NA 531, Records of the SCTIEA, Minutes of Annual General Meetings and Executive Committee Meetings, Fourth Emergency Meeting of eleventh term on 3 December 1939.
8. NAS, Microfilm No. NA 531, Records of the SCTIEA, Minutes of Annual General Meetings and Executive Committee Meetings, Seventh Staff Meeting of eleventh term on 13 December 1939.
9. NAS, Microfilm No. NA 531, Records of the SCTIEA, Minutes of Annual General Meetings and Executive Committee Meetings, Fifth Emergency Staff Meeting on 12 November 1940.
10. NAS, Microfilm No. NA 531, Records of the SCTIEA, Minutes of Annual General Meetings and Executive Committee Meetings, Executive Committee Meeting on 19 December 1940.
11. Although the minutes of the SCTIEA Emergency Meeting recorded the meeting as a call by Tan Kah-kee to all Singapore Chinese organizations, the meeting was actually convened by Sir Shenton Thomas, the last pre-war Governor of Singapore. See C.F. Yong, *Tan Kah-kee: The Making of An Overseas Chinese Legends* (Singapore: Oxford University Press, 1987), p. 282.
12. NAS, Accession No. A002915/02, oral history interview with Gan Tiong Siew, reel 2. In a conversation with Mr Gan, he mentioned that no merchant would have supported the communists.
13. For more about Lim Keng Lian, see Jason Lim, "The Education Concerns and Political Outlook of Lim Keng Lian (1893–1968)", *Journal of Chinese Overseas* 3, no. 2 (November 2007): 194–219.
14. NAS, Microfilm No. NA 531, Records of the SCTIEA, Minutes of Annual General Meetings and Executive Committee Meetings, Emergency Meeting on 22 January 1950; and NAS, Microfilm No. NA 531, Records of the SCTIEA, Minutes of Annual General Meetings and Executive Committee Meetings, Chairman's Report, AGM on 11 August 1950.

15. NAS, Microfilm No. NA 531, Records of the SCTIEA, Minutes of Annual General Meetings and Executive Committee Meetings, Chairman's Report, AGM on 7 January 1951.
16. NAS, Microfilm No. NA 531, Records of the SCTIEA, Minutes of Annual General Meetings and Executive Committee Meetings, Executive Committee Meeting on 10 May 1950. Shantou is a city in Guangdong Province and the home of some Teochew migrants.
17. NAS, Microfilm No. NA 531, Records of the SCTIEA, Minutes of Annual General Meetings and Executive Committee Meetings, Chairman's Report, AGM on 7 January 1951.
18. NAS, Microfilm No. NA 531, Records of the SCTIEA, Minutes of Annual General Meetings and Executive Committee Meetings, Executive Committee Meeting on 10 November 1951.
19. NAS, Microfilm No. NA 531, Records of the SCTIEA, Minutes of Annual General Meetings and Executive Committee Meetings, Executive Committee Meeting on 24 October 1952. To this day, Taiwan is claimed by both the ROC and PRC.
20. NAS, Microfilm No. NA 531, Records of the SCTIEA, Minutes of Annual General Meetings and Executive Committee Meetings, Executive Committee Meeting on 1 March 1954.
21. NAS, Microfilm No. NA 531, Records of the SCTIEA, Minutes of Annual General Meetings and Executive Committee Meetings, Executive Committee Meeting on 9 July 1954.
22. NAS, Microfilm No. NA 531, Records of the SCTIEA, Minutes of Annual General Meetings and Executive Committee Meetings, Executive Committee Meeting on 7 June 1956.
23. Liu Hong, "Organized Chinese Transnationalism and the Institutionalization of Business Networks: The Singapore Chinese Chamber of Commerce and Industry as a Case Analysis", *Southeast Asian Studies* 37, no. 3 (December 1999): 410.
24. NAS, Microfilm No. NA 531, Records of the SCTIEA, Minutes of Annual General Meetings and Executive Committee Meetings, Executive Committee Meeting on 4 June 1957.
25. NAS, Microfilm No. NA 531, Records of the SCTIEA, Minutes of Annual General Meetings and Executive Committee Meetings, Executive Committee Meeting on 20 June 1957.
26. NAS, Microfilm No. NA 531, Records of the SCTIEA, Minutes of Annual General Meetings and Executive Committee Meetings, Executive Committee Meeting on 17 July 1957.
27. For more information about Lim Keng Lian's role in the Trade Mission, see Chapter 8.
28. NAS, Microfilm No. NA 531, Records of the SCTIEA, Minutes of Annual General Meetings and Executive Committee Meetings, Executive Committee Meeting on 17 July 1957.

29. Ibid.
30. NAS, Microfilm No. NA 531, Records of the SCTIEA, Minutes of Annual General Meetings and Executive Committee Meetings, Emergency Meeting on 20 July 1957. The Central Trust of China was established in Shanghai in 1935 to handle deposits and savings, insurance underwriting, and conducted the selling and purchasing of products for the Government during the Sino-Japanese War. In 1949, it moved to Taipei.
31. *Nanyang Siang Pau*, 24 July 1957.
32. NAS, Microfilm No. NA 531, Records of the SCTIEA, Minutes of Annual General Meetings and Executive Committee Meetings, Executive Committee Meeting on 16 October 1957.
33. NAS, Microfilm No. NA 531, Records of the SCTIEA, Minutes of Annual General Meetings and Executive Committee Meetings, Executive Committee Meeting on 7 April 1958.
34. NAS, Microfilm No. NA 531, Records of the SCTIEA, Minutes of Annual General Meetings and Executive Committee Meetings, Executive Committee Meeting on 12 August 1958.
35. NAS, Microfilm No. NA 531, Records of the SCTIEA, Minutes of Annual General Meetings and Executive Committee Meetings, Executive Committee Meeting on 14 December 1958.
36. Chinese Newspaper Division, Information Resource Centre, Singapore Press Holdings (SPH-CND), *Yinliao Gongye* [Beverage industries], newspaper clippings from 1950 to 1996, "Zhongguo Chunchan Lücha Xiayue Shuxing Yingxiao" [Spring green teas from China to be exported and sold in Singapore from next month], *Nanyang Siang Pau*, 21 May 1958.
37. SPH-CND, *Yinliao Gongye* [Beverage industries], newspaper clippings from 1950 to 1996, "Zhongtai Chunchan Cha Shuruliang Youxian Pan Jiawang Qiding" [Limited imports of spring teas from China and Taiwan leads to an anxious wait for confirmation of prices], *Nanyang Siang Pau*, 30 May 1958.
38. SPH-CND, *Yinliao Gongye* [Beverage industries], newspaper clippings from 1950 to 1996, "Chashi Fengguang" [Overview of the tea market], *Nanyang Siang Pau*, 19 September 1958.
39. SPH-CND, *Yinliao Gongye* [Beverage industries], newspaper clippings from 1950 to 1996, "Zhongguo Chaye Shoujia Yidi" [Chinese tea prices lowered], *Nanyang Siang Pau*, 27 October 1958.
40. NAS, Microfilm No. NA 531, Records of the SCTIEA, Minutes of Annual General Meetings and Executive Committee Meetings, AGM on 1 March 1948.
41. NAS, Microfilm No. NA 531, Records of the SCTIEA, Minutes of Annual General Meetings and Executive Committee Meetings, Meeting called to discuss changes in the name and Constitution of the association, 8 March 1948.
42. NAS, Microfilm No. NA 531, Records of the SCTIEA, Minutes of Annual General Meetings and Executive Committee Meetings, Meeting called to discuss changes in the name and Constitution of the association, 15 March 1948.

43. NAS, Microfilm No. NA 531, Records of the SCTIEA, Minutes of Annual General Meetings and Executive Committee Meetings, Meeting called to discuss changes in the Constitution and other matters, 8 April 1948.

44. NAS, Microfilm No. NA 531, Records of the SCTIEA, Minutes of Annual General Meetings and Executive Committee Meetings, Executive Committee Meeting on 13 May 1948.

45. NAS, Microfilm No. NA 531, Records of the SCTIEA, Minutes of Annual General Meetings and Executive Committee Meetings, Emergency Meeting on 23 June 1950; and NAS, Microfilm No. NA 531, Records of the SCTIEA, Minutes of Annual General Meetings and Executive Committee Meetings, Executive Committee Meeting on 10 July 1950.

46. NAS, Microfilm No. NA 531, Records of the SCTIEA, Minutes of Annual General Meetings and Executive Committee Meetings, Executive Committee Meeting on 10 July 1950.

47. NAS, Microfilm No. NA 531, Records of the SCTIEA, Minutes of Annual General Meetings and Executive Committee Meetings, Executive Committee Meeting on 12 September 1950.

48. NAS, Microfilm No. NA 531, Records of the SCTIEA, Minutes of Annual General Meetings and Executive Committee Meetings, AGM on 7 January 1951.

49. NAS, Microfilm No. NA 531, Records of the SCTIEA, Minutes of Annual General Meetings and Executive Committee Meetings, Executive Committee Meeting on 10 November 1951.

6

MYANMAR'S RELATIONS WITH CHINA FROM TAGAUNG THROUGH HANTHAWATI-TAUNGNGU PERIODS

Goh Geok Yian

The study of China-Myanmar relations has largely been undertaken from the Chinese point of view; this can partially be attributed to the fact that more work has been done on Chinese historical sources, and secondly to the general consensus among scholars working on Southeast Asia–China interactions that Chinese sources are more reliable than their Southeast Asian counterparts. It is not the aim of this chapter to counteract the latter view; it argues instead that rather than discrediting certain texts by highlighting their inaccuracies, a more important goal may be to treat these texts as media which reflect the perceptions of their creators and by extension, the people for whom they wrote. Southeast Asian primary texts have only recently been perceived as informative sources, partially because of the language barrier; most Southeast Asian languages, especially Burmese, are not easily learned. There are fewer English translations of Burmese texts than other major Southeast Asian languages.[1] To date, there are only two English translations of Burmese chronicles: the *Glass Palace Chronicle* (English translation of a relatively brief section of the *Hmannan Yazawindawgyi*, compiled in 1829) and the *Zinmeh Chronicle* (the Burmese version of the *Chiangmai Chronicle*). A number of Burmese chronicles, some still on palm-leaf manuscript (*pe sa*), remain untranslated. The primary sources used for this paper are: U Kala's

Mahayazawingyi, Twinthin Taikwun Mahasitthu's *Mahayazawinthit,* and the *Hmannan Yazawindawgyi.* These texts will form the focus of the discussion of Myanmar-China relations.

Other Burmese sources such as the *Bagan Yazawin, Yazadharit Ayedawpon,* and the *Yazawunthalini* [New Bagan Chronicle] will be used when necessary to inform discussion of a particular theme or event. Even though most of these chronicles can only be dated to the eighteenth and nineteenth centuries, descriptions of Burmese perceptions of their relations with Tarup (China) extracted from these sources represent invaluable reflections of indigenous views of their foreign neighbour. These views can contribute to a more balanced observation of Myanmar-China relations over a period of several centuries from Tagaung (mid-first millennium CE) to Hanthawati-Taungngu of the sixteenth century.

This chapter is divided into two main parts. In the first section, a collection of Burmese accounts of their interactions with Tarup (China) is presented chronologically, and diverse descriptions, where they exist, are also discussed. The second part determines whether there are any distinct stages of interaction between Myanmar and Tarup (China) during the period under discussion. The issue of periodization is discussed and problematized, particularly in terms of its relationship to the general subject of historiography.

DEFINITIONS AND BRIEF INTRODUCTION OF THE BURMESE CHRONICLES

In this chapter, Tarup, a modern Burmese referent to China and Chinese ethnic group is used to refer specifically to the geopolitical entity with a geographical boundary approximating that of modern China. I am not using Tarup to describe the (Han) Chinese ethnic category, as it is often defined; Tarup does not refer to the same group of people over this long span of time, and it is beyond the scope of this chapter to discuss the issue of ethnicity.

In the case of the Burmese kingdoms, Myanmar is used both to refer to the territory now held by the modern nation-state and the ethnic majority, often referred to as the Burmans. The Burmese classification of dynasties is used to organize discussion in this chapter. As a general rule, the names of the kingdoms will be given in lieu of Myanmar. In cases where ethnic minorities are referred to, such as the Shan, Myanmar will be generally used to refer to Burmese kingdoms inclusive of Burman Ava and Mon Hanthawati, for example. The main objective is to determine the nature of Myanmar-China relations as they developed over a few centuries.

The earliest extant Burmese chronicle, the ရာဇဝင်ကျော် *Yazawingyaw* [Celebrated Chronicle] begun by Shin Thilawuntha (Silavamsa) in 1502, does not describe Anawrahta's expedition to Tarup, but refers to Taruppye Min's reign (1254–87) as signalling the end of the Bagan dynasty (Shin Maha Thilawuntha 1965). The most elaborate accounts of Burma's relations with the Tarup appear first in the early eighteenth-century chronicle by U Kala (c. 1678–1738), the မဟာရာဇဝင်ကြီး *Mahayazawingyi* [Great Chronicle]. The *Mahayazawinthit*[2] [Great New Chronicle] completed by Twinthin Taikwun Mahasitthu (1726–1806) in 1798[3] contains much abbreviated descriptions of the same events. Scholars such as G. H. Luce, Pe Maung Tin, U Thaw Kaung, and Dr Yi Yi have regarded this chronicle as a critical history, representing "a serious attempt to check history by means of inscriptions" (Luce and Pe Maung Tin 1960, p. xvii; see also Thaw Kaung 2005; Dr Yi Yi 1963). The မှန်နန်းရာဇဝင်တော်ကြီး (*Hmannan Yazawindawgyi*, hereafter referred to as *Hmannan*) [Great Glass Palace Chronicle] was commissioned in 1829, and the compilers replicated *almost* verbatim the elaborate descriptions of figures, events, and kingdoms found in U Kala's chronicle at least up to the Inwa period which marks the end of volume three of U Kala's work. The *Hmannan* brings the narrative of Myanmar's history up to the Konbaung period, ending the account prior to the outbreak of the first Anglo-Burmese War in 1824. The *Hmannan* also varies from U Kala's chronicle in the following areas: organization of narrative sequence, insertions of certain short statements justifying the sequence of events, and the commentaries inserted by the compilers. The *Bagan Yazawin* has not yet been published and appears only on palm-leaf manuscript.[4] This chronicle contains some elaborate embellishments of events which were also described in the three main chronicles.

Another interesting work, which unfortunately bears no date, is the *Yazawunthazalini* (otherwise also known as *Bagan Yazawinthit* [New Bagan Chronicle]). The compiler's name is however given as U Bhe. The *Yazadharit Ayedawpon* (ဗညားဒလ၏ရာဇာဓိရာဇ်အရေးတော်ပုံ) was likely compiled during the reign of King Bayinnaung (1551–81) by Bannya Dala, a minister in the king's court. It is probably the earliest *extant* copy of a text illustrating the history of the Mon in Lower Burma [*italics* by Aung-Thwin] (Aung-Thwin 2005, p. 133). Bannya Dala was purportedly a very powerful figure in the court, acting as the chief advisor to the king, simultaneously a writer-scholar and general between the years of 1518 and 1572 (Aung-Thwin 2005, p. 134).

MYANMAR-CHINA RELATIONS FROM MID-FIRST MILLENNIUM THROUGH SIXTEENTH CENTURY

For this chapter, discussion will be limited to Myanmar's relations with Tarup-China beginning with the foundation of Tagaung around the fifth century CE and ending with the reign of Bayinnaung, the founder of the Second Myanmar Empire. The accounts will be presented in a chronological manner following the classification of Burmese dynasties by the chroniclers.[5] Dynasties are discussed only when there are existing records of Burmese contact with Tarup-China. In cases where an alternative or different description is known, the variant account is presented for comparison if there are notable differences in the description.

Tagaung and Tharehkettara Dynasty

The first reference to Tarup appears in connection with the destruction of Tagaung kingdom. The *Hmannan* states:

ထိုမင်းတို့. အဆုံးစွန် ဖြစ်သော အိန္ဒကရာဇာ မင်းကြီး လက်ထက် သဃ်သသရ မည်သော တကောင်းပြည် ကြီးကို ဂန္ဓာလရာဇ်တိုင်း စိန်ပြည်က တရုတ်တရက်တို့. နေ၁င်ယှက်လာ၍ သဃ်သသ္ဃ မည်သော တကောင်း ပြည်ကြီး:ပျက်စီး:လေလျှင် အိန္ဒကမင်းကြီး:သည် ရဲ:မိသမျှသော မိမိဗိုလ်ရေ အလုံ:အရင်:နှင့် မလည်ချောင်:သို့. ဝင်၍ နေတော်မူ၏ [During the reign of King Bheinnaka, the last of those kings of Tagaung country called Sanghassaratha, the Tarups and Tayeks from Sein country (စိန် is an archaic word used to refer to China), Gandhalaraj division came to disrupt and destroy the great country of Tagaung named Sanghassatha. King Bheinnaka assembled all his remaining troops and they entered Malaykhyaung where they remained.] (*Hmannan* 1992, vol. 1, p. 156; Pe and Luce 1960, p. 3).

This reference to the destruction of Tagaung by the Tarups is surprisingly not found in either U Kala's *Mahayazawingyi* or Twinthin's *Mahayazawinthit*; both texts pre-date the *Hmannan*. At least Twinthin indicated that he was more interested in the founding of Tharehkettara kingdom. Another point to note is that the editor of the *Mahayazawinthit* places Tagaung kingdom under the general category of Tharehkettara dynasty, whereas the editor of the *Hmannan* sees Tagaung and Tharehkettara as two separate dynasties (*Hmannan* 1992; Twinthin 1968).

Bagan

There are numerous references to Tarup in the section on Bagan history in the Burmese chronicles, beginning with events which occurred during the reign of the legendary king Pyuminhti, and ending with the aftermath of the supposed Mongol invasion of 1284. The first description of this period appears under the list of the king's twelve great festivals, which includes celebrations of the legendary slaying of the four great enemies of Bagan: the giant bird, the giant boar, the giant tiger, and the giant flying squirrel. The *Mahayazawingyi* states:

> နိုင်ငံတော်ကျေး:ဖြစ်သော ကောသမ္ဘီမြို့.သို့. ကုရွှေအရာမကသောတရၢ၆စစ်သည်တို့.ရောက်သောအခါ မင်:ကြီ:ကိုယ်တော်တိုင် ဆင်လှံ:မြင်:ရင်:အများ:နှင့် ရှိတော်မူ၍ နိုင်နင်:လုပ်ကြံတော်မူသောပွဲ:လည်:တကြိမ် ... [It is one festival (to commemorate) the time when the great king on elephant marched with his cavalry and elephant troops to do battle as a unified whole against more than ten million and hundreds of Tarup soldiers arrived at Kawthambhi town, which had formerly been a village in the country.] (U Kala 1960, vol. 2, p. 142; Twinthin 1968, p. 55; *Hmannan* 1992, p. 203; see also Pe and Luce 1960, p. 41).

The *Bagan Yazawin* contains an elaborate account of the battle, describing the actual fighting and noting that the battle took place over a period of three months (*Bagan Yazawin* 1895: leaves ၈–ကျာ to ၇–၀၆:; leaves ၇–၀၆: to ၇–ကျာ).

The Burmese chronicles next describe Bagan King Anawrahta's (1044–77) expedition to Tarup country in Gandhalaraj division to request the Buddha's tooth relic. The mission was unsuccessful as the tooth relic refuses to descend from the sky to which it soared upon hearing the king's pleas to take it back to Bagan (U Kala 1960, vol. 1, pp. 184–88; Twinthin 1968, pp. 86–88; *Hmannan* 1992, pp. 250–53; Pe and Luce 1960, pp. 80–83; U Bhe n.d., p. 115). The *Mahayazawingyi* describes Anawrahta who "assembles the elephants, horses, and soldiers in the whole nation and [once he] gathers [all] 36 million [soldiers] by water route, 36 million [soldiers] by land route together with the four spirit horses [implying that it would include his four warriors, Kyansittha, Ngahtweyu, Ngalonlekhpek, and Nyaung U Bhi] and the Shwephyin brothers, to march to Tarup country" (U Kala 1960, vol. 1, p. 185). The *Yazawunthalini* also asserts that he "marches towards Tarup kingdom once the weapons and artillery for the purpose of besieging are assembled" (U Bhe, p. 115). In spite of the description of large numbers of forces, no fighting occurred between the Burmese king and the Tarup Utibhwa, leader of the Tarups. This account highlights the main theme of Buddhist devotion and zeal, and ends with a description of the golden and silver objects such as bars and pots which Anawrahta offered as items of worship for the tooth relic.

This description of Anawrahta's offering of gold and silver items is important in establishing a foundation of Myanmar-Tarup relations for succeeding kings and kingdoms. Even though the items were purportedly presented as offerings to the Buddha's tooth relic, the implication is that these can be perceived as tribute to Tarup-China. This is particularly significant as Alaungsithu (1112–65), grandson of Anawrahta, continued this tradition of offering gold and silver items to the tooth relic in Tarup country. Alaungsithu's expedition to Tarup resembles that undertaken by Anawrahta several decades earlier. Similar to the experience of his grandfather, the tooth relic refused to be taken citing the reason that the religion must flourish in Tarup country for the duration of 5,000 years before the relic could be taken (see relevant sections in the Burmese chronicles).

The offering of gold and silver objects became the pretext for Tarup-China's attack on Bagan during the reign of Narathihapate, who earned himself the infamous epithet, *Taruppye* [he who fled from the Tarup] when he abandoned his capital to avoid the attacking Tarup. The Tarup of this period were Yuan-dynasty China or the Mongols. The reason which brought about the Mongols' attack was given as the Burmese king's execution of the Tarup envoys sent to demand tribute of gold and silver for the Tarup Utibhwa. The description is as follows:

ထိုအခါ တရုပ်ဝင်တည်ဘွား:ထံက သံစေ၍ ဆင်ဖြူ နှင့် နေ့ရထာမင်း:စော လက်ထက် ဆက်မြဲသော ရွှေထမင်း:အိုး ငွေထမင်း:အိုး:များ:ဆက်ကောင်:သည်ဟု တောင်:လှာသော တရုပ်မင်း:က စေသော သံတို့သည် မင်း:ကြီး ရွှေ့တော်ဝယ် သဇ္ဇလီ နေ့ရာမြင့် ထက် ခြေဘွဲ့နေသည်ကို "တယောက်မကြွင်: သတ်လေ"ဟု မိန့်တော်မူလျှင်ရာဇသင်္ကြံတို့က တမန်သုံ့. သေး:တို့.ကို သတ်ထုံး:မရှိရေ"လျှောက်သော်လည်: အယူတော်မရှိ တယောက်မကျန် သတ်လေ၏။ [At the time, an embassy sent from the Utibhwa came requesting the sending of golden and silver rice bowls with a white elephant, a practice which had been carried out since Anawrahtaminsaw's reign. As the envoys sent from Tarup king stood in front of the raised ornamented chair of the king and showed respect, the king gave the order to "kill them all and not spare one". Yazathingyan and the other ministers advised: "it is not the custom to kill diplomatic messengers", the king refusing to believe them ignored their advice and ordered that the envoys be all killed, none spared.] (Twinthin 1968, p. 154)

The king's massacre of the embassy was the catalyst which brought about the attack by the Tarup soldiers; the king Narathihapate fled to Dala before moving on to Puthein (Bassein).

There are two notable differences between the account of U Kala and the *Hmannan* on one hand, and Twinthin's description of the Tarup attack on the other hand. The *Mahayazawingyi* and *Hmannan* both contain a more elaborate description of the encounter between the Tarup embassy and King Narathihapate, especially in terms of a detailed rendition of Minister Yazathingyan's plea to Narathihapate. In the case of the *Hmannan*, the minister was not Yazathingyan, but Anantapyissi (see U Kala 1960, vol. 1, p. 298; *Hmannan* 1992, vol. 1, p. 173). The minister suggested that if the envoys had behaved badly, their actions should be recorded and sent to the Utibhwa. He cautioned the king to exercise tolerance just as a king who manages the affairs of the country and villages should do. The minister also added that past kings were never known to kill ambassadors (Pe and Luce 1960, p. 173; U Kala 1960, vol. 1, p. 298; *Hmannan* 1992, vol. 1, pp. 351–52).

The second difference occurs in the section describing the ensuing confusion in the Bagan palace following news that the Tarup soldiers were on their way to Bagan; the chronicles all agree on the point that the palace female attendants (ဖောင်းဖွဲ့သည်), all 3,000 of them,[6] should be drowned, since it would not be possible to transport them all to the place of refuge. Twinthin added a character description of the Tarup soldiers which cannot be found in U Kala's chronicle. He described the Tarup soldiers as ပန်းသော (Twinthin 1968, p. 155), identifying them as Muslims. It is not clear where Twinthin obtained this knowledge.

In the aftermath of the Tarup attack, the king Narathihapate went into exile, and a contest for the Bagan throne ensued between two of Narathihapate's sons, Uzzana and Thihathu. Uzzana, who had plans to usurp the throne, captured Thihathu, placed him in shackles, and put him in jail in Puthein. However the latter escaped. Thihathu eventually died, shot by his own arrow. His half-brother, Kyawswa, became the new king. It is suggested that Kyawswa was a vassal of Tarup. The reference can be found in the next section on Myinsaing dynasty.

Myinsaing

The Myinsaing period (1298–1312) is significant not only for the shifting of the Burmese capital from Bagan to Myinsaing, but it also marks the beginning of a new dynasty founded by three brothers. This period has sometimes been referred to as the Shan interregnum, emphasizing the three brothers' Shan ethnic identity. Aung-Thwin, however, disagrees with the factuality of this assessment, and argues that the characterization of these brothers as Shan was a misinterpretation perpetuated by Arthur Phayre (Aung-Thwin 1996; 1998). Since the matter of whether the three brothers were Shan or not has little bearing on the nature of Myanmar-China relations during this period, suffice it to note that Tarup interaction with the three brothers of Myinsaing represents another episode in which Tarup-China intervened in the indigenous politics of Myanmar. It is described in the *Mahayazawinthit*:

မင်းညီနောင် သုံးယောက်တို့. မြင်စိုင်းကို နေလေသော် မင်းစောနှစ် နှင့် မိဖုရားဖွားစောက တရုပ် ဥတည်ဘွားသို့. ရှိပင့်လေ၍ ဥတည်ဘွားက ဆုံးမရေ ဟု စစ်သူကြီး: သံစိန်တိန်စင်, ယော်ဓာတိန်စင်, မော်ရှာတိန်စင်, မော်ရှာဒိန်စင် တို့ကို စိုလ်ပါ များစွာနှင့် ရှိလှာစေ၍ မြင်စိုင်းသို့. ရောက်လျင် ပုဂံ မင်းကျော်စွာကိုနှန်:တင်ခဲ့ရမည် ဟု ဆောင်:လှာ၏။ [Min Sawhnit and Queen Pwasaw after paying reverence to the Tarup Utibhwa, requested that he punished the three brothers in Myinsaing. The Tarup Utibhwa also sent the great generals, Thanseinteinsin, Yawdhateinsin, Mawyateinsin, and Mawyadheinsin and their troops to Myinsaing. When they reached Myinsaing, they demanded that Bagan king Kyawswa be placed on the throne.] (Twinthin 1968, p. 164)

Tarup preference for Kyawswa signifies a departure from Myanmar-Tarup relations which had up to this point been carried out along the lines of a tribute system. The implications of the Tarup/Mongol invasion and Tarup direct intervention in Burmese affairs will be discussed in detail in the second part of this chapter.

Why did the Tarup interfere? Part of the reason was offered by the Tarup assertion that the three brothers did not have legitimate claims to the throne. However the Tarup were willing to ignore the transgression and depart if the three brothers paid tribute to them. This obviously suggests that Tarup interference on behalf of the "legitimate" heir of the previous Bagan dynasty was just a pretext for making sure that the rulers at the new capital would continue to send tribute to Tarup-China. The episode is described as follows:

တရုပ်တို့.လည်: – "နန်:ရှိ: မရှိပြီး:ကား: အသူ.ကို နန်:တင်ရမည်နည်:၊ လက်ဆောင် သာ ပေ:တော့၊ ငါတို့. ပြန်တော့မည်" ဟု ဆိုလျင် – "ဥဒါန်:နောက်နောင် ပြောပစရာ ဖြစ်ရစ်အောင် မြောင်:တူ:"ဟု ဆိုသဖြင့် တရုပ်တို့. အား:ပြုလိုသောကြောင့်အလျင်: အတာ ခုနှစ်ရာ အနံနှစ်တာ ထိုမြောင်:ကိုလည်: သင်:တွဲမြောင်:ဟု တွင်၏။ မင်းညီနောင်တို့.က ပေ:သောလက်ဆောင်ကို ခံ၍ ထိုနှစ် ပင် တရုပ်တို့. ပြန်လေ၏။ [The Tarup also said: "Since there is no longer any royal descendant, who will ascend the throne? Give us the gifts and we will go back." (The three brothers replied): "To set a precedent for a future tradition is the same as digging a drain." Having said that, they explained to the Tarup that "therefore they (will) dig a drain with the length of 700 *tar*, width of two *tar*, and a depth of two *tar*, and complete the drain by night time". That drain came to be called "Thintwei Drain". The Tarup after accepting the gifts given by the three brothers also returned (to their country).][7] (Twinthin 1968, p. 165).

When the Tarup left, it was said that the three brothers began to compete among themselves for the throne (Twinthin 1968, p. 166). The notes presented in the published *Mahayazawinthit* state that there were variant dates given for the Tarup attacks and other matters in the *Yazawin Asaungsaung*. It is also mentioned that in the *Sagaing Sawumma* inscription sponsored by the queen of Minkyiswa, 90,000 Khansit arrived in Myanmar Era 662 (1300 CE). Khansit apparently refers to Tarup soldiers (Twinthin 1968, p. 166).

Inwa

During the Inwa period (1364–1555), the Tarup relationship with Burmese polities was further transformed. The change could well be a consequence of the Burmese political situation. Unlike the earlier period of seemingly centralized control by the Bagan Empire, Inwa represents a continuation of the rather unstable state of affairs which characterized the Myinsaing period. In addition, further complications arose as peripheral areas such as those governed by Shan hereditary chiefs, commonly referred to as *sawbwas*, appealed to Tarup-China for assistance in negotiating with their Burmese overlords. The Inwa period sees increasing numbers of competing factions and capitals, including rivalry between Mon ruler Yazadharit and Myanmar leaders, Minkhaung and Minyekyawswa. Tarup tributary system also extended to the lesser political entities such as the Shan chiefdoms.

Only three accounts of Tarup-China's interactions with Myanmar during this period will be discussed here. These three examples symbolize a change in the way the Burmese saw their more powerful neighbour, Tarup-China. Myanmar's willingness to engage in battle with Tarup-China and their subsequent successes over Tarup (at least from the Burmese point of view) show they were no longer intimidated by Tarup prowess. It is important to point out that only the first account relates warfare conducted on a large scale. The two later accounts focus instead on single combat situations between two warriors representing each side.

The first account refers to Inwa king Minyekyawswa's attack on the Shan *sawbwa* of Theinni. The *sawbwa* requested Tarup's assistance to defend his city against Burmese attack.

The following is described in U Kala's *Mahayazawingyi*:

> Theinni *sawbwa*'s sons and sons-in-law also requested military assistance from Tarup and when they successfully completed work to strengthen their city, [even] if there were no more rations they [were able to] hold out [within

their city]. Minyekyawswa attacked Theinni city a number of times over the duration of approximately five months, but he was unsuccessful. When Minyekyawswa heard of the arrival of military reinforcements comprising 2,000 horses and 20,000 foot soldiers from Tarup, he formed a plan and [waited] until the depths of night when no one was awake in Theinni city to pull out of Theinni city. With [his] 200 battle elephants, 3,000 horses, and 40,000 soldiers, [he] stayed in Sinkhan forest. They destroyed Tarup military reinforcements by splitting them into three groups, and [then] attacking them as they came out through the forest. [He] captured [many] prisoners-of-war including five Tarup officials and close to 1,000 horses and almost 2,000 persons. An estimate of 500 horses died. As he was victorious over the Tarup, he returned to besiege Theinni city as before. (U Kala 1960, vol. 2, p. 10)

This account of Tarup-China's rendering of assistance to the Shan *sawbwa* can be found in the *Ming Shi-lu*, except the Chinese name given was "Mu-bang" or Hsenwi[8] (Wade 2004, p. 14). In addition, though the dates listed in the Burmese and Chinese sources differ by two years, they both describe the same event. "When the Ming intended to attack Ava-Burma in 1409, Mu-bang was ordered to prepare its troops for an overland attack, while the Ming forces were to attack from the sea. Mu-bang (Hsenwi) was a frequent pawn in the Ming-Burma machinations, as it lay between the two and was subject to demands by both polities" (Wade 2004, pp. 23–24). This statement about the precarious position of smaller minority polities such as Mu-bang/Theinni acting as both tributary states and buffer zones between two powerful polities forms the basis of Myanmar-China interactions throughout the Inwa and possibly much of Taungngu period. Tarup-China was often called upon to assist these minority polities in dealing with their Burmese overlord.

The second reference to Tarup involvement in Myanmar relations with the Shan chiefs occurred in the year 1412, when Tarup was again asked to intervene on behalf of the Shan *myosa* (literally "town-eater", an official appointed by the Burmese king), Mawtonmawkaysa (for a full account, see U Kala 1960, vol. 2, pp. 15–21; Twinthin 1968, pp. 308–09; *Hmannan* 1992, vol. 1, pp. 21–30). The Shan chief and his brother had earlier fled to Tarup after the Burmese attack on their city. Their wives, sons, elephants, horses, and people were captured and taken as spoils by Prince Minyekyawswa back to Inwa. The Tarup Utibhwa acceded to the brothers' pleas for help and sent a missive to the Burmese king demanding the release of the Shan chief's family and people. The Tarup forces marched to Inwa and in an interesting metonymical characterization, the battle and victory was determined by a joust between Burmese Thameinpayan and Tarup soldier, Kammani. In a dramatic end to the mortal combat, Thameinpayan used his elephant goad to hook Kammani's body, cut his head off, and drop it into a basket before re-entering the city. The Tarup soldiers, in awe, exclaimed, "no longer a human, [he] became a *nat*".[9] With this outcome, the Tarup also returned to their country. There is interestingly no corroborating account in the *Ming Shi-lu*.

The final account describes a Tarup expedition sent in 1444 CE to capture Tho Ngam Bhwa, who sought refuge with the Burmese king, Narapati. As usual there was some internal conflict between Burmese leaders, this time between Narapati and Minngeh Kyawhtin. The Tarup reached Yamethin, but Tho Ngam Bhwa had already gone to Ava with the king. The king fearing that the already volatile situation might escalate into an irresolvable scenario which might involve numerous other Shan polities who had already pledged allegiance to the Tarup, decided to resolve the conflict with Tarup-China. He poisoned Tho Ngam Bhwa, and sent his body to the Tarup. The Tarup, having received the corpse of Tho Ngam Bhwa, chopped off his head, and placed it on an iron spit. They roasted his head, dried it in the sun, and took it with them back to Tarup-China (U Kala 1960, vol. 2, p. 82). An account of this altercation between Myanmar and Tarup-China is corroborated in the *Ming Shi Lu*:

> A further major Ming military expedition which was to greatly affect the upland Southeast Asian polities was that launched in 1448 to capture Si Ji-fa, a son of Si Ren-fa [a Tai-Mao political leader]. At a date equivalent to April/May 1448, Imperial instructions were issued to Wang Ji requiring him to capture Si Ji-fa and the chieftains of Meng-yang. The surrounding polities of Ava-Burma, Mu-bang, Nan Dian, Gan-yai and Long-chuan were also required to provide troops for deployment against Si Ji-fa. (Wade 2004, p. 16)

The Burmese chronicles' view of Myanmar-China relations would naturally focus on diplomatic contact and warfare, and often fail to describe other forms of exchange between the two countries. Sun Laichen believes that in the fifteenth century, China played a key role in distributing military technology throughout northern mainland Southeast Asia in two ways. The first way describes Chinese deserters who helped Southeast Asians to make the weapons, and this is substantiated by a 1444 memorial issued by Wang Ji, Minister of War and commander-in-chief of the campaigns against the Maw Shan. The document reveals that "profit-seekers on the frontier, carrying weapons and other goods illegally, sneaked into Mubang (Hsenwi), Miandian (Ava), Cheli (Sipsong Panna), Babai (Lan Na), etc., and communicated with the aboriginal chieftains and exchanged goods" (Sun 2003, p. 501). The second means by which Southeast Asians gained military technology was through trade with Ming China as verified by "Ava's frequent contacts with the Ming, especially via the frontier trade..." (Sun 2003, p. 503). It is likely that Ava (Inwa) and the Shan chiefdoms represent two separate categories of tributary states.[10]

Taungngu

The second Hanthawati period (1486–1752) began with the founding of a new capital by Minkyinyo in Taungngu. Minkyinyo was the father of Tabinshwehti who began a territorial expansion campaign, which extended to Ayutthaya. However it was only during the reign of his brother-in-law, Bayinnaung, that Taungngu was able to expand its political control over an area more extensive than that of Bagan at its peak. Bayinnaung's reign is still referred to as the Second Myanmar Empire.

Interestingly there are few references to Tarup during the Taungngu period. Two possible inferences can be made from this fact. Firstly, by the reigns of Tabinshwehti and Bayinnaung, Myanmar-Taungngu had become a force to contend with. During the initial years of Tabinshwehti's and Bayinnaung's reigns, they had to contend with rebellions, but these were put down and the kings soon carried out territorial expansion campaigns establishing control beyond the borders of Myanmar into north and central Thailand. It is very likely that the Burmese chroniclers chose to focus on the campaigns conducted by the kings to the east and south, rather than with their neighbour, Tarup. Ming China by the mid-1500s had also weakened considerably, opening their trading ports to foreigners by 1567. In fact, by Bayinnaung's reign, Myanmar's capital had shifted to Bago, closer to the coast. Myanmar-China relations were no longer restricted to tribute trade missions, but rather focused on trade in items, such as weapons and gunpowder.

MYANMAR AND TARUP-CHINA RELATIONS: CHARACTERIZATION AND PERIODIZATION

There is no simple way of determining distinct stages of development in Myanmar-China relations as they were described in the Burmese sources. Part of the difficulty is compounded by the problem that some aspects of their relations continue largely unchanged, except for some minor variations.

One way of periodizing Myanmar-Tarup relations from the Tagaung through Taungngu periods may be along the following demarcations:

- Tarup as simply a neighbouring country which attempted to exercise control over Bagan but failed. Bagan under the reign of Pyuminhti saw itself as an equal to Tarup, and this is demonstrated by the festival celebrating Pyuminhti's victory over the Tarup army.
- Myanmar as a tributary of Tarup-China. The beginning of Myanmar's tributary status as illustrated in the chronicles was established during the reign of Anawrahta (1044–77). The chronicles describe the king's sending of gold and silver bowls, bars, and other items as supposed objects for worshipping the tooth relic then residing in Tarup. Although disguised under Buddhist terms, Anawrahta's sending of these items was considered by the Chinese as tribute, and to some extent, this view is reiterated in the chronicles. As described in the first part of this chapter, Tarup often cited Anawrahta's sending of items as the reason for requesting tribute from later Burmese kings. As in other known cases in other parts of Southeast Asia which were tributaries of the Chinese, new kings or rulers did not necessary feel obliged to send tribute unlike their predecessors. The Chinese saw the tribute system as a testament to their status as a suzerain to whom the tributary states of Southeast Asia were obliged to send tribute in return for the Chinese emperor's recognition of their rights to rule their polities. Southeast Asian rulers, including the Burmese and even the Shan chiefs, did not perceive their tributary status as permanent nor did they see their sending of tribute as obligatory. The Southeast Asian rulers deemed it their right to send and withhold tribute as they saw fit, and in many cases, minority chiefs, such as the Shan *sawbwas*, became tributaries of China in order to extricate themselves from having to submit to another overlord, usually an indigenous ruler. (For further discussion on the differences in the way the Southeast Asians and the Chinese perceived the tribute system, see Wolters 1970, Chapter 5.) During Narathihapate's reign, the Tarup had to send forces to demand that the Burmese king sent tribute to the Utibhwa. This would happen again later during the Myinsaing and Inwa periods.
- Rival overlord and semi-equal relations. The Inwa period is especially marked by Chinese intervention in local affairs. During this time, competition and warfare occurred amidst the continuation of the tribute system. However it is also important to note that the Burmese view of their Tarup "overlord" was transformed into something more negative as warfare became the standard form of Myanmar-Tarup relations, especially during the Inwa (Ava) period. By the Taungngu period, Myanmar had

likely established itself as an equal to Tarup-China. Trade became an important feature of Myanmar-China interactions.

In some ways, this way of periodizing the history of Myanmar-China appears to parallel the Chinese sources' perceptions of the Burmese.

It is possible to distinguish two main periods of Myanmar-China relations according to the Chinese sources, apart from the usual way of examining relations between polities along chronological time frames divided along dynastic lines. The first, which covers China-Myanmar relations until the Mongol invasion of the Yuan dynasty, describes friendly tributary relations between Piao and Pugan (Bagan) on the one hand and China on the other. For example, the *Lingwai Daida* states that: "In the second month of the fifth year of the Chongning reign of Emperor Huizong (March/April 1106) a mission arrived [from Pugan] to offer tribute." (Zhou Qufei 1984, vol. 2, p. 22; see also Chau Ju Kua 1911, p. 59.) The *Song Hui Yao Ji Gao* also states that: "On the twenty-seventh day of the seventh month in the sixth year of Emperor Gao Zong's Shaoxing reign (26 August 1136), the countries of Dali and Pugan offered local products in tribute." (Xu Song 1957, p. 7862).

The second main period is characterized by warfare at the beginning of the Mongol dynasty, including the invasion of Bagan and continuing through the Ming dynasty. The Ming sources have already been briefly discussed in connection with the Burmese sources' accounts of the same events or personalities. As for the Yuan period, *Yuan Wen Lei* contains a section on the "Mian" which describes a detailed account of the Yuan-Burmese wars between 1271 and 1301 (Sun Laichen 1997, vol. 2; see also *Yuan Wen Lei* 1889). The *Yuan Shi* contains numerous detailed records of Yuan-Burmese war and diplomatic missions (Song Lian 1935). Folio 210 of Yuan Shi gives an account of an embassy sent by Dali, Kunming, and Du Yuanshuai Fu (Military Affairs) to the Mian:

> In the eighth year of Shizu Zhiyuan reign (1272), Dali and Shanchan (Kunming) [one of the eight *fu* or administrative district of Dali] Offices of Xuanweisi (Religious or Buddhist Affairs) and Du Yuanshuai Fu (Military Affairs) send an embassy led by Qijiaotuoyin and others to the country of Mian, to summon the country's main Office of Interior Affairs. Fourth month, Qijiaotuoyin and his companions led the embassy with much invaluable [tribute], as it is known. (Song Lian 1935, *juan* 210, p. 1423).

Though this period is marked by successive war campaigns between Myanmar and China, diplomatic missions continued to be sent by both parties.

The parallel between a Burmese and a Chinese periodization of Myanmar-China relations indicates that it is possible to find correlation in the way the two polities perceive their neighbour. Perhaps the only account which appears to contradict China's overlord status over Bagan would have been the description of Pyuminhti's victory over the Tarup. However considering that this victory festival constitutes one among twelve other celebratory festivals, which include the slaying of a giant boar, a giant bird, a giant tiger, and a giant flying squirrel (!), it is hard to take Pyuminhti's legendary defeat of the numerically superior Tarup seriously.

The *Yuan Shi*'s description of diplomatic missions amidst the countless war campaigns also adds to the problem of periodizing Myanmar-China relations. A period of rampant warfare does not necessarily result in the discontinuation of tribute relations, just as a period of friendly tributary missions might be succeeded by refusal to continue diplomatic relations, as demonstrated in the example of Narathihapate.

Rather than creating periods of interactions which seemingly coincide with time frames marked by the rise and fall of dynasties and sometimes kings, it may serve our purpose of examining Myanmar-China relations better to identify themes such as the tribute system, trade, and warfare as representative of long-term features characterizing the relations between the two polities, and examine these in terms of whether relations were stable, fluctuating or unstable over time.

CONCLUSION

In terms of the Burmese perception of their relations with Tarup-China, it is undeniable that Myanmar's recognition of its tributary status to Tarup-China continued in spite of the increase in warfare between the two polities. Myanmar-China relations can be characterized as changing from stable to unstable and hence more volatile, friendly to more antagonistic, and compliant to defiant. Even though it is problematic to characterize the two countries' relations into two distinctive periods of interaction, there is a clear turning point which led to a transformation in Myanmar's relation with Tarup-China. This break occurs in the Bagan period with the Mongol invasion of 1284, which signalled a change in the Burmese perception of Tarup-China. It was Tarup-China's demand for tribute and their attack on Bagan which brought about a negative Burmese perception of their powerful neighbour. Burmese negative view of Tarup-China was further exacerbated by Tarup's continuous intervention in Myanmar's domestic affairs on the pretext of helping the minor polities, especially the Shan chiefdoms.

The initial aftermath of the Mongol invasion saw the Burmese affirming their vassal status, but by the end of the Myinsaing period, Burmese rulers during periods of warfare between Myanmar and Tarup continued to assert their autonomy and sovereignty. At least from the Burmese point of view, though biased in many ways as perhaps the Chinese sources themselves were, they defeated Tarup-China. The fact that the *Ming Shi-lu*'s accounts of numerous altercations with Burmese rulers show inconclusive outcomes suggests that perhaps China did not win in all cases. In addition, as Wade has argued, Ming China's intervention in Southeast Asian affairs including that of Myanmar was aggressive, and the threats were not veiled, but real in terms of threatening physical hostility (Wade 2004). Myanmar-China relations to a great extent are determined by the internal state of affairs within Myanmar; it should be noted that warfare appears to have increased in volume during the Inwa period which was plagued by instability, but during the Taungngu period, the powerful Hanthawati-Taungngu empire appeared to experience minimal interference from and altercation with Tarup-China.

Notes

1. It is important to note that I am only referring to the major Southeast Asian language groups such as Thai, Tagalog, Bahasa Indonesia, Malay (Melayu), etc. There are certainly texts belonging to ethnic minority groups which have not been translated for various reasons, with language proficiency as one possible factor.
2. Note that volume 1 of the 1968 edition of Twinthin's chronicle bears the title, "Myanmar Yazawinthit", which is not used, however, in 1998 editions of volumes 2 and 3 of the same text. For consistency, in this chapter I use *Mahayazawinthit* to refer to Twinthin's chronicle.
3. Although there is some controversy over the date of the chronicle, most scholars, such as U Tin Ohn, U Thaw Kaung, and Victor Lieberman, concur on 1798 as the date of the completion of Twinthin's chronicle. See: U Tin Ohn, "Modern Historical Writing in Burmese, 1724–1942", in *Historians of South East Asia*, edited by D.G.E. Hall, p. 88; U Thaw Kaung, "Two Compilers of Myanmar History and Their Chronicles", paper presented at the Universities Historical Research Centre Golden Jubilee Conference, Yangon, January 2005, p. 9; and Victor Lieberman, *Strange Parallels: Southeast Asia in Global Context, c. 800–1830*, vol. 1, p. 198.
4. It is not clear when the *Bagan Yazawin* was first compiled, the recension used in this chapter bears the date Myanmar Era 1257 (1895), when it was copied.
5. It is important to note that this classification is based on printed versions of the *Yazawinthit* and *Hmannan Yazawindawgyi*. U Kala's *Mahayazawingyi* does not contain such formatting; the 1960 edition is published in the same format

as the original palm-leaf version, except for the introduction of sub-headings. Clearly the division of the long narrative into subdivisions organized along dynastic lines was introduced by the editors of the printed versions.

6. This figure is given in Twinthin's chronicle, but not in U Kala's chronicle or the *Hmannan*.
7. The textual reference drawing an analogy between digging a drain and establishing a tradition is obviously symbolic like many Burmese idiomatic sayings. Further research into the symbolism of Burmese proverbial and idiomatic sayings is required before one can make an informed explanation of the meaning of this particular account. At the most basic level, the drain acts as a physical manifestation reminding the Burmese of their obligation to send tribute. On a metaphorical level, the fact that the three brothers by stating that they would dig the drain overnight, demonstrated their recognition that like the drain they just dug, they had committed to begin and continue a tradition of sending tribute to Tarup, which was new to them.
8. Theinni can alternatively be rendered as "Seinni", which very likely refers to Hsenwi.
9. *Nat* is a Burmese term referring to spirits and deities. There are three categories of *nats*: (1) *devas* or deities, (2) spirits of royalty and people who died green deaths or unnatural deaths; in this case, the people were usually killed by members of Burmese royal families (see Burmese pantheon of the 37 *Nats*), and (3) nature spirits, such as tree, river, and local village spirits.
10. China's tributary system is a hierarchical system in which different Southeast Asian kingdoms were ranked differently according to Chinese perception of their importance, including strategic significance, to the Chinese empire.

References

Burmese language

ပုဂံရာဇဝင်။ *Pugam Yazawin*, palm-leaf manuscript Accession no. 585. Yangon: Universities Historical Research Centre.

ဘညားဒလ၏ရာဇာဓိရာဇ်အရေးတော်ပုံ။တတိယအကြိမ်၊၁၉၇၄။
Bhannya Dala's Yazadharit *Ayedawpon*. 3rd ed. 1974.

တွင်းသင်း၏မြန်မာရာဇဝင်သစ်။ပဌမတွဲ၊ရန်ကုန်မြို့၊မင်္ဂလာပုံနှိပ်တိုက်၊၁၉၆၈။
Twinthin's *Myanmar Yazawinthit*. Vol. 1. Yangon: Mingala Publishing Co., 1968.

တွင်းသင်းတိုက်ဝန် မဟာစည်သူ ဦးထွန်းညို၊မဟာရာဇဝင်သစ်။ဒုတိယတွဲ၊ရန်ကုန်မြို့၊မြတ်မိခင်၊၁၉၉၈။
Twinthin Taikwun Mahasitthu U Htun Nyo. *Mahayazawinthit*. Vol. 2. Yangon: Myat Mi Khin, 1998.

မှန်နန်းမဟာရာဇဝင်တော်ကြီး။ပထမတွဲ။ရန်ကုန်မြို့၊မျိုးချစ်စိတ်ဓာတ်ထက်သန်ရေး၊၁၉၉၂။ဒုတိယအကြိမ်။
Hmannan Mahayazawingyi. 1st vol. 2nd ed. Yangon: Myokhyit Seikdhat Htekthanye, 1992.

ဘိရိစတုရဂ်ဗလသွဲ့ခံ။အငြိမ်းစားကျောက်စာရုံးစာရေးကြီးမြန်မာပညာရှိဦးဘေ။ရာဇဝံသဓာလိနီမည်သောပုဂံရာဇဝင်သစ်။
U Bhe. Yazawunthalini Bagan Yazawinthit.

ဦး:ကုလား:။မဟာရာဇဝင်ကြီး:။ပထမအုပ်။ဆရာပွါ:–တည်းဖြုင့်သည်။ရန်ကုန်မြို့၊မြန်မာသုတေသနန
အသင်:။၁၉၆၀။သုံး:အုပ်ရှိသည်။

U Kala. *Mahayazawingyi*, edited by Saya Pwa. Yangon: Burma Research Society, 1960. Vols. 1 and 2.

Chinese-language Sources

Song Lian (宋濂). 元史 (*Yuan Shi* [Yuan History]). 上海 [Shanghai]: 中华书局 影印 [Zhonghua Book Image and Print], 1935.

Xu Song (徐松辑). 宋会要辑稿 (*Song Hui Yao Ji Gao*). 北京 [Beijing]: 中华书局 [Chinese Book Bureau], 1957.

元文类 (*Yuan Wei Lei*). 10 vols. 江西 [Jiangxi]: 江西书局 [Jiangxi Publishing House], 1889.

Zhou Qufei (周去非). 岭外代答 (*Ling Wai Dai Da*). 10 vols. 台北 [Taipei]: 新文丰出版公司 [Xinwenfeng Publishing Company], 1984.

English language

Aung-Thwin, Michael. *The Mists of Rāmañña: The Legend That Was Lower Burma*. First ed. Honolulu: University of Hawaii Press, 2005.

———. *Myth and History in the Historiography of Early Burma: Paradigms, Primary Sources, and Prejudices*. Ohio and Singapore: Ohio University Center for International Studies and Institute of Southeast Asian Studies, 1998.

Chau Ju Kua. *Chau Ju-Kua: Chu-fan-chi* [His Work on the Chinese and Arab Trade in the Twelfth and Thirteenth Centuries]. Translated by Friedrich Hirth and W.W. Rockhill. St. Petersburg: Printing Office of the Imperial Academy of Sciences, 1911.

Lieberman, Victor. *Strange Parallels Southeast Asia in Global Context, c. 800–1830: Volume 1: Integration on the Mainland*. Cambridge: Cambridge University Press, 2003.

Luce, G.H. and U. Pe Maung Tin, eds. *The Glass Palace Chronicle of the Kings of Burma*. Rangoon: Rangoon University Press, 1960.

Thaw Kaung, U. "Two Compilers of Myanmar History and Their Chronicles". Paper given at the Golden Jubilee International Conference of the Myanmar Historical Commission. Yangon, Myanmar, 2005.

Thingyan, Sithu Gamani. *Zinme Yazawin* [Chronicle of Chiang Mai]. Translated by Thaw Kaung and Ni Ni Myint. First ed. Yangon: Universities Historical Research Centre, 2003.

Sun Laichen. "Military Technology Transfers from Ming China and the Emergence of Northern Mainland Southeast Asia (c. 1390–1527)". *Journal of Southeast Asia Studies* 34, no. 3 (2003): 495–517.

———. *The Journal of Burma Studies*. Special issue. *Chinese Historical Sources on Burma: A Bibliography of Primary and Secondary Works*. Vol. 2. Dekalb: Northern Illinois University, Center for Southeast Asian Studies, 1997.

Wade, Geoff. "Ming China and Southeast Asia in the 15th Century: A Reappraisal". ARI Working Paper 28. Singapore: ARI, 2004.

Wolters, O.W. *The Fall of Srivijaya in Malay History*. Ithaca: Cornell University Press, 1970.

Yi Yi, Dr. "A Bibliographical Essay on the Burmese Sources for the History of the Konbaung Period, 1752–1885". *Bulletin of the Burma Historical Commission*, vol. III (1963): 143–70.

Part II
The Cultural and Chinese Identity

7

CAPITAL ACCUMULATION ALONG MIGRATORY TRAJECTORIES
China Students in Singapore's Secondary Education Sector

Yow Cheun Hoe

Students from Mainland China have made an increasingly pronounced presence in Singapore's drive to internationalize its education market and become an important academic hub. They demonstrate distinct features vis-à-vis other members of new Chinese migrants, who left Mainland China after the inception of economic reform and the open-door policy in 1978,[1] and also in their relations with the local Chinese communities that have settled down in Singapore over a few generations.[2] Among the Chinese new migrants, China students are different from professionals, businesspeople, and study mamas, in terms of migratory trajectory and assimilation direction.[3] In the area of life experience in the local communities, China students differ from other students in terms of their outstanding academic performance and cultural characteristics.

This chapter examines the questions surrounding the position of China students in Singapore, with special focus on the secondary education sector. The findings are derived from a number of sources. These include social contacts with China students since 1999 as well as newspapers and magazines coverage. A substantial part of the research was conducted in one of Singapore's secondary schools, with a questionnaire survey in August 2007 and in-depth interviews with the students in February 2008.

In order to uncover and conceptualize China students' behaviour and thinking in terms of connections with China and Singapore, this chapter is structured in five main parts. The first section is a review of the theories of capitals, assimilation, and transnationalism to see how these devices may be used to dissect China students as migrants in the making. The second and third sections attempt to situate China students within Chinese new migrants and also in relation to local communities in Singapore. The fourth section discusses the findings derived from the survey done in a secondary school where China students constitute one of the major groups in the student population. The fifth section concludes the study.

THEORETICAL TOOLS: CAPITALS, ASSIMILATION, TRANSNATIONALISM

In moving along trajectories, from one place to another, migrants have to overcome a myriad of barriers in a new environment and the linkages in the prior localities. Both before and after emigration, they need to manoeuvre all sorts of resources to ensure a smooth crossing of many kinds of boundaries to the degree that they can. So as to understand the impediments they encountered and the strategies they employed, it is useful to divide their disposable resources into three forms, as Pierre Bourdieu did in his study of social activities: (1) economic capital (material property), (2) social capital (networks and connections), and (3) cultural capital (prestige).[4] For the purpose of this study, cultural capital can and should be modified to include language competence and historical knowledge.

Two more points have to be emphasized here. First, a form of capital can be converted into another, depending on the need and capability of the owner of the capital. Second, capitals can be accumulated for inter-generation reproduction.[5] Some studies have adapted the capital theory and demonstrated that only immigrant families with substantial financial and social capitals succeed in entering the mainstream, while those lacking resources were caught in the underclass.[6]

Assimilation and transnationalism are two important issues confronting migrants. They decide which forms of capitals migrants intend to acquire, accumulate, and convert. They are interrelated and at times in conflict. As they vary in degree from one country to another, local realities engage immigrants in the process of assimilation. Given the variation from one place to another, local requirements limit transnational linkages that migrants have with their original countries. The more abundant capitals they have, the higher capability and flexibility they have in dealing with questions associated with assimilation and transnationalism.

A noteworthy point about assimilation is that it is often more than a linear and uniform process. It entails the possibility of taking diverse directions into the local environment. This leads to the need to employ the concept of segmented assimilation, which sheds light on the conundrum as to how and why some migrants experience upward assimilation while others move horizontally and even downwards in the local social stratification order.[7] Segmented assimilation happens as a result of inequality of resources, in the context of exit and reception. More particularly, the context of exit involves pre-migration resources, such as money, skills, and knowledge, which immigrants bring along with them, their social class status in the homeland, and means of migration. On the other hand, the context of reception includes positions in the system of racial stratification, government policies, labour market conditions, public attitudes, and the strength and viability of ethnic communities.[8]

One of the major factors possibly holding migrants up from smooth assimilation is transnationalism, the linkages with their native lands. As an academic field, transnationalism has become increasingly important, provoking theoretical discussion and case studies by many scholars from various disciplines. The consensus reached is that transnational linkages prevail among contemporary migrants, facilitated by globalization of capitalism and innovation in transportation and communication.[9] Still controversial, however, is how sustainable and frequent the social contacts across national borders are.

There are a slew of factors affecting the magnitude and content of transnationalism as well as assimilation. This study will examine how China students are involved in transnationalism and assimilation, and in so doing, see how these two processes have defined and are defined by manipulation of various capitals.

EARNING POSITIONS IN SINGAPORE: CHINA STUDENTS AS POSSIBLE MIGRANTS AND SETTLERS

In the lexicon now prevalent among the local communities and media in Singapore, China students are regarded as part of Chinese new migrants (*xin yimin*), a term that has increasingly gained currency to refer to those hailing from Mainland China after 1978. In reality, however, China students are different from others under the rubric of Chinese new migrants. While many new migrants aspire to be Singapore's citizens or permanent residents from the outset of emigration, China students are everything but possible migrants and settlers.[10] As the subsequent discussion will show, China students have not yet developed close links or permanent attachment to

Singapore as a place for working and living. The decision to settle down in Singapore is contingent on the degree which they can covert the resources invested in education into economic capitals that can earn a better position in the social stratification.

Singapore started to receive Chinese new migrants in 1990, the year when it established diplomatic relations with the People's Republic of China. The numbers have since been growing and the presence of Chinese new migrants became more pronounced after 2000. In 2004, it was estimated that new Chinese migrants totalled between 200,000 and 300,000.[11] Of Singapore's total population of 4.2 million in 2004, 800,000 were foreigners. Thus, new Chinese migrants are numerically significant, not only as foreigners per se, but also in relation to the local community.

Three distinctive groups can be identified from Chinese new migrants in Singapore: (1) Chinese professionals and executives, (2) China students, and (3) study mamas, who are accompanying their children studying in Singapore. In addition, Mainland Chinese are also noticeably working in hawker centres, food courts, restaurants, and construction sites.[12]

Out of the three major groups, China students are the easiest to track down in terms of numbers. As Table 7.1 shows, in 2005, there were approximately 30,000 China students in Singapore: roughly 10,000 were pursuing tertiary education in two universities and five public polytechnics; 10,000 were

TABLE 7.1
China Students in Singapore, 2005

Education Institution	Number of China Students

• Tertiary institutions
  – National University of Singapore
  – Nanyang Technological University
  – Nanyang Polytechnic
  – Ngee Ann Polytechnic
  – Republic Polytechnic
  – Singapore Polytechnic
  – Temasek Polytechnic
	10,000

• Private schools	10,000
• Primary and secondary schools	10,000
Total	30,000

Source: "Xinjiapo zhenglan Zhongguo xuesheng" [Singapore Competes for China's Students], Wen Wei Po (Hong Kong), 5 September 2005.

in private schools providing training in language and other skills, and the remaining 10,000 were in primary and secondary schools. Apparently, this was a spectacular jump from 2000, a year when China students amounted to 11,000.[13]

Some of the China students are studying on scholarships offered by Singapore's government, companies, and social organizations. However, an increasingly number of the students are supported by their parents, who are from the rising middle class back in China. In Singapore's increasingly internationalized education environment, China students have in recent years become the largest group. In 2005, China students, numbering around 33,000, overtook the estimated 8,000 Malaysians and 8,000 Indonesians, who had traditionally been the two largest foreign student groups in Singapore.[14]

Given that their status before and after migration remains the same as students, China students are moving horizontally in the assimilation process. Chinese professionals and executives are moving upwards while study mamas are moving downwards. Transnationally, China students maintain their relations with China because many of their family members are still in China. Chinese professionals and executives are the most mobile and capable in transcending national boundaries and keeping transnational linkages, while study mamas are mired in local realities adverse to them.[15]

CREATING DISTANCE IN CLASSROOMS: ACADEMIC PERFORMANCE AND CULTURAL CHARACTERISTICS

China students as well as other members of Chinese new migrants have distinctive social and cultural boundaries in their living spaces in Singapore. They share the same race with the local Chinese communities that were established over generations from various waves of migration before 1949. However, they are at times labelled with a national marker, being referred to as the People's Republic of China where they came from. This national descriptor can be a carrier of good implication or a negative stereotype, depending on the context and people involved.

Two factors have drawn the lines of demarcation between China students and their counterparts from other nationalities in Singapore's schools. First, the cultural differences and social habits that they have carried from China are roadblocks to overcome when making contacts with their classmates. Second, the outstanding academic performance that they often deliver is the gap that other students need to close.

For China students, horizontal movement across national borders is the best way to depict their social mobility; their status as students still remains the same after moving into Singapore, albeit that the new schooling environment is different from the one in China. The money expended in education in Singapore usually takes up much of the saving and income of their parents, but they hope the horizontal movement will only be temporary and that the inter-generational reproduction will subsequently translate into capitals pushing them upward socially.

This explains why many China students, particularly those in primary and second schools, work harder and spend more time in study than the local students. They expend great efforts to overcome the language barrier in the English learning environment. Nevertheless, they are catching up very fast. In 2002, for instance, six out of seventeen top Primary School Leaving Examination scorers were China students.[16] The better education attainments of China students in classrooms has stirred emotions ranging from jealousy and envy to awe and admiration among local parents and local students.[17] The education gap between China and local students as well as the lukewarm reception of some local parents may impede the assimilation into local society. Many cases, however, reveal that the longer they study in Singapore, the deeper they acculturate to the local environment and the weaker their bonds to China.

CONNECTING WITH SINGAPORE AND CHINA: A SURVEY AT A SECONDARY SCHOOL

China students constitute an important cohort in the St. Francis Methodist School (SFMS), where a questionnaire survey and in-depth interviews were conducted as a case study to show how China students relate to and connect with Singapore as well as China. Annually, pursuing education in the SFMS requires approximately S$12,000, covering school and examination fees, which is expensive in the considered context. Across the spectrum of Singapore secondary education in Singapore, in terms of the cost needed, acclaimed international schools are at the high ends while in the low end are mainly public secondary schools and junior colleges.

The SFMS is home to an annual cohort of 700–750 students, both local and foreign, hailing from more than twenty countries, including China, Vietnam, Thailand, Indonesia, Myanmar, and Korea.[18] China students make up about 20 to 25 per cent of the student population. For the purpose of this study, forty China students were surveyed randomly in August 2007 and asked to answer a questionnaire containing sixty-five questions, divided into six major components: (1) personal particulars, (2) family background, (3) China's linkages, (4) local connections, (5) everyday activities, and

(6) future directions. This was followed by in-depth interviews with a number of students in February 2008.

Founded in 1960, the SFMS is one of Singapore's leading private academic schools. The first Methodist School to be privatized, it is currently managed by the Methodist Church of Singapore as a non profit-making organization. As a pan-Asian institution with an international mix of staff and students, the SFMS offers a host of programmes, including IGCSE, the Lower Secondary and Singapore-Cambridge GCE "O" and "A" Levels. In addition, the St. Francis Academy, a division of SFMS, is the centre for pre-degree programmes offering the AUSMAT (Year 11 and 12), St. Francis Baccalaurate, and BTEC Higher National Diploma (Business).[19] All these programmes and examinations are internationally recognized, preparing students for enrolling into Singapore's tertiary institutions as well as leading universities in other parts of the world.[20]

The findings show no significance in gender preference in the trajectory of pursuing secondary education in Singapore. Out of the 40 surveyed students, 16 were males and 24 females. The eldest were born in 1987 while the youngest were born in 1991. Thus, the students aged between 21 and 17 in 2008. Their home towns and villages were scattered across China from coastal to inland provinces, including Guangdong, Fujian, Zhejiang, Shanghai, Hebei, Shanxi, Shaanxi, and Hubei. This diversity in origin is in fact consistent with other members of Chinese new migrants and is a departure from the traditional emigration patterns, before World War II, which was confined predominantly to Guangdong and Fujian provinces.[21]

It appears that the students counted on their own family for education fees and living expenses in Singapore. Table 7.2 shows that families are the

TABLE 7.2
Question 14: Sources of Support for Education Fees

Sources	Number of China Students
(a) Family	40
(b) China's government	—
(c) Singapore government's scholarship	—
(d) Singapore government's loan	—
(e) Scholarship from Singapore social organizations	—
(f) Loan from Singapore social organizations	—
(g) Others	—
Total	40

single source of payment of education fees for all forty surveyed students. This is in stark contrast to the case of the tertiary education sector, where a considerable number of China students are on scholarships and loans offered by Singapore's government.[22] As demonstrated in Table 7.3, on average, the students surveyed had to depend on their families for 99.5 per cent and on part-time jobs for 0.5 per cent of the living expenses. The main reason for not relying on scholarships and loans is the fact that many of them were from middle-class families in China where their parents can afford to invest in overseas education. As Table 7.4 shows, in terms of average monthly family income in China, half of them (22) came from the cohort of above RMB10,000 and many from RMB5,000–9,999 (5) and RMB4,000–4,999 (6). The decision to coming to Singapore, the questionnaire and interviews show, was made as either a family strategy or the student's own intention. Their studies in Singapore in fact involve inter-generational reproduction, with the hope of securing a better future for both families and students.

TABLE 7.3
Question 17: Sources of Support for Living Expenses

Sources	Percentage
(a) Family	99.5
(b) Scholarships and loans	—
(c) Part-time job	0.5
Total	100

TABLE 7.4
Question 21: Average Monthly Family Income in China

Monthly Income	Number of China Students
(a) no income	0
(b) Below RMB1,000	0
(c) RMB1,000–1,999	0
(d) RMB2,000–2,999	3
(e) RMB3,000–3,999	4
(f) RMB4,000–4,999	6
(g) RMB5,000–9,999	5
(h) Above RMB10,000	22
Total	40

Regardless of which geographical point and social cohort they came from, Singapore was not considered the most desirable destination for them to receive education. What can be gleaned from conversations with the students is that the favourable countries for education, in descending order, were the Untied States of America, the United Kingdom, Australia, and Singapore.[23] What brought them to Singapore was the limited capitals they have with them. While their families could afford to support them financially in the pursuit of an education in Singapore, they were not rich enough to study in more expensive countries such as the United States and the United Kingdom. Where academic background is concerned, only top talent students would be offered scholarships in the United States and the United Kingdom; many in Singapore are the second best among the China students dispersed across the world. From another perspective, as an informant student coined, Singapore is a "transient" place, particularly so for those in the secondary education sector.[24] With a confluence of Chinese and Western cultures, Singapore is an ideal place from them to learn and catch up before deciding the next destination. In Singapore, they can convert economic capital into competence in English and certificates conferred by Singapore's schools so that they will be more valuable in the next stage.

All forty surveyed students have family ties with China; 38 have a father, 39 have a mother, 20 have at least a brother, 9 have at least a sister. On the contrary, few have family connections in Singapore; only 2 have a father, 1 has a mother, 1 has at least a brother, 2 have at least a sister. This means that while family bonds keep them in touch with China, there are not many family ties to help them to expand social networks in Singapore. They still maintain linkages with China to a considerable extent. What can be gleaned from the questionnaire survey is that on average they returned to China twice a year, not following Chinese festivals such as the New Lunar Year celebration, but according to the school's timetable for holiday. When in Singapore, they send an average of 1.3 letters a year back to their families in China. As a matter of fact, their contacts with home in China were mostly facilitated by telecommunications. Every month, they made telephone calls 10.9 times with 26.3 minutes each time and sent five e-mails to their homes in China.

The students are more concerned with what happened in China than in Singapore. As Table 7.5 shows, of the news that all the surveyed students read everyday, 67.9 per cent was about China, only 18.8 per cent about Singapore and 13.3 per cent about elsewhere. This is partly because of the family ties and other linkages they still keep with China. This is also partly because of the problems they have in the process of blending into the local society. On

TABLE 7.5
Question 50: News Read Everyday

Coverage	Percentage
(a) China	67.9
(b) Singapore	18.8
(c) Elsewhere	13.3
Total	100

the other hand, not reading enough about local happenings may in turn be a hindrance towards closer ties with Singapore.

Table 7.6 shows that the majority of them (21) regard the language problem as the biggest obstacle for them to assimilate into local society. Others deemed cultural and habit (5) and insufficient time outside study (4) as the major roadblocks in mixing with the local people. A point to note here is that over the decades Singapore has evolved into an English-speaking nation, particularly in schools where English is the medium of instruction. In such an environment, the cultural capital of the exit, in the form of competence in Chinese language and knowledge about China, does not help China students. They have to strive to master English, making it a capital useful to them.

A combined picture from Tables 7.7 to 7.11 tells how the students cast their future directions. After their current studies, only 12 students planned to stay on in Singapore and 7 wanted to returned to China, but as many as 21 wished to go elsewhere (Table 7.7). When asked what they would want to do in Singapore after completion of their study, 28 decided not to stay on while 7 wished to work and 5 wanted to do further studies (Table 7.8). Even for those who wanted to stay put in Singapore, the duration they intended to do so appeared relatively short; only one chose to stay put as long as possible, while only 3 students planned to stay for 1–3 years, 2 for 4–5 years, and 3 for 6–10 years (Table 7.9). Neither was China a favoured destination. After

TABLE 7.6
Question 44: The Biggest Obstacle to Assimilating into Local Society

Obstacle	Number of China Students
(a) Language problem	21
(b) Insufficient time outside study	4
(c) Culture and habit	5
Total	30

TABLE 7.7
Question 52: Where to Go after Completion of Study in Singapore?

Plan	Number of China Students
(a) Stay on in Singapore	12
(b) Return to China	7
(c) Go elsewhere	21
Total	40

TABLE 7.8
Question 53: What to Do in Singapore after Completion of Study?

Plan	Number of China Students
(a) Further studies	5
(b) Working	7
(c) Will not be staying on	28
Total	40

TABLE 7.9
Question 55: How Long Do You Plan to Stay on in Singapore?

Duration	Number of China Students
(a) 1–3 years	3
(b) 4–5 years	2
(c) 6–10 years	3
(d) as long as possible	0
(e) will not stay on	28
(f) do not know	4
Total	40

pursuing secondary education in Singapore, 32 would not return to China, 8 would find jobs in China, and none would further studies at universities in China (Table 7.10). Of the 21 students setting their eyes beyond Singapore and China, 17 planned to further studies while 4 wanted to work in other countries (Table 7.11).

While China may no longer expect all its overseas students to return for the purpose of helping the country, Singapore does hope to absorb foreign students into its drive for economic growth. Much of the criticism imposed

TABLE 7.10
Question 56: What to Do in China after Completion of Study?

Plan	Number of China Students
(a) Further studies	0
(b) Work	8
(c) Will not be returning	32
Total	40

TABLE 7.11
Question 58: If Going to Other Countries, What Will You Do?

Plan	Number of China Students
(a) Further studies	17
(b) Work	4
Total	21

on China students has been that they only treat Singapore as a "springboard", from where they can jump to other destinations for better opportunities. One of the surveyed students dismissed such stereotyping of China students. He contended that the presence of China students was as beneficial to Singapore as it was to the students. This is because the students gain knowledge and degrees from the schools, whereas Singapore taps a source of both talent and money from them. In his hometown, Shanghai, he added, Singapore was advertised by education agencies with a slogan of "Singapore is more than a gold springboard". In fact, Singapore can mean a place for working, living, or settling down, after the completion of studies. When asked to describe how he related to Singapore, he said in a metaphorical way,

> I would prefer to see myself as a bee and Singapore a place where I am now picking up nectar from flowers. I may move on to other countries for new source of nectar, but I may also stay on to continue with honey making. I may choose this place to build up my own hive, but I may also consider other places for such purpose. It all depends on where can provide me with the best conditions for setting up a home.[25]

CONCLUDING REMARKS

The foregoing discussion clearly shows China students take up a distinctive position among Chinese new migrants and also among the student population in Singapore. Along migratory trajectories in arriving from mainland China to Singapore, they have demonstrated remarkable features where capitals, assimilation, and transnationalism are concerned. More specifically, China students pursuing secondary education are the most dynamically situated with the highest tendency to move on to other countries for further studies. In Singapore's context, their position is temporarily fixed as foreign students. Their future directions, however, are still unfolding and vacillating between becoming settlers with roots in Singapore or passengers en route to other destinations to embark on another stage of life.

It is obvious that the investment in and capital reproduction from education is still ongoing for them. The fruits from education are yet to be borne and revenue will probably yield only a few years after they have finished tertiary studies. The economic capital they have transferred from China and poured into Singapore is now in the process of converting into knowledge and skills. This is the capital that is not yet ready to cash out, but China students are eagerly accumulating with the hope of translating into social capital, in the form of degrees and social status, in the future.

Since their status remains fixed as students after coming to Singapore — their living space is confined to a large extent to schools and their social connections are mainly with their classmates — they are undertaking horizontal assimilation. Their transnational linkages, predominantly in the form of family ties, have been facilitated by telecommunication. It is, however, still early to predict whether the transnationalism that they have with China will be sustained or break down in the future.

Puzzles abound as to whether China will remain a point of ultimate return, or whether Singapore will become a place for settlements or if other countries are the next destination. This is subject to a host of factors that are and will continue to cfhange. Nevertheless, the chosen destination is definitely a place that will promise to optimize the conversion and usage of capital.

Notes

1. For a pioneering effort in putting Chinese new migrants in historical perspective, see Wang Gungwu, "New Migrants: How New? Why New", in *Diasporic Chinese Ventures: The Life and Work of Wang Gungwu*, edited by Gregor Benton and Hong Liu (London and New York: RoutledgeCurzon, 2004), pp. 227–38. For analysis of China-centric consciousness among these migrants, see Liu Hong, "New Migrants and the Revival of Overseas Chinese Nationalism", *Journal of Contemporary China* 14, no. 43 (May 2005): 291–316. Succinct studies on Chinese new migrants in Singapore have yet to be fully conducted. For a snapshot, see Zhou Zhaocheng, "Shicheng xin yimin de san xin liang yi" [Three News

and Two Olds among Chinese New Migrants in Singapore], *Yazhou Zhoukan*, 1 April 2007, p. 27.

2. There is a huge literature on Singapore Chinese communities grown out of various waves of immigration before World War II. A good place to start on the formation and evolution of Singapore Chinese communities is Cheng Lim-keak, *Social Change and the Chinese in Singapore: A Socio-Economic Geography with Special Reference to Bang Structure* (Singapore: Singapore University Press, 1985).

3. "China" is used as an adjective to specifically modify the people from the People's Republic of China. This is to avoid the ambiguities arising from the adjective "Chinese", which may serve as either a racial or nationality reference point. In fact, as the subsequent discussion shows, new Chinese migrants are often labelled with a "national" marker.

4. Pierre Bourdieu and Loic Wacquant, *An Invitation to Reflexive Sociology* (Chicago: University of Chicago Press, 1992).

5. Craig Calhoun, "Pierre Bourdieu", in *The Blackwell Companion to Major Contemporary Social Theorists*, edited by George Ritzer (Malden: Blackwell, 2003), pp. 274–309.

6. Victor Nee and Jimmy Sanders, "Understanding the Diversity of Immigrant Incorporation: A Form of Capital Model", *Ethnic and Racial Studies* 24, no. 3 (2001): 386–411; Richard D. Alba and Victor Nee, *Remaking the American Mainstream: Assimilation and Contemporary Immigration* (Cambridge, MA: Harvard University Press, 2003); Martin N. Marger, "Transnationalism or Assimiliation? Patterns of Sociopolitical Adaptation among Canadian Business Immigrants", *Ethnic and Racial Studies* 29, no. 5 (September 2006): 882–900.

7. For case studies on Western countries, see Alejandro Portes and Zhou Min, "The New Second Generation: Segmented Assimilation and its Variants Among Post-1965 Immigrant Youth", *The Annals of the American Academy of Political and Social Sciences* 530 (1993): 74–96; Mary C. Waters, "Ethnic and Racial Identities of Second-Generation Black Immigrants in New York City", *International Migration Review* 28 (1994): 795–820; Alejandro Portes and Ruben G. Rumbaut, *Immigrant America: A Portrait* (Berkeley, CA: University of California Press, 1996); Alejandro Portes and Ruben G. Rumbaut, *Legacies: The Story of the Immigrant Second Generation* (Berkeley, CA: University of California Press and Russell Sage Foundation, 2001).

8. Min Zhou and Yang Sao Xiong, "The Multifaceted American Experiences of the Children of Asian Immigrants: Lessons for Segmented Assimilation", *Ethnic and Racial Studies* 28, no. 6 (November 2005): 1123.

9. Nina Glick Schiller, Linda Basch, and C. Blanc Szanton, "Towards a Transnational Perspective on Migrants: Race, Class, Ethnicity, and Nationalism Reconsidered", *Annals of the New York Academy of Sciences* 645 (1992): 125–43; Michael Peter Smith and Luis Eduardo Guarnizo, eds., *Transnationalism from Below* (New Brunswick: Transaction Publishers, 1998); Alejandro Portes, Luis E. Guarnizo,

and Patricia Landolt, "The Study of Transnationalism: Pitfalls and Promise of an Emergent Research Field", *Ethnic and Racial Studies* 22, no. 2 (Special Issue: Transnational Communities) (March 1999): 217–37; Peter Kivisto, "Theorizing Transnational Immigration: A Critical Review of Current Efforts", *Ethnic and Racial Studies* 24, no. 4 (July 2001): 549–77.

10. For a discussion, from a global perspective, on how China students can take part and contribute to Chinese migration, see Wang Gungwu, "Liuxue and Yimin: From Study to Migranthood", in *Beyond Chinatown: New Chinese Migration and the Global Expansion of China*, by Mette Thuno (Denmark: NIAS Press, 2007), pp. 165–81.

11. Lu Fangsi and Xiao Jiwei, "Tamen gaibian le Xinjiapo, ye gaibian le Zhongguo" [They Changed Singapore and also China], *Yazhou Zhoukan*, 25 April 2004, pp. 14–18.

12. For the purpose of this study, it is not analytically plausible to treat the Mainland Chinese working in the culinary sector and other service businesses as one group because a considerable number of them are students and study mamas. Mainland Chinese in construction sites are seasonal guest workers and thus their contacts with the larger society are relatively limited.

13. Pan Xinghua, "Woguo da zhong xiao xue Zhongguou xuesheng chaoguo wan ming" [More than 10 thousand China's Students in Our Country], *Lianhe Zaobao* (Singapore), 30 September 2000.

14. Sandra Davie, "Foreign Students in Singapore A Class Apart", *Straits Times* (Singapore), 3 December 2005.

15. For a more detailed discussion on segmented assimilation and transnationalism across the Chinese new migrants in Singapore, see Yow Cheun Hoe, "More or Less Distinctive? Chinese New Migrants in Singapore", presented at the Africa Regional Conference of the International Society for the Study of Chinese Overseas, "Diversity in Diaspora: The Chinese Overseas", Department of Historical and Heritage Studies, University of Pretoria, South Africa, 4–6 December 2006.

16. Chua Mui Hoong, "Foreign Bright Sparks Help Kids Here Shine", *Straits Times* (Singapore), 18 February 2005.

17. Tracy Quek, "China Whiz Kids: S'pore Feels the Heat", *Straits Times* (Singapore), 13 February 2005.

18. St. Francis Methodist School website, <http://www.sfms.edu.sg/01about.asp> (accessed 10 February 2008).

19. Ibid.

20. The IGCSE (International General Certificate of Secondary Education) provides a foundation for higher lever courses. The Singapore-Cambridge GCE "O" and "A" Levels are both two-year programmes; the former serves as an entry requirement for college, overseas university foundation and professional courses worldwide, while the latter is the culmination of secondary education and a gateway to tertiary education. Also a two-year programme, the AUSMAT (Australian Matriculation) is administered by the Curriculum Council on behalf of the Government of

Western Australia as a pre-university programme, equivalent to the GCE "A" Level. The St. Francis Baccalaureate is specifically linked to Southeast College, Kansas, United States, where the latter will admit students who pass the programme in St. Francis to complete studies in a specialist or generalized field. The BTEC Higher National Diploma is administered by Edexcel, which was formed in 1996 by the merger of the Business and Technological Education Council (BTEC), the United Kingdom's leading provider of vocational qualifications, and the University of London Examinations and Assessment Council (ULEAC), one of the major examination boards for general certificate of secondary education and "A" Levels. It is a two-year programme, providing students with knowledge and skills in the business environment for prospective employment or progression to an undergraduate degree.

21. For the formation of traditional Chinese communities, see Cheng Lim-keak, *Social Change and the Chinese in Singapore*, and Yen Ching-hwang, *A Social History of the Chinese in Singapore and Malaya, 1800–1911* (Singapore: Oxford University Press, 1986).

22. For a comparative study, in more respects, between China students in secondary education and those in tertiary education in Singapore, see Yow Cheun Hoe, "En Route to the World: China Students in Singapore", presented at the Sixth Conference of the International Society for the Study of Chinese Overseas on "Recent Trends in the Relations between Chinese Abroad and Their Ancestral Homeland", Peking University, Beijing, 21–23 September 2007.

23. In fact, throughout almost the entire history of China students' going abroad for education, the United States of America has been the favourite choice. See Cheng Xi, *Dangdai Zhongguou liuxuesheng yanjiu* [Studies of Contemporary China Students Overseas] (Hong Kong: Xianggang Shehui Kexue Chubanshe, 2003).

24. Interview with student SFMS02, 22 January 2008.

25. Interview with student SFMS01, 22 January 2008.

8

CHINA AND THE CULTURAL IDENTITY OF THE CHINESE IN INDONESIA

Aimee Dawis

INTRODUCTION

The ethnic Chinese in Indonesia have lived in a complex web of social, political and historical conditions of the country for generations. Most Chinese in Indonesia regard China as a "mythic homeland" (Ang 2001) that most have never visited. Scholars who have studied the Chinese in Indonesia document the experiences of the Chinese with respect to shifts and fluctuations in their cultural identity (e.g. Thung 1998), as well as their changing political relationship with China (e.g. Suryadinata 1992). However, no specific case study analysed the role of the media in the identity formation and maintenance among the Chinese in Indonesia, specifically those who grew up during the Soeharto era.

This chapter focuses on the cultural identity of the Chinese in Indonesia in the Soeharto era (1966–98) and current watershed events in the revival of Chinese culture post-1998. I have chosen the Soeharto era because it is the period in Indonesian history when the environment is most restrictive with respect to Chinese culture and language. The analysis of the cultural identity of the Chinese in Indonesia during the Soeharto era is based on a case study of how the Indonesian Chinese used imported media from Hong Kong, Taiwan and China to inform their cultural identity formation and maintenance.

In sharp contrast to the restrictive cultural and linguistic environment that the Indonesian Chinese experienced during the Soeharto era, the Indonesian government has been more open to Chinese culture and language following the fall of Soeharto in May 1998. While much of the literature on this period, also called *Reformasi*, has centred on the changing role and identity of the Chinese in Indonesia, especially in the political arena and nation-building (e.g. Tan 2004 and Budiman 2005), no study has been conducted on how recent cultural events specifically demonstrate the link between China, Chinese culture and the identity of the Chinese in Indonesia. For this reason, I have chosen to examine two cultural events in 2007: the Chinese New Year celebration on 28 February 2007, held at the Jakarta Fair Ground in Kemayoran and attended by President Susilo Bambang Yudhoyono, and the Miss Chinese Cosmos Pageant Indonesia, held at Mulia Hotel, Jakarta, on 1 August 2007. Both events are significant because they illustrate the intermingling of Indonesian and Chinese cultural identities. The fact that both events received the support of both Indonesian and Chinese governments is also noteworthy because it pertains to the increased cooperation and mutual understanding between the two countries.

This chapter approaches cultural identities as "the points of identification and the unstable points of identification or suture made by a group (or groups) of people within the discourses of history and culture" (Hall 1990, p. 226). Specific to the Chinese in Indonesia, cultural identities involve identity formations which cut across and intersect natural frontiers, and which are composed of people who have been dispersed forever from their ancestral homelands (Hall 2000). As we will see in the analysis of the three case studies, the Indonesian Chinese are obliged to come to terms with the indigenous cultures of Indonesia without wholly assimilating to them and completely losing their own identities. Their cultural identities are shaped by traces of Indonesian and Chinese cultures, traditions, languages and histories. Thus, they are irrevocably the product of several interlocking histories and cultures.

Before the case studies may be discussed, it is important for us to learn about the social, political and historical situations of the Chinese in Indonesia. Moreover, as Stuart Hall (1990) reminds us,

> Cultural identities come from somewhere, have histories. But, like everything which is historical, they undergo constant transformation. Far from being eternally fixed in some essentialized past, they are subject to the continuous "play" of history, culture and power. (p. 225)

Therefore, in order for us to understand the cultural identity of the Indonesian Chinese, we must first begin with a historical overview of the Chinese in Indonesia to provide the context for the three case studies.

THE CHINESE IN INDONESIA: PERENNIAL STRANGERS IN THEIR OWN COUNTRY

The question of Indonesian Chinese identity goes back to the time when Indonesia was called the East Indies and the Dutch were the colonial masters of the region. During this era,[1] the Dutch built their East Indies empire on the principle of "divide and rule" which gave rise to a tripartite racial classification system (Coppel 2002). According to this system, Europeans were placed on the highest social rung whereas Foreign Orientals (i.e. the Chinese) and the Natives (i.e. the indigenous Indonesians or the *pribumi*)[2] were placed on subsequent rungs.

The arrangement was designed to segregrate the Chinese from the indigenous population and pitted the two groups against one another. Thus, the indigenous Indonesians resented the Chinese because the latter were accorded special privileges and served as "middle men" and tax collectors for the Dutch. Because the Chinese managed to accumulate some capital through their role as tax collectors and middlemen,[3] the Dutch were determined to suppress the development of domestic bourgeoisie among the Chinese and the possibility of an alliance between the Chinese and the *priyayi* (the indigenous aristocratic class) (Kemasang 1985). Consequently, they proceeded to "cut the Chinese down to any size they wished" (Kemasang 1985, p. 72) in a horrendous bloodshed widely known as the 1740 Chinese Massacres in Java. The massacres served as a harsh reminder to the Chinese that they could never go against the Dutch. Unfortunately, despite the massacres and restrictions placed on the Chinese to enter and leave their residential compounds, most of the indigenous population continued to resent the Chinese for their perceived "higher position".

In the post-colonial period, the Chinese continued to be resented for their perceived dominance in Indonesia's private economic sector. The Chinese have been envied and vilified for their economic prowess as they are believed to control 70 per cent of the country's private economic sector and make up only 3 per cent of the 240 million people who reside in Indonesia (Suryadinata 1999). It is partly because of this imbalance of economic power relative to their size that the Chinese often become targets of violence during the political upheavals in Indonesia's history. One such event occurred in

1965. In the aftermath of an alleged PKI (Partai Komunis Indonesia or Indonesian Communist Party) coup to overthrow the Soekarno government in 1965, anti-Chinese riots erupted in major cities of Indonesia. During the riots, mobs attacked buildings and Chinese community organizations and destroyed automobiles, motorcycles, houses, and shops belonging to the Chinese in order to express their hostility to China, the Chinese, or to the Communists[4] (Coppel 1983). In the course of this destruction, hundreds of Chinese were killed, violently assaulted or arrested (Coppel 1983). It is also important to note that Sino-Indonesian relations deteriorated in 1965–67 because the Indonesian government accused China of backing a Communist plot with the PKI, even though there was no credible evidence to support this accusation (Nadesan 1980).

As a consequence of this political turbulence, a 1966 tract[5] issued by the government stipulated that the Chinese would have to substitute Indonesian for Chinese names in order to convince Indonesians of their commitment to Indonesia (Suryadinata 1999). Consequently, the Chinese in Indonesia use Indonesian names in place of their Chinese ones. Instead of providing a robust sense of self-identity,[6] the Indonesian names lend a sense of ambiguity to the Indonesian Chinese. They look Chinese, but their primary means of identifying themselves (i.e. their own names) are rooted in a complex historical and political background.

The language spoken by the Indonesian Chinese population is also mired in complexities. Another consequence of the failed coup in 1965 was the policy of assimilation implemented by the Soeharto government, which was in place until 1998.[7] According to this policy of assimilation,[8] the government closed all Chinese-language schools and ruled that children of Chinese descent must enroll in Indonesian-language schools. In these schools, the Chinese were to learn Indonesian history, politics, and social practices alongside their Indonesian peers. Aside from closing the schools, the use of Chinese characters in public spaces, the import of Chinese-language publications,[9] and all forms and expressions that can be traced to a Chinese cultural origin, such as the public celebration of the Lunar New Year, were prohibited[10] (Tan 1999). As a result of these restrictions, most Chinese children born after 1966 speak, write, and read only the Indonesian language (Bahasa Indonesia).

Despite the fact that most of the Indonesian Chinese born after 1966 speak only Bahasa Indonesia and regard Indonesia as their country where they were born and raised, they are still viewed as "the other" by the rest of the population. Speaking the national language does not mean that they may attain a true sense of identity in the modernist sense[11] because they are still not completely assimilated into the Indonesian society. Furthermore, they are always reminded of their position as a marginalized group in the country during anti-Chinese riots/massacres that have occurred throughout Indonesia's history at times of political turbulence. The most recent example occurred in May 1998. During these riots, hundreds of Chinese homes, office buildings, and other establishments were pillaged and burned. In addition, many Chinese individuals were robbed, injured, killed or raped. The mass rape, harassment, molestation, and killing of dozens of Chinese women and girls evoked anger from women's groups and Indonesian Chinese intellectuals (Budianta 2000).

In his article, "Citizenship, Inheritance, and the Indigenizing of 'Orang Chinese' in Indonesia", Aguilar (2001) contends that the Chinese "are fixed as perennial first-generation immigrants in a static landscape set against a tormented, contentious, and changeless past" (p. 527). Aguilar (2001) further asserts that the Chinese would always be seen as aliens by the *pribumi* because they are attributed a definite and knowable place of origin — China — and a first set of ancestors from "outside" who set foot and descended on Indonesia. Thus, the May 1998 riot, along with other violent events, reminds the Indonesian Chinese as being forever alienated in their own country. Like the survivors of the Holocaust, these events become a form of "collective traumas" (Eber and Neal 2001, p. 175) that have become embedded in the social heritage of the Indonesian Chinese. They are always caught between their duty to remember their origins and their desire to forget the suffering they encountered during those violent incidents.

In light of the intricate position of the Indonesian Chinese in Indonesia's socio-economic and political conditions, we must move away from the modernist tradition of fixing an absolute identity (cf. Giddens 1991) to better understand how this group of people grapple with their sense of identity. For a tiny minority that allegedly controls a tremendous part of the country's economy, the Indonesian Chinese need to comply with the government's assimilationist policies not only because of their vulnerable position, but also the lucrative opportunities that they reap from the business networks that they have established for centuries, beginning from the Dutch colonial period when they served as middlemen. The Indonesian Chinese thus reflect some of the postmodern characteristics of the *pastiche personality*, "a social chameleon, [that is] constantly borrowing bits and pieces of identity from whatever sources are available and constructing them as useful or desirable in a given situation" (Gergen 2000, p. 150) instead of the modern notion of the bounded, autonomous individual.

Globalization further complicates the notion of Indonesian Chinese identity because it brings up issues of transnationality and provokes questions about the place of the Indonesian Chinese within the Chinese diaspora, a "transnational, spatially and temporally sprawling sociocultural formation of people, creating imagined communities whose blurred and fluctuating boundaries are sustained by real and/or symbolic ties to some original 'homeland' " (Ang 1993, p. 5). Moreover, "modern communications, mass media, global mass culture, and flexible capitalism — the constituent elements of globalization" (Hall 1991, pp. 22–23) — have intruded to the body-politic of the nation-state to create "transnational publics" (Nonini and Ong 1997, p. 25) such as the Chinese diaspora. By imagining oneself as part of a globally significant, transnational Chinese diasporic community, a minority Chinese subject (e.g. an Indonesian Chinese) can "rise, at least in the imagination, above the national environment in which (s)he lives but from which (s)he may always have felt symbolically excluded" (Ang 2001, p. 78). In this sense, transnationalism differs from nationalism because, "unlike the nationalism of the nation-state, which premises itself on a national community which is territorially bound, [transnationalism]…produces an imagined community that is deterritorialized" (Ang 2001, p. 83). Thus, the world can no longer be understood as "being made up of independent, separate nations with solid boundaries. Instead it has become a transnational, interdependent system where national borders are increasingly permeable" (Sorensen 1997, p. 107). It is in this globalized setting that "the constituent elements of globalization" provide opportunities for members of the Chinese diaspora to provide alternatives to state ideologies for (re)making identity; mixing and transferring Chinese values, beliefs, and images across nations.

In her book, *Flexible Citizenship: The Cultural Logics of Transnationality*, Aihwa Ong (1999) also notes that there is an ever-growing pluralization of Chinese identities as a result of global capitalism:

> The multiple and shifting position of "Chineseness" has been formed and embedded within the processes of global capitalism — production, trade, mobility, consumption, dislocation/relocation — and subjected to various modes of governmentality that fix them in place or disperse them in space. (Ong 1999, p. 24)

Ong's mention of "governmentality" is significant because the identity of Chinese diasporan subjects is very much dependent on the *politics* of the countries they choose to settle in. As noted, the Indonesian Chinese have been cut off from their Chinese culture due to the political and socio-economic conditions of Indonesia. However, they are still part of a diasporan community of *huaqiao* (Overseas Chinese), sharing the same cultural values such as *guanxi* (or maintaining network connections in business relationships), traditional

Chinese familialism, business acumen, and talent for wealth-making (Ong 1999). It is interesting to note that these Chinese folk values, long vilified by people of Mainland China because they embody the stereotypical Overseas Chinese who are concerned only with building their own businesses, are now valorized. As more and more Overseas Chinese (e.g. Liem Sioe Liong, one of the wealthiest Indonesian Chinese) contributed large amounts of money to rebuild their ancestral hometowns and invest in various projects, they gained the respect of their peers in China and opened up investment opportunities. Indeed, government officials and corporate representatives of Mainland China imbue cultural solidarity, filial piety, and everlasting loyalty to the motherland at investment-scouting meetings to persuade Overseas Chinese (especially those from Indonesia) to commit to their proposals (Ong 1999).

In the age of globalization, the above values may be transmitted to the Overseas Chinese communities via mediated forms of communication such as films and television serials that feature Chinese actors and actresses from Hong Kong or Taiwan. Ong (1999) asserts that the rise of transnational media markets has paved the way for a new sense of translocal Chinese cultural identity that is established not so much by language or national origin as by kinship rituals and cultural values that are variously represented in the mass media. Therefore, even though the audience members of a certain Chinese film do not live in the same country, they may still be able to relate to the elements that they see in the films and television serials because they share the same cultural values and beliefs. In a sense, then, they become part of an "imagined community" because even though they may never know the people in places such as Hong Kong or Taiwan, or even visit those places, the "image of their communion" (Anderson 1998, p. 6) is conveyed through the media.

The transnational consumption of Chinese series and films also brings up "imagined memories" or "imagined nostalgia" (Appadurai 2000, p. 77) of a mythical homeland (i.e. China) for diasporic Chinese communities that have settled in other countries for generations and who have never been to Mainland China. These "memories" are essential for the Chinese to understand concepts of selfhood and collective conscience because the core meaning of any individual or group identity is sustained by remembering; and what is remembered is defined by the assumed identity (cf. Gillis 1994). Like identities, memories are subjective, socially constructed representations of reality that shape who we are. We are constantly revising our memories to suit our current identities; the realities of the past take on special meaning through our current perceptions of them, and the future becomes a mixture of present fears and aspirations (Eber and Neal 2001).

In modern society, we belong to several different groups simultaneously, each with its own collective memory. In order to assert our sense of identity within these groups, we turn to mechanical repositories of the past such as the media. As Ong (1999) has pointed out, the increasing mobility of goods, images, and ideas, in addition to migratory practices all over the world, more people (e.g. diasporic Chinese communities) assume multiple identities and memories that transcend national boundaries. The media are thus the social tools that may allow them to traverse the trajectories of their personal, cultural, and national identities.

Despite the powerful potential of the media in representing and shaping memories and identities, little theoretical and empirical work has been conducted to link the media with memory and identity. Unlike the experiences of the South Asian community studied by Gillespie (1995), however, the Chinese media texts do not convey images of pre-immigrant pasts to the Indonesian Chinese. They are, instead, a form of "imagined nostalgia" which contains images that diasporic Chinese communities (e.g. the Indonesian Chinese) have never directly experienced but are still relevant to their concept of "Chineseness" because they convey shared beliefs, values, and norms. As Appadurai (2000) notes, the notion of "imagined nostalgia" (p. 77) is one that has not been applied by scholars to analyse media's ability to create feelings of loss and longing for things that audiences have never actually experienced. To be more specific, "imagined nostalgia" refers to a form of mass advertising which creates experiences of duration, passage, and loss that teach consumers to miss things that they have never lost. "Imagined nostalgia" is thus distinct from memories that are derived from lived experiences.

The Indonesian Chinese generation born after 1966 presents an excellent opportunity for researchers to examine the role of "imagined nostalgia" in the meaning-making processes of a particular diasporic group. Furthermore, the conditions of forced assimilation, perpetual identity crisis, and unique media environment under which this generation grew up in not only provide the opportunity for scholars to situate media texts and audiences within meaningful historical, social and cultural contexts, but also to explore the emerging terrain of memory, media and identity.

IDENTITY, MEMORY AND THE MEDIA: THE CASE OF INDONESIAN CHINESE

Throughout my study, I endeavoured to discover how members of a particular Indonesian Chinese generation grapple with their sense of cultural identity through their memories of growing up in a restrictive media environment.

In order to examine the process of their identity maintenance, I conducted seven focus groups to learn how my twenty-five respondents interacted with imported Chinese media, mostly kung fu or martial arts series that originated from Hong Kong, Taiwan and China. In keeping with the policy of assimilation, these programmes were dubbed in English and featured subtitles in Bahasa Indonesia. From 1988 onwards, the kung fu serials were shown on Indonesia's national television, but they were dubbed in Bahasa Indonesia. The only form of media featuring Chinese characters speaking in the Chinese language was Hong Kong films shown in movie theatres located mainly within and around Chinatown. According to Philip Pus, a director of Cinekom, a company that specializes in importing Chinese-language video compact discs (VCDs) and films into Indonesia, these Chinese films were allowed to be shown in Chinese without dubbing because of an agreement made by theatre owners and importers of Chinese films with the LSF or the Lembaga Sensor Film (Indonesia's Censor Board). As long as these films met the censorship standards of the LSF, they could be shown in Chinese. Mr Pus added that a rationale behind this exception could be that unlike videotapes and television, audiences needed to pay the price of admission to watch the movies. Thus, these films reached a smaller audience than other forms of media.

During the focus group sessions that I conducted as part of my study and subsequent analysis of the sessions, I discovered that some of my respondents look to Chinese media as a source of "imagined security" where their identity as Chinese is unquestioned and they would not be discriminated against. In the words of Irman, one of my respondents, the Indonesian Chinese are always "*kalah dan salah*" (always losing, always in the wrong). He was referring to his own difficulties as an Indonesian Chinese whose identity is always linked with his fear of safety not only during the country's political upheavals such as the May 1998 riots, but also in his everyday life. No matter what he does, he believes that he is always seen as "the other" in Indonesian society. Irman's views are shared by his friend, Hendra, who said that even though he does not speak Chinese and his family hardly celebrates Chinese cultural celebrations such as Chinese New Year, he is constantly reminded of his identity as a Chinese from the prejudices that he has experienced in his life. In order to illustrate his point, Hendra shared with me that his two attempts to open a chicken farm were thwarted by *preman* or thugs because of his ethnicity. He maintained that in Indonesia, a Chinese individual can only dream of achieving the safe and orderly situation that the films from Hong Kong portray.

Hendra's story, along with Irman's, show how identity formation can only be understood within the intersection of our everyday lives with the economic and political relations of subordination and domination (Rutherford 1990). Living in Indonesia means that Hendra and Irman must grapple with the stifling role of being scapegoats in times of political turmoil while accepting the assimilationist policies that the government have imposed on them and other Indonesian Chinese members of their generation. According to Hall (1990), "there is always a politics of identity, a politics of position" in the construction of cultural identity (p. 226). For people like Hendra and Irman, the political decisions made by the government and the resulting socio-cultural environment that is created from those decisions have an inexorable impact on their lives. This is where the very particular nature of identity formation, that is, when they struggle with questions of who they are, and what they are becoming (cf. Weeks 1990), clash with the universalist character of government policies that shape the social structure of Indonesia.

While Irman and Hendra's experiences show the contradictory struggles and the trappings of being Indonesian Chinese, they also reflect the notion of "imagined nostalgia" — longing and desire to live within the "imagined security" of a society that they have never directly experienced (cf. Appadurai 2000, p. 77). Both Irman and Hendra also garnered information such as lifestyle and socio-economic and political conditions of places such as Hong Kong and Taiwan through imported Chinese media. Irman even expressed his desire to live in such places and his preference for Asian cities over Western ones. The fact that they have never been to those places is significant because it illustrates a way in which the media have become the bridge connecting the diasporic Chinese communities in Indonesia, Hong Kong, and Taiwan through their power to convey and share values, images and impressions. In this respect, according to Thompson (1995), the media perform the function of a "mobility multiplier": they make available to individuals such as Hendra and Irman a vast array of experiences that otherwise would have been unavailable to them, and they do so while obviating the need for physical travel. Moreover, "precisely because mediated experience is vicarious experience, it cultivates the individual's faculty of imagination" (Thompson 1995, p. 189) — in this case, Hendra and Irman's longing for the "imagined security" at places such as Hong Kong and Taiwan.

The images of Chinese culture, history, people, and "style" were all part of my respondents' construction of their identity as Chinese adolescents in Indonesia. The transnational transmission of these images from places that most of my respondents have never been to (i.e. Hong Kong, Taiwan, and China) not only created a longing and desire to experience living in those places, but also allowed other respondents such as Ferry and Handy to learn gender roles and expectations that they variously translated into their lives as they were growing up. For example, the "cool" gangsters in *Gangland Boss* or *A Better Tomorrow* taught my male respondents a "show of greatness" by emphasizing blood brotherhood and loyalty. In fact, the characters in "gangster" movies left such a deep impression on them that they formed gangs with other Chinese boys as they were growing up. During a focus group session, Handy's eyes lit up as he enthusiastically reminisced about his membership and initiation into the *Flying Tiger* gang in Biak, Papua, which sealed his fate as one of the "coolest" boys in his area:

> Well, we had sort of a group... like in films... we lived in a small city so it's easy to get people together... I remember when I was still a young kid, when I was only about 9 or 10 years old, I looked up to those older than me — who were 15 to 17... and I remember them forming a group that is so *kompak* (close-knit) that they named themselves the *Flying Tiger* gang... made up of the Chinese boys in my area... All of the boys in my area wanted to be part of the gang... because it was so *keren* ("cool")....
> We'd ride motor bikes and speed on the streets but we were so powerful that no police officer dared to give us speeding tickets. Our gang leaders knew all of the police officers well... Well, what can I say? We Chinese need to maintain good relationships with those officers... We'd get into fights and the police wouldn't interfere... Those other gangs were no match for us... I mean, our parents were involved in business, so... economically, we're stronger than them... We could have our own motor bikes and *Flying Tiger* jackets... We were so serious about that gang... We'd go to Buddhist temples to make ourselves sworn brothers... yes... sworn brothers... sort of like an initiation rite, I guess... we'd prick our fingers... just like in those films... and mix our blood together in a bowl of water and drink the liquid... We'd promise to always help each other in times of hardship because we're blood brothers... I mean... come to think of it... where'd we get such ideas if not for those films?

From Handy's story, we may infer that by the time a Chinese boy reached the age of 9 or 10 in Biak, he would learn that he needed to be one of the *Flying Tigers* to assure his social status. When I asked him what the criteria for membership were, all he said was that the boy must be of Chinese descent. This may be seen as one of the outward displays of how the Chinese also regard other ethnic groups as "the other" as they created and asserted boundaries[12] between themselves and other ethnic groups. It also serves as an example where Soeharto's assimilationist policies did not affect the ways in which these young Chinese boys affirmed their sense of identity as Chinese adolescents. More significantly, as Ong (1999) suggests, the transnational cultural values transmitted by the films gave rise to a translocal Chinese identity that was established not by language or national origin but through the kinship rituals that are represented within the films. Even though Handy and his fellow gang members neither spoke Chinese nor read Chinese characters, they bonded with each other through initiation and kinship rituals inspired by the scenes that they saw in the films. The "blood brotherhood" initiation ritual at the Buddhist temple not only symbolizes a rite of passage for the boys to graduate into manhood, but also indicates how young Chinese boys in one of the most remote regions of Indonesia rearticulated their Chinese identity. In this sense, *Flying Tiger* provides Handy and his friends with a strong sense of solidarity and brotherhood in the process of growing up while also allowing them to negotiate facets of their "Chineseness" through their own interpretations of kinship rituals presented in the films.

The "imagined dreamland" depicted by the Chinese media, specifically the kung fu films/series, also kept my respondents in awe of ancient Chinese dynasties, values, history, and tradition. They all expressed immense pride in Chinese culture and being Chinese as they marvelled at the grandeur and majesty of the dynasties ruling ancient China in the kung fu films/series that they watched. It is through these kung fu films/series that China as a mythical homeland is constructed and remembered. As Ferry, a respondent from Manado, North Sulawesi, said:

> ... it all depends on the director... how he wants to present the movie to us. If he wants to bring us into the forbidden city, we'd be very happy to see what those huge jars look like in olden times and utensils made of pure gold... that's what I call knowledge... How else can we see people eating using golden spoons?

Ferry, who has never been to China, Hong Kong or Taiwan, admitted that it is only through Chinese films/series that he was able to see the forbidden city in Beijing and the various cutlery and utensils made of gold. In watching those depictions of opulent relics from a thousand-year-old culture, he felt tremendous pride in his heritage. Sunni, who was born in Aceh, North Sumatra and lived at three different places: Rangkasbitung, West Java, Medan, North Sumatra, and Jakarta, echoed Ferry's sentiments:

> I was drawn to the very interesting and engaging storylines... Beautiful scenery and costumes... I liked that those Chinese films include many words of wisdom... especially the kung fu ones... those that feature ancient heroes and heroines, along with stories told to me by my parents about those characters... I even thought of learning more about Chinese literature in Beijing...

China, to Ferry and Sunni, is a form of "imagined nostalgia" that they have never directly experienced but one that they have a deep emotional connection with. The images of China transmitted by the Chinese media also bring them together as part of an "imagined community" (Anderson 1998, p. 6) in their symbolic sharing of the same cultural values and history. Hence, these media offer Ferry and Sunni a way of recovering and, indeed, inventing traditions which reconnect them to China — a place of origin that is simultaneously real and imagined.

CHINA AND THE CULTURAL IDENTITY OF THE INDONESIAN CHINESE IN POST-1998 INDONESIA

During the Soeharto era, it is clear that the Chinese endured more than three decades of government policies that aimed to suppress Chinese culture, language and expressions. From the above discussion, we learn that the generation of Indonesian Chinese who grew up in the Soeharto era experienced struggles in their cultural identity partly because of these constraints. However, restrictions against Chinese culture, language and expressions were lifted following the fall of Soeharto in 1998.

When Abdurrahman Wahid came into power as the President of Indonesia from November 1999 to August 2001, he spearheaded efforts to end discriminatory regulations against the Indonesian Chinese population. The first step that he took was to abolish the Presidential Instruction Number 14, signed in 1967 by Soeharto, which restricted the practice of Chinese customs and religions to private domain. He formalized this act by signing the Presidential Instruction Number 6, stipulated in the year 2000, which allows the public celebration of the Chinese New Year. Under Megawati, who headed Indonesia's government from August 2001 to September 2004,[13] Chinese New Year has been made into a national holiday starting 1 February 2003.[14]

Following the abolition of the government policies, various cities and places throughout Indonesia such as Jakarta, Surabaya, Medan and Palembang celebrated Chinese New Year with aplomb and great festivities. As I have been living in Jakarta since August 2002, I was amazed to see Jakarta come alive in the weeks preceding 1 February 2003 with vibrant colours of red and gold — not just in the Chinatown areas of Glodok and Gajah Mada, but also in the posh shopping malls such as Plaza Senayan in south Jakarta and Plaza Indonesia in central Jakarta. Displays of cherubic dolls wearing traditional Chinese costumes appeared in the windows of Sogo department stores at Plaza Senayan and red ribbons fluttered down from the high, domed ceilings of the mall. I remembered that I could only listen to Chinese New Year songs in Chinatown or at my home during the festive season, but that year, I realized that most stores at malls outside Chinatown played the same songs that I listened to during my childhood from their stereo systems.

Other than public spaces such as malls and stores, the Indonesian media were filled with "*Gong Xi Fa Cai*" or "Happy Chinese New Year" messages — from television stations to newspapers. The newspapers also included articles[15] on the meanings behind Chinese New Year, festivities that were planned all around Jakarta, and how popular Indonesian Chinese actors and actresses such as Ferry Salim, the male protagonist in *Cau Bau Kan* (a film chronicling the romance between a wealthy Chinese man and a poor *pribumi* woman that won critical acclaim within Indonesia and abroad), celebrated the holiday. Other articles[16] discussed how the Chinese could celebrate in safety — as vouched by the head of the police department in Jakarta and featured several photographs of the Chinese praying at Buddhist temples. There were also many advertisements promoting *barongsai* (lion dance) performances at housing complexes and various stores offering discounts on the occasion of Chinese New Year. The Chinese characters *fu* for luck and *xi* for happiness were also used in many of these advertisements, which used the prosperous colours of red and yellow in the background.

The Chinese New Year celebrations between the years 2003 and 2007 became progressively more festive as more and more Chinese organizations (e.g. the Fuqing Association, the Hakka Association, the Hokkien Association, INTI (Perkumpulan Indonesia Tionghoa or Association of Indonesian Chinese) and NABIL (Nation Building)) collaborate with the Chinese embassy and other Indonesian cultural groups to organize large-scale cultural events. According to Siu (2005), diasporic communities often form transnational organizations to maintain ties with a distant "homeland" and to create "safe spaces" and a sense of community. By organizing many cultural events, organizations such as the ones that were established in post-1998 Indonesia help maintain and perpetuate their cultural identity as Chinese individuals in Indonesia. Furthermore, their close relationship with the Chinese embassy, especially with the cultural attaché, promotes not only a smooth exchange of ideas, but also showcases aspects of Chinese culture in terms of dances and musical performance by both Mainland Chinese and Indonesian Chinese artists that are presented during the events.

Along with the revival of Chinese organizations in Indonesia, Chinese media have also flourished in the post-Soeharto era. Between 1965 and 1998 only one Chinese-language newspaper was allowed to circulate (i.e. *Harian Indonesia,*[17] which was heavily controlled by the government). Unlike

Harian Indonesia, the Chinese-language newspapers that are currently in circulation have little or no government control. These newspapers include *Guo Ji Ri Bao* (*The International Daily News*), *Shang Bao Ri Bao* (a business-oriented newspaper), *Wen Wei Po* (a Hong Kong-based newspaper), and most significantly, *People's Daily Overseas Edition* (the overseas edition of People's Republic of China's official newspaper). Of these publications, *Guo Ji Ri Bao* is the most successful, with circulation figures that have jumped from 20,000 in 2002 to 50,000 in 2007. It obtains most of its revenues from congratulatory notices for various events in the Chinese community, ranging from weddings to large-scale public events.

Other than newspapers, the Indonesian Chinese and others who are interested in Chinese language and culture may also turn to television and radio. Since 1999, Metro TV has begun broadcasting news in Chinese. Cable providers such as Cable Vision and Indovision widen the options of Chinese-language television channels by transmitting programmes and shows directly from China and Taiwan. There are also channels such as the Celestial Channel on Cable Vision that feature Hong Kong serials and films throughout the day. These television and cable channels are further complemented by Mandarin programmes and songs that are broadcast from a radio station called Cakrawala.

The Chinese media widely reports the Chinese cultural events that have been held by the Chinese organizations. In 2007 alone, there were hundreds of festivities all over Indonesia during the Chinese New Year. As a form of official government support for the Chinese New Year celebrations, the revival of Chinese culture and the Indonesian Chinese community, President Susilo Bambang Yudhoyono attended several of the most prominent celebrations. One such celebration was held at the Jakarta Fair Ground in Kemayoran, Central Jakarta, on 28 February 2007.[18]

THE "UNION" OF INDONESIAN AND CHINESE CULTURES: THE CHINESE NEW YEAR CELEBRATION AT THE JAKARTA FAIR GROUND, 28 FEBRUARY 2007

Along with the President, important members of the Indonesian government and society were also present at the momentous occasion. They were: House of Representatives Speaker Agung Laksono, cabinet ministers such as Trade Minister Dr Mari E. Pangestu and Minister for Culture and Tourism, Mr Jero Wacik, Jakarta Governor Sutiyoso, Indonesian Chamber of Commerce Chairman M.S. Hidayat, Indonesian Association of Entrepreneurs (APINDO) Chairman Sofyan Wanandi, representatives of 152 ethnic Chinese organizations in Indonesia, revered religious leaders, the

Indonesian Ambassador to China, Sudrajat and the Chinese Ambassador to Indonesia, Lan Lijun.

During the event, aptly titled, *Indonesia... Bersatu* (Indonesia... Unite), the President declared that the enactment of the Presidential Decree Number 12, signed in 2006 means that legal discrimination against non-indigenous Indonesians, which mostly affects the Indonesian Chinese, was no longer acceptable. There was now only one way to refer to citizens of Indonesia: as Indonesians. He also stressed that Indonesia should be seen as a home to many ethnic groups that have worked together hand in hand to build a better future. He talked about how, in Indonesia, informally and factually, the ethnic Chinese and people of other ethnicities have interacted for centuries and have had trade, cultural and political links for centuries. He also provided pertinent examples of how the two cultures have fused and created new culinary dishes and styles of celebrating that are now uniquely Indonesian. One example of this is the tradition of eating *Lontong Cap Go Meh* among many ethnic Chinese living in Indonesia on the fifteenth day of the Lunar New Year (*Cap Go Meh*). It is common knowledge in Indonesia that *lontong* (rice cakes) is a quintessential Indonesian dish used to accompany *sate* (skewers of chicken, beef or mutton). However, it has now become an indispensable part of the festivities surrounding the Lunar New Year for the Chinese in Indonesia, providing an example of how the two cultures have melded together.

The theme of reconciliation and blending of Indonesian and Chinese cultures is also showcased in the use of both Indonesian and Chinese languages in the performances that were staged during the event. The opening dance, *Tarian Nusantara* (The Dance of the Nation), was a fusion of Chinese-Indonesian song and dance. Three ladies of different ethnicities sang together harmoniously in Javanese, Bahasa Indonesia and Mandarin, while dancers in ornate costumes danced to music emanating from both traditional Indonesian and Chinese instruments. Afterwards, an adapted version of the widely known Indonesian song, *Jali-Jali*, was performed by the famous Indonesian Chinese singer, Titiek Puspa. She sang in a controlled voice and playful manner backed by distinctive Indonesian strings, Chinese zithers (*gu zheng*) and other musical instruments. For many of the audience members, the highlight of the performances was the exceptional *Butet* serenade and its Mandarin version, *Zhuan Ke*. Indonesian male singer, Victor Hutabarat started robustly with the Bahasa Indonesia version while a female singer who flew in from China for the evening, Ren Jian, continued the song in Mandarin. The performance was a seamless blending of two languages, two countries and two cultures.

The dances, speeches and songs performed and delivered during the event all reflect Ien Ang's (2001) assertion that

> being Chinese outside of China cannot possibly mean the same thing as inside. It varies from place to place, moulded by the local circumstances in different parts of the world where people of Chinese ancestry have settled and constructed new ways of living. (p. 38)

The performances suggest that the Chinese in Indonesia have integrated "local circumstances" into their lives to construct a cultural identity that is the result of an undeniable fusion of Indonesian and Chinese traditions. To me and the other audience members, the evening symbolizes a nation that is ready to embrace a future full of hope and optimism. It also ushers in an era where members of both the Indonesian Chinese and the larger Indonesian communities may resolve their centuries-old tensions and arrive at a mutual understanding and appreciation of one another's cultures.

The event was also seen as a watershed moment in Indonesian Chinese history by cultural historians and activists. A cultural historian, Benny G. Setiono, who is also the current leader of INTI, wrote in an editorial in *Suara Pembaruan*, a daily newspaper, on 5 March 2007 that President Yudhoyono's purposeful use of the word *"Tionghoa"* in his speech instead of *"Cina"*, which has a derogatory connotation for the Indonesian Chinese community, is a symbolic act which shows the Indonesian government's support for the Indonesian Chinese community. Setiono's views are shared by Eddie Kusuma, a Chinese political activist who put together a book based on the Chinese New Year event entitled *Chinese New Year 2007: Indonesia... Unite — An Event Marking 50 Years of Cultural Exchange between Indonesia and China*. In his book, Kusuma included the full text of the speeches made by President Yudhoyono and Lan Lijun, the Chinese Ambassador to Indonesia. The ambassador's speech, which emphasizes enriching and promoting "cultural exchanges between [China and Indonesia], hence further deepening China-Indonesia strategic partnership" shows that China is committed to maintaining a smooth working relationship between the two countries. Lan reiterated China's stance towards Indonesia in a written message in the *Jakarta Post* on 1 October 2007 (China's Fifty-eighth National Day). In the message, he states:

> China has long been supporting Indonesia's efforts to safeguard territorial integrity and national unity, as well as to invigorate the economy. China attaches great importance to developing long-term, stable, mutually-trusted and mutually-beneficial strategic partnership with Indonesia.

As evidence of the successful bilateral relationship between the two countries, especially in the economic area, Lan mentions that two-way trade volume reached US$19.06 billon in 2006, a 13.5 per cent increase from 2005. From January to July in 2007, bilateral trade increased by 39.5 per cent, reaching US$14.1 billion; and the annual trade volume is expected to exceed US$20 billion by the end of the year.

Just a few days before the message was published, Lan formally endorsed the building of a Chinese-language and cultural centre in Jakarta on 29 September 2007.[19] According to Lan, the new institute aims to introduce Chinese languages and cultures so as to enhance bilateral relations between the two countries. He further revealed that the institute would be established by Beijing Hanban — a Beijing-based organization appointed by the Chinese government to build Chinese language centres worldwide — and *Bina Terampil Insan Persada* (BTIP), a Jakarta-based Chinese language school. The Ambassador's speech during the Chinese New Year event, his Independence Day message and formal endorsement of the Chinese language and cultural centre reinforce China's commitment and contribution to the economic and Chinese cultural developments within Indonesia.

These developments, especially the evident educational support from China, are significant to the overall cultural identity of the Chinese in Indonesia because they help to strengthen China's presence not only in Indonesia but also within themselves and their families. In *China and the Chinese Overseas*, Wang Gungwu (1991) argues that the "Chineseness" of Southeast Asian Chinese involves the sharing of universal cultural norms such as the learning of the Chinese written language. Therefore, Chinese language maintenance is important in the enhancement of a Chinese cultural identity among the Indonesian Chinese community. As more Chinese in the post-1998 era learn the Chinese language, they will have the keys to unlock the mysteries of Chinese culture and history, unlike their predecessors who were denied the chance to study the language during the Soeharto era.

Nevertheless, not all Indonesian Chinese believe that learning the Chinese language or practising Chinese culture is relevant to their lives. In early 2007, I surveyed the recent developments of Chinese education in Indonesia.[20] In the course of my research, I interviewed young Chinese parents regarding their preferences on Chinese education for their children. While some believe that Chinese education is essential to compete in today's business world, which regards China as a tremendous commercial empire, some prefer their children to be cultivated in a purely Indonesian environment, with Bahasa Indonesia as the main language used in the curriculum. Coming from a family that hardly spoke Mandarin and rarely celebrated Chinese festivals as they were growing up, these parents do not see the importance of learning Mandarin. They said that it is more essential for their children to know what it means to be Indonesians because they live in Indonesia and have never been to China. Learning and excelling in Bahasa Indonesia is thus a priority for them instead of learning Chinese. The differences in attitudes and preferences with respect to Chinese education reveal the polyphonic and complex nature of the Indonesian Chinese cultural identity and its relationship to China. The multifaceted dimensions of Indonesian Chinese identity and their connections with China are both celebrated and challenged in the Miss Chinese Cosmos Pageant, which I discuss below.

CONTESTING IDENTITIES: THE MISS CHINESE COSMOS PAGEANT OF 2007

A few months after the Chinese New Year celebrations, on 1 August 2007, another cultural event, the Miss Chinese Cosmos Pageant (MCCP) Indonesia, deepened the relationship between the Chinese in Indonesia, the Indonesian government, and China. Like the Chinese New Year celebration on 28 February 2007, Jakarta Governor Sutiyoso and Indonesian cabinet ministers such as Dr Mari E. Pangestu and Mr Jero Wacik were in attendance. They shared the same table as Yang Lingzhu, the Minister-Counsellor of the Chinese embassy. Lan Lijun could not attend the event because he was in China at the time. Numerous leaders and members of Chinese organizations also came to support the event.

In the month preceding the event, 20 finalists were chosen from 482 applicants to represent cities and provinces in Indonesia with the most number of ethnic Chinese, namely Jakarta, West Java, Central Java, East Java, Kalimantan, the Riau Islands, Northern Sumatra and Southern Sumatra. One of the deciding criteria for selecting finalists is that candidates must be proficient in Bahasa Indonesia, English and Mandarin. This is because the mission of the pageant is about

> promoting Indonesia's diverse ethnic cultures and tourism to the world. This event also endeavours to optimally develop the potential of Chinese individuals as Indonesian ambassadors to compete on an international level. Armed with the understanding that they are citizens of a nation that highly respects unity and diversity, the Chinese contestants may have the opportunity through MCCP to promote this notion of Indonesia worldwide. (Excerpted from the official press release of the Miss Chinese Cosmos Pageant Indonesia, 2007.)

Since the winner of the pageant would be sent to Beijing at the end of August 2007 and Japan in September 2007 to compete with candidates from different parts of the world, it was of paramount importance for the finalists to be proficient in English and Mandarin. In actuality, however, it was difficult for the organizers of the pageant to find candidates who were proficient in Mandarin. As the contestants were all between 18–28 years of age, most did not receive formal Chinese education in Indonesia due to Soeharto's assimilationist policies. Those who did study Chinese went to foreign countries such as Singapore, Malaysia and Taiwan for their education. Out of the twenty finalists, there was only one who could read and write in Chinese. The others were selected based on their varying abilities to converse in Mandarin.

Before the actual pageant was held on 1 August 2007, the finalists participated in a one-week quarantine. During the quarantine, they met with Mrs Triesna Wacik, the wife of Tourism Minister Jero Wacik. Mrs Wacik not only provided many words of encouragement and advice for the twenty finalists, but also arranged for the finalists to have traditional dancing lessons at her residence. According to Mrs Wacik, the winner of the pageant must be cognizant of the rich cultural diversity of Indonesia. Therefore, it is important for the winner, while ethnically Chinese, to also promote Indonesia's varied cultural heritage while abroad. This stress on Indonesia's traditions is further emphasized when the finalists visited Bali and had dinner with Dewa Made Beratha, the spouse of Bali's Governor, and Mrs Sylvia Agung Laksono, the spouse of the Speaker of the House, Mr Agung Laksono. Mrs Sylvia Agung Laksono was also the head of the organizing committee of the pageant. Her involvement with the pageant is noteworthy because it signals the Indonesian government's support of Chinese culture. The Indonesian government's support is further reinforced by the finalists' visit to Bandung's Regional Administrative Officials at the Asia Africa Conference Building, and their meeting with Jakarta's Governor, Sutiyoso.

On 1 August 2007, on the day the actual pageant was held, various media representatives covered the event. The event received extensive coverage in the Indonesian media such as the television stations Metro TV and RCTI and newspapers such as the *Jakarta Post*,[21] *Indopos*, *Guo Ji Ri Bao*, *Shang Bao Ri Bao* and the MRA Media Group (which owns influential fashion and lifestyle magazines such as *Harper's Bazaar*, *Cosmopolitan* and *Spice*). The influential and most highly-circulated daily in Indonesia, *Kompas*, also ran a profile[22] on the winner of the pageant as a follow-up to the event. The pageant was thus seen as an "Indonesian" rather than an exclusively "Chinese" event by the media. Organizers of the pageant also emphasized that proceeds from the pageant (from donors and contributors) would be donated to charities. Some of the funds had already been channelled to several orphanages before 1 August 2007. In doing this, the organizers hoped to dispel the myth that Indonesian Chinese were "takers" rather than "givers" in the Indonesian society.

Like the organizers of the Chinese New Year Celebration at the Jakarta Fair Ground, the organizers of the pageant inserted various examples of Indonesian and Chinese cultures during the event itself. Even though not all of the twenty finalists could speak fluent Mandarin, they all practised diligently during their quarantine to smoothly deliver their introductions in Mandarin. They wore three different outfits: Western cocktail dresses by Susy Lucon, an Indonesian Chinese designer who married a French man, *kebaya encim* (a *peranakan*-style long-sleeved blouse worn with a *sarong* or *batik*-printed cloth) designed by Ghea Panggabean (a *pribumi* designer) and the *qipao*, the tight-fitting, high-necked traditional Chinese dress designed by Adjie Notonegoro, a *pribumi* designer who is famous not for his *qipao* but for his ornate *kebaya*, the traditional Javanese sheer blouse worn with *batik* or plain fabric. The contestants introduced themselves in the cocktail dresses, danced in a traditional Javanese manner in the *kebaya encim* and answered questions from the jury in their *qipao*. Members of the jury also reflected the organizers' concern with diversity. They included: Tatang Rukhiyat, the Director for International Promotion at the Indonesian Ministry of Culture and Tourism; Indira Soediro, the inaugural Miss Indonesia (she won the title in 1994); Claudine Jusuf, a designer with Chinese, Vietnamese and French backgrounds; Aaron Liao, a representative from Phoenix TV, the organizer for the international Miss Chinese Cosmos Pageant; Hendro Setiawan, an Indonesian Chinese entrepreneur; and Dian M. Soedarjo, the President-Director of the MRA media group.

As the evening progressed, it was clear that Suyenti, a twenty-year-old finalist from Medan, North Sumatra, would win the title. She was calm, poised and exuded self-confidence and intelligence, befitting the pageant's theme of "Love and Care: The Charm of Inner Beauty". By winning the pageant, she shows that beauty is not the only prerequisite to win the pageant. One also needs to speak fluent Mandarin and have an extensive knowledge of current affairs to compete. These requirements are a far cry from Myra Sydartha's (1987) study on Indonesian Chinese women before 1945. According to her study, the ideal Indonesian Chinese girl before 1945 was timid, reticent and adaptable. As an unmarried girl she should obey her father and eldest brother, when married she should obey her husband and when widowed her son. More than five decades after Myra Sydartha's study, Suyenti symbolizes some enlightening changes in gender expectations among the Indonesian Chinese women and Chinese women in general as the holder of the Miss Chinese Cosmos Pageant Indonesia title.

Suyenti is also a symbol of acculturation in Indonesia. She is part Batak (an indigenous ethnic group) from her mother's ancestral line. Although she speaks fluent Mandarin because it is her mother tongue, she cannot read and write Chinese characters because she never received proper instruction at school. Despite her inability to read and write in Chinese, her fluency in three languages enables her to sing and perform Batak, Indonesian and Chinese songs. Hence, Suyenti's mixed background pertains to the changing perceptions of cultural identities within and beyond the Indonesian Chinese community.

Following the Miss Chinese Cosmos Pageant Indonesian contest, she was sent to Beijing at the end of August to receive extensive Mandarin training and participate in the quarantine arranged by the international organizing committee for the Miss Chinese Cosmos Pageant. The quarantine prepared her and fellow contestants for the semi-final in Tokyo, Japan on 11 September 2007.

Prior to winning the contest, Suyenti had never been to China. By bringing contestants from all over the world to Beijing, the pageant's international nature speaks to the power of diasporic Chinese ties across the world that bring them together to the place of their ancestral origin (i.e. China). In my personal interview with Suyenti after she had returned to Indonesia, she told me that she enjoyed the camaraderie that she experienced with her fellow contestants. Although they originated from various parts of the world, they came together in the shared understanding that they had a common legacy of Chinese history and culture. Suyenti was thus delighted to have the opportunity to visit world-famous sights such as Tiananmen Square and the Great Wall of China while in Beijing. Nevertheless, Suyenti acknowledged that her command of Mandarin was far below the level of her fellow contestants:

> I realized that the level of my Mandarin proficiency was far below all of the other contestants'. This is especially true during the various interview sessions that we had to undergo during the quarantine and semi-final. The interviewers would ask simple questions (e.g. "What is the meaning of beauty?") and I answered their questions as best as I could. However, the other contestants who were born and raised in China or those born in China but decided to stay on overseas after their tertiary education could embellish their answers with ancient Chinese poetry, which they learned at school. Of course their answers sounded so much better than mine! I never had formal education in Chinese language. Ancient Chinese poetry is thus way beyond my reach.

She also regretted not knowing how to read and write in Chinese:

> Not knowing how to read and write in Chinese was a tremendous
> disadvantage during the contest. For instance, we went to the beach one
> evening and there were already many lit candles there when we arrived.
> The atmosphere was romantic and delightful. Then we were asked to write
> our dreams and wishes in Chinese on pieces of paper and wrap the paper
> around a glass jar containing a candle. I was fully aware that additional
> points were given by the organizers if we wrote our dreams and wishes
> eloquently in Chinese. As I couldn't write Chinese characters, I had no
> choice but to write my dreams and wishes in English. I also remember that
> throughout the contest, we were given many pamphlets and instructions
> in Chinese and I could not read them. I had to ask my fellow contestants
> to translate them into English. It's also very important to know how to
> write well in Chinese because when the contestants advanced into the
> finals, they had to write detailed computer-generated reports of their
> activities and training.

As a consequence of her inability to read and write in Chinese, Suyenti
did not advance to the final. The final, held on 3 November 2007 in Hong
Kong, was eventually won by Zhen Guang from the Shanxi province in China.
Suyenti revealed that Zhen Guang was the clear favourite from the first day
of the quarantine in Beijing and the semi-final in Tokyo, Japan. Everyone
admired her combination of beauty, elegance and intelligence. Indeed, during
the interview session of the final, her confident answer to one of the most
difficult questions given by the jury ("How does the *pipa*, a traditional Chinese
musical instrument, represent beauty, culture and your identity as a Chinese
woman?"), clinched the title. In her answer, she explained that it is an honour
for a Chinese woman to be able to play the *pipa* because it is a combination
of elegance and Chinese culture. In order to play the *pipa*, one needs skill
and patience, which are two qualities that a Chinese woman should have. A
woman playing the *pipa* is thus beautiful because she represents and exudes
high levels of cultural understanding. Suyenti herself is not familiar with the
pipa. She told me that she has never seen it in her life and does not know
how it should be played. She admitted that only someone like Zhen Guang,
who has an extensive knowledge of Chinese culture and who has an excellent
command of the Chinese language, may answer such a question gracefully.
    Suyenti's experiences during the Miss Chinese Cosmos Pageant reflect
the various expectations and conflicts that come along with the reaffirmation
of "Chineseness" in the Chinese diaspora. As Cohen et al. (1996) have
argued, "Beauty contests are places where cultural meanings are produced,

consumed, and rejected, where local and global, ethnic and national, national and international cultures, and structures of power are engaged in their most trivial but vital aspects" (p. 8). The Miss Chinese Cosmos Pageant is an international beauty contest that emphasizes "Chineseness" above all. While contestants come from all parts of the world, they soon learn that there are "universal cultural norms" (cf. Wang 1991) that make up the cultural identity of the Chinese. First and foremost of these norms, as Suyenti discovered, is the mastery of the Chinese language. Before she left for Beijing, Suyenti was optimistic about promoting the culture and diversity of Indonesia abroad. She was even prepared to perform a Batak dance for the talent show that was part of the semi-final. Although she did perform the dance, she encountered difficulties in expressing her thoughts and beliefs in Mandarin at the high level of proficiency that her fellow contestants commanded. Her struggles exacerbated when she discovered that her inability to read and write in Chinese put her at a clear disadvantage. Hence, while she was selected as the best person to represent the Chinese in Indonesia when she won the Miss Chinese Cosmos Pageant Indonesia, her "authentic" cultural identity as a Chinese was problematized during the international competition because she was unable to read and write the Chinese language.

CONCLUSION

The notion of Chinese cultural identity among the Indonesian Chinese is intricate and multifaceted. From the historical overview of the socio-political conditions of the Indonesian Chinese, we may see that identity conflicts occur in their efforts to assimilate into the social fabric of Indonesia. When they arrived on Indonesian soil thousands of years ago, the Chinese knew that they had to intermingle with the host country and meld their culture with the indigenous way of life. As time moves on, however, they are still considered to be perennial strangers in their own country and have to live within a position of marginality in spite of their economic successes. Throughout Indonesia's history, they have to endure policies designed to restrict Chinese cultural expressions and become repeat targets of violence in times of political unrest. It is not until Soeharto stepped down from his position of power in 1998 that firm steps were taken to eradicate the prejudices against the Indonesian Chinese, including the erasure of Soeharto's assimilationist policies.

The first case study that I discussed in this chapter shows how my respondents created new meanings about themselves, Chinese culture, and their position in Indonesia as they interacted with the transnationally transmitted images of places that most of them have never been to. It is through their stories of media interaction that I discovered their longing for role models, "security", and other aspects of Chinese culture when they were growing up in the Soeharto era. In this way, the media functioned as a "mobility multiplier" — allowing them to "experience" a China, Hong Kong, and Taiwan without the need of physical travel (cf. Thompson 1995). This is especially significant when we consider the political constraints placed on Chinese cultural expressions, education, and the media during the Soeharto era. The various meanings that my respondents derived, constructed and transformed from the Chinese media show the function of the media as social tools that allowed them not only to maintain and strengthen cultural boundaries, but also to create new, shared spaces where they could redefine their social experiences. In so doing, they demonstrated their resourcefulness as media consumers in (re)constructing their own identities. Through my respondents' collective memory of growing up in the Soeharto era, we are able to observe the melding of the very personal process of identity maintenance and (re)construction and the macro politics of structural change.

In the second and third case studies, we see how certain events such as the celebration of Chinese New Year on 28 February 2007 and the Miss Chinese Cosmos Pageant on 1 August 2007 were well received by the Indonesian society, especially by the Indonesian government. In both events, the blending of Indonesian and Chinese cultures was celebrated and enjoyed by the audience, performers and contestants. They also fostered a good relationship between the Chinese and Indonesian governments.

While the events are meant to be positive signs of the Indonesian government's acceptance with respect to Chinese culture and language, there are some who warn against the "exclusive" connotation of these events. Prominent members of the Indonesian Chinese intellectual circle, such as Harry Tjan Silalahi,[23] a member of the Board of Trustees at the influential Center of Strategic and International Studies, is steadfast in his opinion that these celebrations are too extravagant. Hence, they may induce jealousy and invoke the idea of "exclusivity" for the Indonesian Chinese society. His views are shared by Benny G. Setiono, the current head of INTI, who cautioned publicly against an "exclusive" image portrayed by events such as the Miss Chinese Cosmos Pageant in an INTI seminar on the role of Indonesian Chinese Organizations in the Globalized World on 25 August 2007.[24] Silalahi's and Setiono's views are important words of caution as the Chinese community celebrates the end of decades-long restrictions on Chinese culture and language. In my own observations, however, the majority of the Indonesian Chinese are optimistic about the revival of Chinese culture and language. Top leaders of Chinese organizations and organizers of the Miss Chinese Cosmos Pageant have revealed that events such as the Chinese New Year celebration and the pageant should not be seen as exclusive. They are events that belong to the Indonesian society as a whole. Eddie Kusuma, the leading Indonesian Chinese political activist mentioned earlier, provides examples in his book where all levels of the society, including the *pribumi*, participate joyfully in Chinese New Year parades in Singkawang, Medan and Yogjakarta. Organizers of the pageant also reminded me that all proceeds of the event were channelled to charities to help fellow Indonesians in need, not just the Chinese.

Although the three case studies discussed in this chapter reflect differences in attitudes with respect to Chinese culture and language as they are based on different eras in Indonesia's history, one common thread weaving through all three case studies is the concept of Indonesian Chinese cultural identity and how it is connected to China. The (re)negotiation, and (re)articulation of "Chineseness" is crucial to understanding the process of cultural identity formation and maintenance in all three case studies. As Ien Ang (1993) points out, "Chineseness" has become an open category "whose meanings are not fixed and pregiven, but constantly renegotiated and rearticulated, both inside and outside China" (p. 5). Therefore, "Chineseness" should be seen as a fluid and flexible concept that is constantly changing due to certain conditions that may affect a particular group of people within China or the Chinese diaspora. During the Soeharto era, the social, political and historical conditions surrounding the Indonesian Chinese community created a generation who cannot read and write Chinese characters. While this phenomenon is largely accepted as an inevitable part of their lives, some members of this generation, such as Suyenti, realize that not knowing how to read and write Chinese constitutes a tremendous loss of cultural heritage. This is especially true when members of Suyenti's generation compete at an international level which requires Chinese language proficiency. For Suyenti, not being able to read and write in Chinese put her at a considerable disadvantage compared to the other contestants. While she has always been proud of her Chinese roots and speaks Mandarin better than her peers in Indonesia, her cultural identity as an "authentic" Chinese is called into question when she was in China itself.

Suyenti's experiences, along with the diverse experiences of my respondents who grew up in a restrictive media environment during the Soeharto era also reflect what Stuart Hall (1990) calls the "diaspora experience":

> the recognition of a necessary heterogeneity and diversity; by a conception of "identity" which lives with and through, not despite difference; by *hybridity*. Diaspora identities are those which are constantly producing

and reproducing themselves anew, through transformation and difference. (p. 235, emphasis in original)

Hall's formulation of diaspora identities is especially appropriate to the Indonesian Chinese in all three case studies because it involves recognition of difference and the notion of *hybridity*. As Ien Ang (2001) suggests, Indonesian Chinese undergo an ongoing process of hybridity or a continuous process of transculturation (two-way borrowing and lending between cultures). In the first case study, my respondents confess that, in order to live in Indonesia, they have to be constantly aware of their status as Indonesian Chinese. Although they have "Indonesianized" themselves to the extent that some do not celebrate Chinese New Year and use Indonesian instead of Chinese, they were still drawn to imported Chinese media to search for the Chinese role models that were absent from Indonesian media during the Soeharto era. Their cultural identity as Chinese individuals in Indonesia is therefore a result of hybridity. In the second case study, a vivid display of hybridity was presented during the Chinese New Year celebration, where the singers, musicians and dancers performed Chinese and Indonesian songs together. Hybridity was even acknowledged and approved by President Susilo Bambang Yudhoyono, as seen from his speech at the event. In the third case study, the explicit portrayal of hybridity is seen in the costumes and dances performed by the contestants at the Miss Chinese Cosmos Pageant Indonesian Contest. Suyenti herself, with her mixed background, symbolized hybridity.

In conclusion, I propose these case studies as the first steps towards understanding the complicated process of cultural identity, (re)construction, and (re)negotiation among the Indonesian Chinese. Thung (1998) argues that the construction of identity among the Chinese in Indonesia is dependent upon several power structures, namely Mainland China as the country of origin, the local government in the country of residence, and the global network of Chinese commercial activities. I would add the media and local Chinese organizations to this list of power structures. As the findings of my first case study show, growing up in a restrictive media environment pushed my respondents to seek images of Chinese culture and people in the form of images imported from China, Hong Kong and Taiwan — places that are simultaneously real and imagined. In the second case study, it is evident that Chinese organizations have the power, resources and ability to promote mutual understanding and a better relationship between China and Indonesia, especially through events such as the Chinese New Year celebration on 28 February 2007. While the Miss Chinese Cosmos Pageant Indonesian contest was not an actual event organized by the Chinese organizations, they supported the event by contributing funds, placing congratulatory notices in the Chinese newspapers and showing up at the event. The support of the organizations was thus instrumental to the success of the event. The findings of the three case studies, however, do not suggest that they should be seen as a comprehensive analysis of how the Indonesian Chinese, as a diasporic community, (re)negotiate and (re)construct their cultural identity. In the years to come, many more events, situations and conditions with respect to Chinese culture and language will occur in Indonesia. China's relationship with the Indonesian government and the Indonesian Chinese community may well be affected by these developments. All these factors deserve more scholarly attention and examination if the continuously evolving and complex nature of the Indonesian Chinese cultural identity is to be explored and understood.

Notes

1. The colonial period began in 1602 when the Dutch founded their East India Company or the VOC (*Vereeniging Oost Indische Compagnie*). The VOC sought to maximize profits by exploiting the natural and labour sources of Indonesia, then known as the East Indies.
2. *Pribumi* literally means "sons of the soil" in Bahasa Indonesia. It reflects the Indonesian nationalist spirit that instills pride in the indigenous population of their motherland. For instance, during the struggle for Indonesia's independence in the 1940s, nationalists called upon their fellow *pribumi* to fight against the Dutch for their motherland's freedom. In Soeharto's New Order, several economic policies favoring *pribumi* capitalists served to buttress the expansion of indigenous industries and corporations. For a more complete discussion on these policies, refer to Richard Robison's *Indonesia: The Rise of Capital* (Sydney: Allen and Unwin, 1988) especially the chapter on "Indigenous Capitalists Under the New Order" (pp. 323–72).
3. When the spice trade became increasingly lucrative in the late seventeenth and eighteenth centuries, the Dutch used the Chinese as an "economic Trojan horse" to penetrate the pre-colonial Indonesian trade that was monopolized by the indigenous aristocracy (*priyayi*) class (Kemasang 1985).
4. Because of their ancestry and connection with China, the Chinese were accused of sympathizing with the Communists.
5. Instruction of the Cabinet Presidium no. 127/U/KEP/1966, *Name Changing Policy for Indonesian Citizens with Chinese Names*, sanctioned in Jakarta on 27 December 1966, and signed by Soeharto as chairperson of the Ampera Cabinet Presidium.
6. Anthony Giddens (1991) argues that a person's name is a primary element in his/her biography. It helps a person to develop a strong sense of self-identity to weather major tensions in the social environment in which he/she moves.

7. Soeharto stayed in power from 1965 to 1998, when a revolution spurred by the Asian economic crisis and Indonesians' increasing dissatisfaction with Soeharto stripped him of his presidency.

8. One of the regulations under this policy of assimilation was the Instruction of the Cabinet Presidium no. 37/U/IN/6/1967, *The Basic Policy for the Solution of the Chinese Problem*, sanctioned in Jakarta on 7 June 1967, and signed by Soeharto as chairperson of the Ampera Cabinet Presidium.

9. The Indonesian Department of Trade and Cooperatives Decree for the Minister of Trade and Cooperatives no. 286/KP/XII/78, *The Prohibition to Import, Trade and Circulate All Kinds of Printed Materials in the Chinese Language and Characters*, sanctioned in Jakarta on 28 December 1978, and signed by Radius Prawiro, the Minister of Trade and Cooperatives.

10. Although this assimilationist policy resulted in an erosion of Chinese language and culture, it may also be seen as a positive effort on the part of the government to diminish prejudice against the Chinese population. It was part of Soeharto's plan to emphasize ethnic and religious harmony and reduce hate-mongering in the nation.

11. Inherent in the modern ideal of identity is the notion of self-accountability and the search for a true identity. One of the ways through which an individual may form a true conception of him/herself is through the language that he/she speaks. According to the modern tradition, language is a fundamental attribute of self-recognition because it provides an individual with a framework to understand reality (Castells 1997).

12. According to Cornell and Hartmann in their book, *Ethnicity and Race: Making Identities in a Changing World* (Thousand Oaks, CA: Pine Forge Press, 1998), identity construction involves the establishment of a set of criteria for distinguishing between members and non-members. This set of criteria signifies a categorical boundary; the line between "us" and "them". This process of boundary assertion involves situating the group in the context of social relations, specifying its position in a set of relationships and statuses.

13. Susilo Bambang Yudhoyono became the sixth president of Indonesia following his success in a national election held in September 2004.

14. Megawati's government declared Chinese New Year as an elective holiday (which means that the Chinese may take that day off to celebrate it) for the Chinese in 2002 but formally declared it as a national holiday in 2003.

15. See Ignatius Wibowo, "Happy Chinese New Year", *Kompas*, 31 January 2003, p. 3 and "Stars Celebrate Chinese New Year", *Kompas*, 31 January 2003, p. 19.

16. See "Police Guarantee A Safe Chinese New Year", *Kompas*, 31 January 2003, p. 1.

17. Since 2006, *Harian Indonesia* has been taken over by the Malaysian group *Xing Zhou Ri Bao* (Xing Zhou Daily News). It is now known as the Indonesian version of *Xing Zhou Ri Bao*.

18. For a complete report of the Chinese New Year celebration on 28 February 2007, refer to the *Jakarta Post* article by Lily Dawis, "A Celebration of Hope,

Friendship; A Window Into the New Indonesia", published on 3 March 2007, p. 6. I was also present at the event.

19. See the *Jakarta Post* article by Desy Nurhayati, "China Sweeps the World with Language" on 21 September 2007, p. 9.

20. More detailed analysis of Chinese education in Indonesia may be found in my paper, "Chinese Education in Indonesia: Developments in the Post-1998 Era", which I presented at the conference on "Ethnic Chinese in Indonesia in an Era of Globalization", organized by the Chinese Heritage Centre, NABIL and the Institute of Southeast Asian Studies in Singapore. The conference was held on 19 July 2007.

21. See the *Jakarta Post* article by A. Junaidi on "Suyenti: I Am Proud of My Chinese Roots" on 10 August 2007, p. 24.

22. See the *Kompas* profile by Iwan Ong on "Suyenti, Miss Chinese Indonesia" on 7 August 2007, p. 32.

23. Personal interview, October 17, 2007.

24. See the *Kompas* article by Iwan Ong, "Indonesian Chinese Community Asked Not to be Discriminative" on 27 August 2007, p. 21.

References

Aguilar, F. V. "Citizenship, Inheritance, and the Indigenizing of 'Orang Chinese' in Indonesia". *Positions* 9, no. 3 (2001): 501–33.

Anderson, Benedict. *Imagined Communities: Reflections on the Origin and Spread of Nationalism.* New York: Verso, 1998.

Ang, Ien. *On Not Speaking Chinese: Living Between Asia and the West.* New York: Routledge, 2001.

————. "To be or not to be Chinese: Diaspora, Culture, and Postmodernism". *Southeast Asian Journal of Social Science* 21, no. 1 (1993): 1–17.

Appadurai, Arjun. *Modernity at Large: Cultural Dimensions of Globalization.* Minneapolis: University of Minnesota Press, 2000.

Budianta, Melani. "Discourse of Cultural Identity in Indonesia During the 1997–1998 Monetary Crisis". *Inter-Asia Cultural Studies* 1, no. 1 (2000): 109–28.

Budiman, Arief. "Portrait of the Chinese in Post-Suharto Indonesia". In *Chinese Indonesians: Remembering, Distorting, Forgetting*, edited by Tim Lindsey and Helen Pausacker. Singapore: Institute of Southeast Asian Studies, 2005, pp. 95–104.

Cohen, Colleen Ballerino, Richard Wilk, and Beverly Stoeltje, eds. *Beauty Queens on the Global Stage: Gender, Contests, Power.* New York: Routledge, 1996.

Coppel, Charles. "The Indonesian Chinese as 'Foreign Orientals' in the Netherlands Indies". In *Studying Ethnic Chinese in Indonesia*, edited by C. Coppel. Singapore: Humanities Press, 2002, pp. 157–68.

————. *Indonesian Chinese in Crisis.* New York: Oxford University Press, 1983.

Eber, Dena E. and Arthur G. Neal. "The Individual and Collective Search for Identity".

In *Memory and Representation: Constructed Truths and Competing Realities*, edited by Dena E. Eber and Arthur G. Neal. Bowling Green, OH: Bowling Green State University Popular Press, 2001, pp. 169–82.

Gergen, Kenneth J. *The Saturated Self: Dilemmas of Identity in Contemporary Life*. New York: Basic Books, 2000.

Giddens, Anthony. *Modernity and Self-Identity: Self and Society in the Late Modern Age*. Stanford: Stanford University Press, 1991.

Gillespie, Marie. *Television, Ethnicity and Cultural Change*. New York: Routledge, 1995.

Gillis, John R. "Memory and Identity: The History of a Relationship". In *Commemorations: The Politics of National Identity*, edited by J. R. Gillis. Princeton, NJ: Princeton University Press, 1994, pp. 1–24.

Hall, Stuart. "The Question of Cultural Identity". In *Modernity: An Introduction to Modern Societies*, edited by Stuart Hall, David Held, Don Hubert and Kenneth Thompson. Malden, MA: Blackwell Publishers, Inc, 2000, pp. 595–634.

―――. "The Local and the Global: Globalization and Ethnicity". In *Culture, Globalization, and the World System: Contemporary Conditions for the Representation of Identity*, edited by A.D. King. London: Macmillan, 1991, pp. 19–39.

Kemasang, A. R. T. "How Dutch Colonialism Foreclosed a Domestic Bourgeoisie in Java: The 1740 Chinese Massacres Reappraised". *Review* 9, no. 1 (1985): 57–80.

Nadesan, A. "Sino-Indonesian Relations 1950–1967 and its Future". *Asian Profile* 8, no. 1 (1980): 25–44.

Nonini, Donald M. and Aihwa Ong. "Chinese Transnationalism as an Alternative Modernity". In *Ungrounded Empires: The Cultural Politics of Modern Chinese Transnationalism*, edited by Aihwa Ong and Donald M. Nonini. New York: Routledge, 1997, pp. 3–33.

Ong, Aihwa. *Flexible Citizenship: The Cultural Logics of Transnationality*. Durham: Duke University Press, 1999.

Rutherford, Jonathan. "A Place Called Home: Identity and the Cultural Politics of Difference". In *Identity: Community, Culture, Difference*, edited by Jonathan Rutherford, pp. 9–27. London: Lawrence & Wishart, 1990.

Siu, Lok C. D. *Memories of a Future Home: Diasporic Citizenship of Chinese in Panama*. Stanford: Stanford University Press, 2005.

Sorensen, Ninna Nyer. "Roots, Routes, and Transnational Attractions: Dominican Migration, Gender, and Cultural Change". In *Ethnicity, Gender, and the Subversion of Nationalism*, edited by Fiona Wilson and Bodil Folke Frederiksen, pp. 104–18. London: Frank Cass, 1997.

Suryadinata, Leo. *Etnis Tionghoa dan Pembangunan Bangsa*. Jakarta: PT Pustaka LP3ES, 1999.

―――. *Pribumi Indonesians, the Chinese Minority and China*. 3rd ed. Singapore: Heinemann Asia, 1992.

Sydartha, Myra. "The Making of the Indonesian Chinese Woman". In *Indonesian*

Women in Focus: Past and Present Notions, edited by Elsbeth Locher-Scholten and Anke Niehof, pp. 59–76. Dordrecht, Holland: Foris Publications, 1987.

Tan, Mely G. "Unity in Diversity: Ethnic Chinese and Nation-Building in Indonesia". In *Ethnic Relations and Nation-Building in Southeast Asia*, edited by Leo Suryadinata, pp. 20–44. Singapore: Institute of Southeast Asian Studies, 2004.

———. "The Ethnic Chinese in Indonesia: Trials and Tribulations". In *Struggling in Hope: A Tribute to the Rev. Dr. Eka Darmaputera*, edited by Ferdinand Sleeman, Adji Ageng Sutama, and A. Rajendra, pp. 683–703. Jakarta: BPK Gunung Mulia, 1999.

Thompson, John B. *The Media and Modernity: A Social Theory of the Media*. Stanford: Stanford University Press, 1995.

Thung, Julan. "Identities in Flux: Young Chinese in Jakarta". Unpublished doctoral dissertation, La Trobe University, Australia, 1998.

Wang, Gungwu. *China and the Chinese Overseas*. Singapore: Times Academic Press, 1991.

Weeks, Jeffrey. "The Value of Difference". In *Identity: Community, Culture, Difference*, edited by Jonathan Rutherford, pp. 88–100. London: Lawrence & Wishart, 1990.

Part III
Economy, Politics and Regionalism

9

THE ECONOMIC EMERGENCE OF CHINA
Strategic Policy Implications for Southeast Asia

Ng Beoy Kui

INTRODUCTION

When China adopted an open-door policy in 1978, Asian countries were not particularly concerned with the policy owing to the unsettled political uncertainties within China.[1] After Deng's visit to Southern China in 1992, a political atmosphere in favour of drastic economic reform emerged in earnest. Foreign direct investment (FDI) started to pour in and reached a peak in 2005. Initial focus on manufacturing activities was directed at light manufacturing such as textiles, clothing, apparels, sport goods and toys. As multinational corporations (MNCs) from Taiwan, Hong Kong, Korea and Japan began to relocate their electronics plants to China, China switched its focus to the manufacturing of electrical, electronics and telecommunication products and was subsequently integrated into the Asian production networks.[2] The rapid expansion of manufacturing exports from China has raised the concern among Southeast Asian countries that their exports might be crowded out by Chinese exports in third-country markets, in particular the U.S. market. This is because China's comparatively cheap labour may wipe out Southeast Asian labour-intensive industries. The concern is further aggravated by the accentuation of China serving as a magnet for attracting

massive FDI at the expense of Southeast Asia as a region. With the accession
of China into the World Trade Organization (WTO) in 2001, such fear of
the "China threat" has caused much anxiety within the region and various
policy proposals were adopted in response to the emergence of China as an
economic powerhouse.

China has attempted to allay the fear by showing its willingness to join
ASEAN's free trade zone as early as December 2000 so as to establish the
ASEAN-China free trade zone by the year 2010. China also participated in
other regional cooperation efforts such as the "Early Harvest Programme" in
October 2003 and Chiang Mai Initiative (CMI) for financial cooperation in
2000. All these economic cooperations were well documented and updated
by a recent book edited by Saw (2007). While the regional approach towards
the rise of China is well documented in the literature, less research has been
conducted on individual national policy responses. The purpose of this chapter
is to assess various policy implications and also evaluate some of the policy
responses adopted by the Southeast Asian countries.

This chapter is divided into four sections. The second section following
this Introduction attempts to ascertain the seriousness of the China threat in
trade and investment. The third section assesses various policy implications
for the Southeast Asian countries from a national strategic perspective. The
final section provides an overview of these policy implications and raises some
issues and concerns for future discussion and research.

DOES CHINA POSE A THREAT?[3]

With the opening of China, its merchandise trade has increased tremendously
over the last three decades. In particular, Chinese exports which accounted
for 1 per cent of the total world exports in 1978, increased significantly to
13 per cent in 2005. Consequently, China is the third largest trading nation
after the United States and Germany in 2006. China's trade structure has,
in the meantime, undergone a profound transformation since its opening in
the late 1970s. Firstly, manufactured exports as a percentage share of total
merchandise exports rose from less than 40 per cent in the late 1970s to
92.4 per cent in 2006, with the rest accounted for by agricultural and mineral
products. Secondly, there was also a structural change within the manufacturing
export sector. In the first and half decade after its opening, manufacturing
exports comprised mainly labour-intensive products such as apparel, footwear,
toys and sport goods. These manufacture goods accounted for half of the
total merchandise exports and two-thirds of manufacturing exports by the
mid-1990s (Athukorala 2007, p. 5). However, the composition of export

trade shifted towards more sophisticated manufactured products, such as electronics and telecommunications products as well as transport equipment and machinery. While sophisticated manufacturing exports recorded a dramatic increase from 17 per cent to 44 per cent between 1993 and 2005, light manufacturing exports, however, showed a decline from 49 per cent in 1993 to 31 per cent in 2005. Notwithstanding such a dramatic shift, the degree of sophistication in these Chinese manufacturing exports is debatable.

Does China Increase Its Market Share at the Expense of Southeast Asia?

In the mid-1990s, Southeast Asian countries' market share in the United States' and Japan's imports already showed signs of weakening, in the face of increasing competition from China. For instance, China's share of U.S. imports has increased from 0.7 per cent in 1987 to 9.2 per cent in 2004, while the share of ASEAN-5 (Indonesia, Malaysia, the Philippines, Singapore and Thailand) in the same market increased from 4.5 per cent in 1987 to 6.7 per cent in 2000 and then declined to 3.8 per cent in 2004. As Ravenhill (2006) observes, China's exports of office machinery, electrical machinery and telecommunications products which were insignificant in 1995 in U.S. and Japanese markets started to exceed that of ASEAN-5 by around 2002. For clothing, apparel and footwear, the negative impact from China in these two markets was even more damaging. For instance, imports of clothing from China by Japan rose by more than 70 per cent between 1995 and 2004 and the share of this market reached 80 per cent. In contrast, ASEAN's share dwindled to 3 per cent from 6.5 per cent in the same period. This "trade competition" paradigm is well supported by empirical evidence provided by A. Bhattacharya, S. Ghosh and W. J. Jansen (2001). Eichengreen, Rhee and Tong (2004) also concur that China's exports to third markets tend to crowd out the exports of other Asian countries. A study by McKibbin and Woo (2003) also show pessimistic results that Southeast Asian industrial exports were facing intense competition from Chinese industrial exports.

In the same vein, a study by Lall and Albaladejo (2004) also shows the extent of competition from China. The authors use correlation analysis between Chinese and regional export structures as indicators of China's competitive threat (see Table 9.1). Between the period 1990 and 2000, they conclude that the Chinese export structure was becoming similar to that of its neighbours. For instance, the export structure of Singapore was hardly similar to that of China in 1990. However, by 2000, the correlation coefficient went up from 0.1 to 0.41. Other Southeast Asian countries also show similar trends. Chia

TABLE 9.1
Correlation Coefficients of Mainland China and
Regional Export Structure
(3 digit SITC)

	Mainland China 1990	Mainland China 2000
Korea 1990	0.38	0.64
Korea 2000		0.43
Taiwan 1990	0.34	0.83
Taiwan 2000		0.53
Singapore 1990	0.10	0.42
Singapore 2000		0.41
Malaysia 1990	0.28	0.24
Malaysia 2000		0.44
Thailand 1990	0.30	0.52
Thailand 2000		0.51
Indonesia 1990	0.38	0.07
Indonesia 2000		0.33
Philippines 1990	0.23	0.38
Philippines 2000		0.33

Source: Lall and Albaladejo (2004), Table 4.

and Sussangkarn (2006, p. 109) calculate Spearman's rank correlations on global exports of ASEAN and China for 2003 which shows R^2 = 0.6149 for the region. Individual countries show correlation between 0.4733 (Singapore) and 0.6663 (Thailand).

Lall and Albaladejo (2004) also compute the technological structure of China and ASEAN-5 (Table 9.2). All countries show an upgrading in their exports' technological structure. China started with a high share of resource-based and low technology exports. Within a decade, China had improved significantly on exports of high technology products. ASEAN-5 also displayed similar trends to varying degrees. The authors also use changes in world market shares as indicators of China's threat. ASEAN-5 is considered as facing a "direct threat" from China if its market share declines while that of China rises. Similarly, if both entities improve their market share, that situation is considered as "no threat" from China. However, if both entities gain market share at the same time but China's gain is faster, then it is noted as a "partial threat". Table 9.3 shows the changes between 1900 and 2000: all ASEAN-5 face an increasingly "partial threat" from China but "direct threat" has gone down significantly. Except for Malaysia, "direct threat" for other ASEAN

TABLE 9.2
Technological Structure of Manufactured Exports 2000
(Percentage)

	China	Singapore	Malaysia	Thailand	Indonesia	Philippines
Resource-based	14.3 9.5	27.8 14.9	31.9 13.1	24.2 18.4	54.2 33.7	37.6 6.5
Low technology	51.9 44.9	9.6 6.5	14.8 9.6	40.1 21.5	32.6 31.3	33.7 11.9
Medium technology	26.9 21.2	23.4 17.4	18.0 17.8	15.1 23.8	11.3 17.5	12.9 11.6
High technology	6.9 24.4	39.1 61.2	35.3 59.4	20.6 36.3	1.9 17.4	15.8 70.0

Source: Lall and Albaladejo (2004), Table 3.

countries shows significant declines. The number for "no threat" from China also increased for all ASEAN-5 except Malaysia. There are two main reasons for such a scenario. One is that ASEAN-5 exports a significant amount of machinery and electronic parts and components to China which later serves as an export platform for these products after their processing or assembly there. That explains the increasing "partial threat" from China and this is misleading. Secondly, "no threat" from China increases because China imports large quantities of primary products and resource-based manufactures as well as capital and intermediate goods to meet its needs in domestic-oriented production. It also imports sophisticated consumer goods to meet increasing domestic demand (Lall and Albaladejo 2004, p. 1457). Studies by Ahearne and others (2003) also observe that there was a co-movement of export growth between China and other Asian economies in the period between 1979 and 2001. Common factors such as economic growth in advanced economies, movements in the world prices of key exports and movements in the yen-dollar exchange rates exerted far more impact on all Asian exports. The implications from their analysis are that competition from China has negligible effects on Southeast Asian export performance.

Ravenhill (2006) also observes that shares of manufactured goods in China's imports from ASEAN increased from a weighted average of 31 per cent in 1990 to 56 per cent in 2004 (see Table 9.4). This confirms the view that China is deeply involved in the triangular trade of the Asian production

TABLE 9.3
China's Threat to NIEs in the World Market 2000
(Percentage of Total Exports)

Category	Singapore		Malaysia		Thailand		Indonesia		Philippines	
	1990	2000	1990	2000	1990	2000	1990	2000	1990	2000
Partial threat	33.6	40.4	47.7	56.5	41.8	61.6	22.8	48.3	30.7	44.0
No threat	12.8	32.0	12.6	5.0	7.5	15.9	5.7	10.7	7.2	44.3
Direct threat	49.0	23.5	10.8	28.7	40.1	15.1	37.1	19.9	34.4	5.8
Reverse threat	2.3	3.4	22.4	6.3	6.5	6.1	5.6	8.9	6.6	3.6
Mutual withdrawal	2.3	0.7	6.5	3.5	4.1	1.3	28.9	12.2	21.1	2.4

Source: Lall and Albaladejo (2004).

TABLE 9.4
Share of Manufactures in China's Imports from ASEAN
(Percentage)

	1990	1995	1996	1997	1998	1999	2000	2001	2002	2003	2004
Indonesia	54.4	29.2	22.5	23.5	34.1	29.0	25.3	27.0	25.0	22.4	22.3
Malaysia	11.9	41.0	48.3	40.9	41.9	49.4	54.5	62.1	54.5	50.8	50.2
Philippines	1.8	6.5	18.6	24.1	45.6	58.4	59.9	69.2	79.3	81.0	92.5
Singapore	28.6	48.5	48.2	50.9	60.5	68.1	66.5	67.1	66.0	66.6	68.4
Thailand	10.4	14.5	21.5	31.7	47.7	45.2	44.5	45.9	53.3	46.7	59.7
ASEAN-5 (weighted average)	31.1	34.9	36.5	39.1	49.2	52.2	51.7	56.0	56.1	54.1	55.5

Source: Ravenhill (2006), Table 2. Calculated from UN COMTRADE data.

networks (Gaulier, Lemone and Unal-Kesend 2005; Haddad and Easpr, March 2007; Athukorala 2006; IMF 2007). In this trade, the newly industrialized economies comprising Hong Kong, Korea, Singapore and Taiwan as well as ASEAN-5 imported parts and components from the United States and Japan and processed them into intermediate inputs. These inputs are then exported to China for final assembly as this last stage of processing is the most labour-intensive. Finally, China exports these final products back to the United States and Japan.

Does China Divert Foreign Direct Investment?

Another Southeast Asian concern is the diversion of FDI away from the region in the face of massive FDI flows into China. Such diversions became evident in Southeast Asia following the 1997 Asian financial crisis. In fact, the region's share of total FDI declined from more than 30 per cent in the mid-1990s to 10 per cent in 2000. With the global IT recession in 2001 and the outbreak of SARS (Severe Acute Respiratory Syndrome) in 2003, FDI inflows into Southeast Asia still hovered around US$20 billion on average between 2000 and 2003 while China was experiencing double the inflows of Southeast Asia, recording almost US$50 billion on average (see Table 9.5). In 2006, FDI flow to China was recorded at US$69.5 billion and that of Southeast Asia recovered strongly to reach US$51.5 billion. This trend shows that the issue of FDI diversion to China is uncalled for. In fact, FDI flows between the two entities grew concurrently with a rapid pace, indicating that the flow of FDI is not a zero-sum game. The so-called diversion was mainly due to the uncertainties arising from the aftermath of the Asian financial crisis (Wu et al. 2002), the global IT recession and the outbreak of SARS. According to Mercereau (2005), there is very little evidence to indicate that China's success in attracting FDI has been at the expense of other countries in the region, with the exception of Singapore and Myanmar. Singapore suffered a decline in FDI due to the global IT recession in 2001 and the outbreak of SARS in 2003. Myanmar suffered a decline in FDI because Singapore, one of its main investing countries, switched its investment focus to China.

Kit, Ong and Kwang (December 2005) believe that the Southeast and East Asian economies of Korea, Taiwan, Singapore, Malaysia, Indonesia and Thailand will continue to draw FDI flows, notwithstanding China's attractiveness for FDI. Their conclusion is based on the notion that MNCs need to diversify their risks in investment among Southeast and East Asian countries, and also that the lack of intellectual property protection in China may deter some MNCs from investing in China.

TABLE 9.5
Foreign Direct Investment (FDI) by Country
(US$ million)

	1980	1990	2000	2001	2002	2003	2004	2005	2006
China	57	3,487	40,715	46,878	52,743	53,505	60,630	72,406	69,468
Southeast Asia	2,756	12,821	23,541	19,582	15,774	19,920	35,245	41,071	51,483
Brunei	−20	7	549	526	1,035	3,375	334	289	434
Cambodia	1	…	149	149	145	84	131	381	483
Indonesia	300	1,092	−4,550	−2,978	145	−597	1,896	8,337	5,556
Laos	…	6	34	24	25	19	17	28	187
Malaysia	934	2,611	3,788	554	3,203	2,473	4,624	3,965	6,060
Myanmar	0	225	208	192	191	291	251	236	143
Philippines	114	550	2,240	195	1,542	491	688	1,854	2,345
Singapore	1,236	5,575	16,484	15,649	7,338	10,376	19,828	15,004	24,207
Thailand	189	2,575	3,350	3,886	947	1,952	5,862	8,957	9,751
Timor-Leste	0	0	0	84	1	5	3	…	3
Vietnam	2	180	1,289	1,300	1,200	1,450	1,610	2,021	2,315

Source: United Nations Conference on Trade and Development, *World Investment Report 2007.*

Secondly, the need for division of labour in the Asian production networks arising from intra-industrial specialization among affiliates of MNCs and supply chain complementarities would lead to concurrent investment in both China and the Southeast Asian region (Giroud 2004; Ravenhill 2006). Chantasasawat et al. (2004) estimate that for a 10 per cent increase in China FDI, East and Southeast Asian countries are able to attract 5 per cent to 6 per cent in FDI. The correlation partly explains the complementary aspect of FDI between China and other parts of East Asia. This is especially so when China is already deeply involved in vertical specialization in the electronics and telecommunication industry. According to Dean, Fung and Wang (January 2007), 35 per cent of the value of China's exports to the world might be attributed to imported inputs. In some sectors, the percentage share is more than 50 per cent.

CHINA'S EMERGENCE AND POLICY IMPLICATIONS

The above discussion is at the aggregate level. Much more insight will be shown if one delves into the industry or product level. The Economic Analytical Unit (2003) uses the Michaely index[4] to show China and East Asian countries' major areas of comparative advantage and disadvantage. From the analysis (Table 9.6), China's major comparative advantage is still in the areas of labour-intensive manufactures. Its major comparative disadvantage is still confined to primary commodities such as crude oil and mineral products. However, China is rapidly moving up the value added chain, as shown in Table 9.7. China is gaining its comparative advantage in electronics and telecommunications products while losing its advantage in light manufacturing products such as clothing and footwear as well as prepared foodstuffs.

Resource-based Industry and Policy Responses

Regionally, Southeast Asia has a comparative advantage in resource-based products, such as timber (Malaysia, Indonesia and Myanmar); crude oil (Indonesia and Malaysia); palm oil (Indonesia and Malaysia); and other food products (Thailand and Vietnam). In this respect, exports of these commodities to China are that of complementary relationships. With an average GDP growth rate of about 9–10 per cent a year since 1978, China has an insatiable appetite for raw materials to the extent that it has been labelled as a "hungry dragon" (*Economist*, 2 October 2004). Its demand for primary commodities, especially energy, metal and food products has increased rapidly. China is now the second largest consumer of oil after the United States. In this case, Southeast Asia's exports of commodities and foodstuff to China are

TABLE 9.6
China's Major Areas of Comparative Advantage and Disadvantage

Top Ten Comparative Advantage Groupings	Top Ten Comparative Disadvantage Groupings
Clothing	Non-office machines
Office machines and parts	Electronic integrated circuits and micro
Footwear	assemblies
Toys and sporting goods	Plastic in primary forms
Furniture	Crude oil
Leather articles	Chemical products
Plastic articles	Steel
Iron and steel articles	Instruments (not timekeeping or musical)
Prepared foodstuffs	Copper and copper articles
Video and digital cameras	Mineral ores
Mobile phones	Aircraft

Source: Economic Analytical Unit (2003), Table 2.1.

TABLE 9.7
China's Changing Revealed Comparative Advantage

Top Five Areas of Strengthening Advantage	Top Five Areas of Improving Disadvantage
Office machines and parts	Non-office machines
Video and digital cameras; mobile phones	Non-rail vehicles
Iron and steel articles	Steel
Video recorders	Fertilizers
Furniture	Synthetic fibres and fabrics
Top Five Areas of Declining Advantage	**Top Five Areas of Worsening Disadvantage**
Clothing	Electronic integrated circuits and micro-
Vegetables product	assemblies
Animals and animal products	Crude oil
Footwear	Organic chemicals
Prepared foodstuffs	Oilseeds
	Diodes, transistors and semiconductors

Source: Economic Analytical Unit (2003), Table 2.2.

considered complementary in nature. However, some Southeast Asian countries are concerned that the higher demand for such products by China and the concurrent decline in manufacturing exports may lead eventually to their "de-industrialization".[5] The term has a negative connotation of "exploitation" and "old colonial division of labour" (Bello, December 2006) of primary commodity-producing countries.[6] The concern was especially widespread among Asian latecomers such as Vietnam, Myanmar, Laos, and Cambodia, and to a lesser extent, Thailand and the Philippines (Bello, December 2006; Cao 2006; Tran, March 2006).

The complementary economic relationship between China and Southeast Asia would inevitably benefit Southeast Asia as a whole. This will contribute to the region's GDP and thereby economic development of the region. As noted by Humphrey and Schmitz (April 2006), China has a substantial economic impact on Asia through its increasing demand for oil. Energy consumption has been driven by China's rapid economic growth, accompanied by its industrialization, urbanization, and increased motorization. This has raised oil prices, contributing a huge amount of oil revenue to the coffers of oil-exporting countries such as Indonesia, Malaysia and Vietnam. However, oil-importing countries, especially the latecomers, will suffer greatly as oil import bills will rise substantially. In addition, rising oil prices will raise inflationary expectations among countries which can turn into intractable macroeconomic problems for all nations. The increasing exports of other raw materials and foodstuff to China also help Southeast Asian development. As to the issue of de-industrialization, it is up to each of the Southeast Asian countries to undertake policy measures to avoid such a process. Export proceeds earned from resource-based industries could be diverted to the effort of restructuring and upgrading their economies. The issues of "exploitation" and the "old colonial division of labour"[7] would not be repeated as Southeast Asian countries also export manufactures and not just primary commodities in a globalized world. The policy issue here is how to exploit one country's comparative advantage and to restructure the economy at the same time so as to be globally more competitive.

Labour-intensive Manufacturing and Policy Implications

A study by the Asian Development Bank (2007) concludes that "Southeast Asia competes in world markets with the PRC in labour-intensive manufacturing but the PRC is largely complementary in natural-based products and human capital- and technology-intensive manufactures." According to the IMF (October 2007, p. 47), "While there remains a clear division of labour among Asian sub-regions, the complementary relationship shows some signs of evolving into a more competitive one." In particular, ASEAN-5 (Indonesia, Malaysia, the Philippines, Thailand and Vietnam) is experiencing rising competition from China. As Rahardja (August 2007) notes, these countries now feel competitive pressure from China in the third markets as well as in their own backyards. For instance, China's exports of machinery to the world in 1993 were at the same level as that of Malaysia. However, by 2004, China's exports of the products were four times more than that of Malaysia. Tham (December 2001) concludes that for high-technology products, Malaysia still has comparative advantage vis-à-vis that of China. Its resource-based products such as wood and wood products, crude oil and palm oil are making significant inroads into the Chinese market. However, Malaysia lost out in terms of export share of labour-intensive products such as clothing and apparel. As for home markets, manufacturers of motorcycles in Indonesia (Rahardja August 2007), Thailand and Vietnam (Intarakumnerd and Fujita 2006) are under severe competition from imported Chinese motorcycles. However, ASEAN increased its market share (value term) in the U.S. apparel market from 17.3 per cent in 2005 to 19.3 per cent in 2006 (ADB 2007, p. 95). In particular, Cambodia, Indonesia and Laos have gained significant market share in the U.S. clothing market.

From the above analysis, it is difficult to ascertain whether China poses a threat to the Southeast Asian countries. In the exports of machinery and electronics products, there seems to be more of a complementary nature. The only concern is that as China upgrades along its technological ladder, other Southeast Asian countries will also need to upgrade themselves to sustain its complementary relationship in the Asian production networks. In fact, the main threat comes from the southern provinces of China which are equally, if not more competitive than many Southeast Asian countries. In the face of increased competition not only between China and the region but also among Southeast Asian countries themselves, each country will have to play a role in the "catching up" process through technology transfers from more advanced economies to less advanced to latecomers (IMF 2007). This is the familiar "flying-geese model" as expounded by Akamatsu (1962). However, one main concern is that unlike NIEs, where they possess a relatively strong indigenous technological base, Southeast Asian countries including Singapore still rely very much on MNCs for technology transfers. Unless MNCs are prepared to help upgrade host country's technological levels, the question of technological upgrading especially among latecomers will become very remote. At the same time, host countries must also facilitate such technology transfers by raising educational standards, the widespread use of English and enhance their research capabilities.

As for labour-intensive and light manufacturing in the third markets and home markets, competition from China is expected to be more severe. Singapore, which is constantly facing labour shortages, has reallocated such

industries to other parts of Southeast Asia in the 1980s. Similarly, Malaysia
has shifted away from labour-intensive industries as it started to face the
pressures of labour shortages in the mid-1990s. With the rise of China,
labour-intensive industries in Southeast Asian countries with the exception
of Singapore and Malaysia are now facing increasingly competitive pressure
from China. One way to avert direct competition from China is to focus on
those labour-intensive industries which are also resource-based such as oleo
chemical products, rubber products and processed foodstuff. As for footwear,
apparels and clothing, Southeast Asian countries need to establish a niche
market with solid branding. Such a strategy will be able to establish a strong
foothold in the third markets. The other alternative is to exploit markets that
China is still not able to penetrate much. For instance, Singapore, Malaysia
and Indonesia can establish hubs for *halal* food for Middle East countries
and even in the China market itself.

Policy Implications for Attracting Foreign Direct Investment

Kit, Ong and Kwan (December 2005) argue that East Asia-7 (Korea, Taiwan,
Singapore, Malaysia, Indonesia, the Philippines and Thailand) will continue
to draw FDI, despite the fact that China has attracted a substantial amount
of FDI inflows since 2003. Firstly, MNCs would like to diversify their risks
as China, while politically stable, may encounter various problems such as
power outages, pollution and supply bottlenecks. The so-called "China plus
one" strategy[8] is to ensure that the supply chain in the Asian production
network would not be disrupted at any point of time. Secondly, manufacturers
in East Asian-7 have moved up the value chain and already established a
niche in high-end products which are complementary to the manufacturing
and assembly of lower-end products. Thirdly, investment in China does not
necessarily mean profitable ventures. China is still at a very early stage of
developing private property rights, general respect for intellectual property
and high hygienic standards. Wages and office rentals in coastal provinces
and cities are also increasing at a rapid rate that may also expand their profit
margins. However, Cross and Tan (2004) conclude that the greatest competitive
pressure will come from China for higher value-added market-oriented FDI
from Triad countries.[9]

The policy implications from the above analysis are threefold. One is
that if Southeast Asian countries are to stay relevant in the Asian production
networks, the region has to always stay ahead of China in a "flying-geese"
pattern (ADB 2007, p. 96). If China were to move up the value chain,
Southeast Asia has to move up as well and must be always way ahead of

China. Then their complementary relationship would be sustainable. In this manner, FDI flows to China will be accompanied by FDI flows to the region. Should any Southeast Asian country fail to keep up the pace, it would eventually fall behind China. Such competitive pressure from China is considered as "healthy" in a globalized world as this will sustain increasing total productivity gains in the region.

Secondly, in order for MNCs to consider the next best alternative after China for their risk diversification purpose, the regional investment climate has to be improved further "through increased legal certainty and strengthened governance to enforce contracts, to protect intellectual property, and to ensure that product standards are met."[10] Specifically, there is a need to introduce customs reforms and improve infrastructure and logistics services to reduce trade cost. In addition, ownership restrictions which are averse to MNCs should be reduced to a bare minimum. For instance, the "New Economic Policy" as implemented by Malaysia will do more harm than necessary in attracting FDI, not only because of its ownership restrictions but also its adverse effect on productivity growth (Ng 1998). Apart from micro-level policies, macroeconomic stability and potential for growth are also important means of attracting FDI flows.

The third strategic step is to avert direct competition with China by exploiting its comparative disadvantages. These disadvantages include relatively low protection of intellectual property rights, private property rights and general disregard for high hygienic standards and environment protection. In this respect, investment policies should be directed at providing a conducive environment for those industries that require stringent rules and regulations on intellectual property rights and hygienic standards, and their enforcement of these rules. The other areas of great potential are those based on technological innovations as well as innovative ideas. Singapore, for instance, has adopted this strategy by attracting FDI which requires stringent patent and intellectual property protection such as the pharmaceutical and multimedia industries.

Huge Chinese Market as an Investment Opportunities

Investment in China to exploit its huge market requires certain core competencies, especially those based on indigenous technology in addition to investible funds. Among Southeast Asian countries, only Singapore, Malaysia and Thailand made strides in investing in China. One main barrier is that local enterprises in the region are not well-capitalized MNCs which should have established their own niche areas or branded products. To overcome this barrier, countries could follow the Singapore model of developing its own government-linked corporations (GLCs) into MNCs. The other alternative is to develop its own local enterprises into MNCs as Japan and Korea have undertaken in the past decades. Moreover, the government can also encourage local enterprises to join MNCs in investing in China. To get involved in this type of joint ventures in China, local enterprises must have a certain niche either in terms of indigenous technology or in terms of local expertise in certain areas. Finally, GLCs can also take the lead in a business group comprising local private enterprises in investing in China, a model that Taiwan has pursued for the last two decades.

The service sector in China represents an enormous potential market for foreign investment. As China takes steps to liberalize its services sector, Southeast Asian investors should take advantage of its services liberalization. China's services sector grew strongly in the 1990s as per capita income rose. However, the development of the services sector in China has been constrained by the country's focus on manufacturing exports. At the same time, barriers were imposed on trade and investment in the services sector. Moreover, the services sector is dominated by many state monopolies such as the banking, insurance, telecommunication, and transport sectors. With its accession to the WTO in 2001, China has decided to speed up the development of its services sector. Steps have been taken to increase foreign participation to promote competition and improve efficiency. For instance, in November 2007 the Chinese government announced that plans to encourage foreign investors to expand into outsourcing services in China have been put in place. Ten cities including Beijing and Shanghai have also been assigned to house centres for outsourcing services. In this regard, China will gradually scrap restrictions on the destination, ownership and business scope of foreign investment in the services sector. With rapid urbanization and industrial development, the services sector in China is expected to expand by leaps and bounds.

Outbound tourism in China is another potential area for exploitation by investors in Southeast Asia. Outbound tourism officially started in 1990, and it has gone from the phase of travel to Hong Kong and Macao, to travel to the border regions, to the phase of travel to other distant foreign countries (World Tourism Organization 2006). Subsequently, outbound travel by private Chinese citizens has been increasing rapidly. From 1994 to 2000, the number of outbound travellers has experienced an increase of one million a year and reached 10 million in 2000. After 2000, the rate of increase was about 3–4 million a year. By 2005, outbound numbers reached more than 31 million, as compared with 3.74 million in 1993. It is estimated that there are more than 200 million Chinese who are financially able to travel overseas. According to a forecast from the World Tourism Organization (2006), China will have 100

TABLE 9.8
Visitor Arrivals from China to ASEAN Countries

Country	1995		2005		1995–2005	
	'000s	Share of China (%)	'000s	Share of China (%)	'000s	Share of China (%)
Brunei	0	0.00	4	0.1	38	0.6
Indonesia	39	0.90	53	1.8	264	0.5
Malaysia	103	1.38	352	11.7	3437	3.0
Philippines	9	0.51	107	3.6	327	1.5
Singapore	202	2.83	858	25.5	5238	6.5
Thailand	376	5.49	762	25.3	6948	6.8
Cambodia	23	10.45	50	2.0	341	5.5
Laos	4	1.16	39	1.3	259	3.6
Myanmar	0	0.00	20	0.7	131	3.8
Vietnam	63	4.66	753	25.0	5999	25.1
ASEAN	818	2.76	3007	5.9	22984	5.5

Source: ASEAN Secretariat. Available at <http://www.aseansec.org>.

million outbound travellers and become the fourth largest source of outbound travel in the world by 2020. To support outbound tourism, nearly 700 licensed outbound travel agencies have been set up in China. In addition, more than 90 countries have been given ADS (Approved Destination Status), and this figure is expected to increase further. In this context, China represents the single greatest growth opportunity in the world for Southeast Asian travel destinations and tourism companies, as 91 per cent of outbound Chinese tourists travelled in the Asia-Pacific region in 2006. Of these, about 3 million arrived in ASEAN countries in 2005, with Singapore, Thailand, Vietnam and Malaysia receiving larger portions of the pie[11] (see Table 9.8). Together with the emergence of low-cost airlines, inbound tourism presents vast potential to Southeast Asian countries. In response to this great potential, Singapore in April 2005 announced its plan to set up two integrated resorts (IR) as a major step towards this direction. According to its Ministry of Trade and Industry, the objective of the integrated resorts is "to broaden our leisure and entertainment options to enhance Singapore's reputation as a premium 'must-visit' destination for leisure and business visitors".[12] Singapore has to act fast as many countries in the region are moving quickly to develop their tourist attractions to entice, among others, the large number Chinese outbound tourists. In addition, Singapore is also trying to attract healthcare tourism, not only from the ASEAN region but also from China.

Strategic Partners in Outward Investment from China

In 2001, the then Chinese premier, Mr Zhu Rongji announced the adoption of "Going Global", i.e. encouraging Chinese companies to invest abroad. In March 2006, the Chinese government reiterated its commitment to invest abroad. The agenda behind this drive is for energy security, geopolitical positioning and promotion of national competitiveness (Lunding 2006). China's outward investment grew at an average of 65.6 per cent per annum from 2000 to 2005. In 2006, outward investment during 2006 amounted to US$16.1 billion vis-à-vis US$2.9 billion in 2003. As of the end of 2006, total stock of outward investment from China totalled US$73 billion, as against US$15.8 billion in 1995. The Chinese government estimates that by the year 2010, the total stock of outward investment will go up to US$120 billion. There are more than 30,000 Chinese companies investing in 160 countries. However, there is a changing focus in these outward investments away from developed countries in North America and Europe towards Asia. About 60 per cent of these Chinese overseas direct equity investments went to Asia. However, Southeast Asia received only an insignificant amount of these outward investments (Chia and Sussangkarn 2006, p. 118). The main recipients were Thailand, Singapore, Indonesia and Cambodia. China's outward investment is a "win-win" strategy for both China and Southeast Asia. Such capital flows not only create jobs at the investment destinations and boost the local economy, but also help Chinese firms to diversify export origins of their products and thus avoid any controversial trade disputes and conflicts with its trading partners, especially the United States and Europe. Bearing in mind that China is expected to amass a total of US$1.4 trillion in foreign exchange reserves in 2007, the main issue is how to attract these Chinese investments to the region. Alternatively, Southeast Asian countries should also seriously consider treating China as a strategic partner in investment and trade in Europe, the United States, India and the Middle East by exploiting their traditional colonial links, as well as cultural and ethnic affinity to these regions. For instance, their Muslim, Chinese and Indian communities can be empowered to be valuable resources for such strategic alliances in the venture.

CONCLUDING REMARKS

From the above analysis, one can safely conclude that China's emergence as an economic powerhouse has benefited most of the Southeast Asian countries. In the Asian production networks, the complementary aspect of the production has given rise to a booming intra-regional and intra-industry trade. The triangular trade among the United States, Japan, NIEs and Southeast Asian countries has resulted in a certain degree of payment imbalances in favour of both China and the Asian region. However, there are concerns that some Southeast Asian countries may fail to catch up as China moves up its technological ladder so much so that such complementary relationships may break down in the future. China's emergence also benefits Southeast Asian countries in another way. With its rapid growth in the past three decades, China's increasing demand for raw materials benefits a number of Southeast Asian countries. However, some of these countries have expressed their concern of de-industrialization and a repeat of old colonial division of labour. Moreover, the labour-intensive industries in Southeast Asia may face the crowding-out effect from China.

However, the huge domestic market of China presents great potential for investment opportunities to the Southeast Asian countries. This is particularly so in the service sector, including outbound tourism from China. Equally important is the outward investment by China which can supplement domestic capital for economic development and employment creation. The main beneficiaries are Southeast Asian latecomers such as Vietnam, Cambodia and Laos.

The chapter also explored various policy implications arising from China's economic emergence. Depending on their respective degrees of economic development, economic structure and comparative advantage, eight strategic positionings have been identified. Of these eight positionings, direct competition is considered as an unwise move because China is richly endowed with relatively cheap labour resources and possesses a huge domestic market that may serve as a magnet for direct foreign investment. Instead, competition based on niche areas through indigenous technology and branding provides a viable alternative. The other alternative is to upgrade and restructure one's own economy, venturing into those areas where China has no comparative advantage. Others may adopt "connecting" strategies such as complementing or supplementing the Chinese economy by meeting China's increasing demand for natural resources or exploiting its huge domestic market. Others may explore the possibilities of forging strategic alliances in the global market or playing the role of a middleman between China and the West.

On the whole, Southeast Asian countries need to constantly upgrade and restructure their respective economies as an effective policy response towards threats from China. They must be able to turn these threats into opportunities. For instance, stiff competition from China's labour-intensive industries should alert the local counterparts in Southeast Asia not to be complacent and increase their productivity constantly. Such competition from China will also allow the region to look beyond exporting traditional products by establishing a niche in mature markets. They must also look beyond the usual traditional markets by exploring those of unexploited ones in the Middle East and Latin America.

Of no less importance is the need to improve Southeast Asian countries' domestic business and investment climate. This is crucial in three respects. One is to be more competitive than China in attracting FDI from the Triad countries, as well as from NIEs and other intra-regional FDI. Secondly, Southeast Asian countries should also serve as the next best, if not the better alternative to China for MNCs to diversify their overall risk in Asian investment. Finally, the better business and investment climate should serve as a key attraction for China's outward investment.

Southeast Asian countries have been adopting export-oriented strategies as the main thrust for economic growth since the 1970s. In the face of the economic threat from China, a two-track strategy stemming from "Thaksinomics".[13] seems to be a more balanced approach as a policy response to the rise of China. The strategy requires a country to continue with the export-oriented approach and at the same time, to look inward to its domestic market as a renewed source for sustaining their economic growth. This strategy is only relevant to those countries which have a large population base in the agricultural sector. Countries like Indonesia, Thailand and Vietnam are possible candidates for such a policy strategy. With this strategy, increase in government expenditure with a view to eradicate poverty and improve rural income will be the most effective way to ensure that the strategy is successful. However, the budgetary implications arising from such a strategy could be enormous and the governance to avoid corrupt practices can be a challenging task to most of the Southeast Asian countries.

Notes

1. There were factions in China then. One led by reformist, Deng Xiao Peng and the other by Chen Yun, a conservative. The two factions fought over the extent and pace of economic reforms for China. It is the ultimate victory for Deng that he decided to accelerate the pace of economic reform in 1992 (Yang 2004).
2. There are three major regional production networks in the world. One is based in Northern America with its base in Silicon Valley. The others are the Asian production networks and the European production networks.
3. For detailed discussion on China's economic rise as threats and opportunities, refer to Ng (December 2007.)
4. The index measures a product's share of exports minus its share of imports. If

the index is positive, it indicates that the country is a net exporter. Otherwise it is a net importer. The index is therefore a revealed comparative advantage (disadvantage) of a country.

5. It is also known as "Dutch disease" arising from reallocation of resources from the traditional industrial sector to the booming sector such that output share from the traditional industrial sector falls as a consequence.

6. This same view was also expressed by a *New York Times* article (29 June 2002) that "China is grabbing much of the new foreign investment in Asia, leaving its once-glittering neighbors — Thailand, South Korea, Singapore — with crumbs... Some Asian officials say they fear that Southeast Asia will be relegated to the role of supplier of food and raw materials to China in exchange for cheap manufactured goods...".

7. In this division of labour, developed countries which were also the colonial masters, imported primary commodities from their colonies at lower prices. They then processed these primary commodities into manufactured goods and exported them back to their colonies at much higher prices.

8. This is an MNC strategy in diversifying their risk in investment in China and other Asian region. If a plant is built in China, another plant will also be set up in other parts of Asia.

9. Triad countries refer to the United States, Japan and Europe.

10. *Asian Development Bank Outlook* (2007b), p. 74.

11. The growth of the Asia-Pacific tourism market is further fuelled by the growing middle class in India, the Middle East and ASEAN region.

12. Ministry of Trade and Industry, <http://app.mti.gov.sg/default.asp?id=585>.

13. Thaksinomics (proposed by the former Thai prime minister, Mr Thaksin Shinawatra) is an eclectic strategy comprising two tracks. The first track is the usual export-oriented strategy in manufacturing spearheaded by multinational corporations (MNCs). The second track provides strong support to local enterprises leveraging indigenous skills and resources. In the short run, the government strategy is to stimulate domestic demand through its expenditure on the rural and agricultural sector. At the same time, the second track also seeks to develop new local industries as part of the diversification away from export-oriented activities. In addition, the track also attempts to implement measures to assist business to move up the value-added chain, thus keeping ahead of direct Chinese competition <http://www.thaksinomics.com/>.

References

Ahearne, Alan G. et al. "China and Emerging Asia: Comrades or Competitors?" Federal Reserve Bank of Chicago, WP 2003–27. Chicago, IL: Federal Reserve Bank of Chicago, 2003.

Akamatsu K. "A Historical Pattern of Economic Growth in Developing Countries". *Journal of Developing Economies* 1, no. 1 (March–August 1962): 3–25.

Asian Development Bank. "Trade and Structural Change in East and Southeast Asia: Implications for Growth and Industrialization". In *Asian Development Bank Outlook, 2007 Update*. Manila: ADB, 2007*a*, pp. 82–99.

———. "Export Dynamics in East Asia". In *Asian Development Bank Outlook, 2007 Update*. Manila: ADB, 2007*b*, pp. 55–86.

Athukorala, Prema-Chandra. "The Rise of China and East Asian Export Performance: Is the Crowding-out Fear Warranted?". ANU Working Papers in Trade and Development, Working Paper No. 2007/10. Canberra: ANU, 2007.

———. "Product Fragmentation and Trade Patterns in East Asia". *Asian Economic Paper* 4, no. 3 (2006): 1–27.

Bello, Walden. "China and Southeast Asia: Emerging Problems in an Economic Relationship". <http://www.focusweb.org/china-and-southeast-asia-emerging-problems-in-an-economic-relationship.html>.

Bhattacharya, A., Swati Ghosh, and W. Jos Jansen. "Has the Emergence of China Hurt Asian Exports?". *Applied Economics Letters* 8 (2001): 217–21.

Cao, Sy Kiem. "East Asian Economic Integration: Problems for Late-Entry Countries". In *East Asian Visions: Perspectives on Economic Development*, edited by I. Gill, Y. Huang, and H. Kharas. Washington, D.C.: World Bank and Institute of Policy Studies, 2006, pp. 91–100.

Chantasasawat, B., K. C. Fung, H. Iizaka, and A. Siu. "Foreign Direct Investment in East Asia and Latin America: Is There a People's Republic of China Effect?". ADB Discussion Paper, no. 17. Manila: ADB, 2004.

Chia, Siow Yue and C. Sussangkarn. "The Economic Rise of China: Challenges and Opportunities for ASEAN". *Asian Economic Policy Review* 1 (2006): 102–28.

Cross, A. and Hui Tan. "The Impact of China's WTO Accession on Southeast Asian Foreign Direct Investment: Trends and Prospects". In *The Future of Foreign Investment in Southeast Asia*, edited by Nick J. Freeman and F. L. Bartels, Chapter 7, pp. 125–54. London and New York: RoutledgeCurzon, 2004.

Dean, J. M., K. C. Fung, and Z. Wang. "Measuring Vertical Specialization in Chinese Trade". Washington, D.C.: U.S. International Trade Commission Office of Economics Working Paper, no. 2007-01-A, 2007.

Economic Analytical Unit (EAU). *China's Industrial Rise: East Asia's Challenge*. Canberra: Australian Government, 2003.

Economist. "A Survey of the World Economy — A Hungry Dragon". 2 October 2004, p. 12.

Eichengreen, B. Y. Rhee and H. Tong. "The Impact of China on the Exports of Other Asian Countries". NBER Working Paper Series, No. 10768. Cambridge, MA: NBER, 2004.

Gaulier, G., F. Lemone, D. Unal-Kesend. "China's Integration in East Asia: Production Sharing, FDI & High-Tech Trade". CEPII Working Paper, no. 2005-09. Paris: CEPII, June 2005.

Giroud, A. "Foreign Direct Investment and the Rise of Cross-border Production Networks in Southeast Asia". In *The Future of Foreign Investment in Southeast*

Asia, edited by Nick J. Freeman and F. L. Bartels, Chapter 6, pp. 104–24. London and New York: RoutledgeCurzon, 2004.

Haddad M. and Easpr. "Trade Integration in East Asia: The Role of China and Production Networks". World Bank Policy Research Working Paper 4160. Washington, D.C.: World Bank, 2007.

Humphrey, J. and H. Schmitz. "The Implications of China's Growth for Other Asian Countries". <http://www.uk.cn/uploadfiles/2006428171612242.doc>.

Intarakumnerd, P. and M. Fujita. "China's Threat and Opportunity for Thai and Vietnamese Motorcycle Industries: A Sectoral Innovation System Analysis". <http://www.globelicsindia2006.org/Patarapong%20Intarakumnerd.pdf>.

International Monetary Fund (IMF). "The Evolution of Trade in Emerging Asia". *Regional Economic Outlook: Asia and Pacific Region*. Washington, D.C.: IMF, 2007, pp. 41–55.

Kit Wei Zheng, J. W. Ong, and K. Kwan. "China's Rise as a Manufacturing Powerhouse: Implications for Asia". MAS Staff Paper no. 42. Singapore: Monetary Authority of Singapore, 2005.

Lall, Sanjaya and M. Albaladejo. "China's Competitive Performance: A Threat to East Asian Manufactured Exports?". *World Development* 32, no. 9 (2004): 1441–66.

Lunding, Andrea. "Global Champions in Waiting". Deutsche Bank Research, China Special, Current Issues, 4 August 2006.

McKibbin, Warwick, J. and Wing Thye Woo. "The Consequences of China's WTO Accession on its Neighbours". Brookings Discussion Papers in International Economics, no. 157. Washington, D.C.: Brookings Institution, 2003.

Mercereau, Benoit. "FDI Flows to Asia: Did the Dragon Crowd Out the Tigers?". IMF Working Paper no. 05/189. Washington, D.C.: IMF, 2005.

New York Times. "Economic Juggernaut: China is Passing US as Asian Power". 29 June 2002.

Ng, Beoy Kui. "The Economic Rise of China: Its Threats and Opportunities from the Perspective of Southeast Asia". *Copenhagen Journal of Asian Studies* 25 (2007): 9–27.

———. "The Economic Rise of China: Its Threats and Opportunities from the Perspective of Southeast Asia". Asia Research Centre, Copenhagen Business School Discussion Paper no. 15. Copenhagen: Asia Research Centre, October 2006.

———. "The New Economic Policy and the Chinese in Malaysia: Impact and Responses". *Journal of Malaysian Chinese Studies* 2, no. 2 (1998): 99–123.

Pamlin, Dennis and Long Baijin. "Re-think China's Outward Investment Flows". Gland, Switzerland: WWF International, April 2007.

Rahardja, Sjamsu. "Big Dragon, Little Dragons: China's Challenge to the Machinery Exports of Southeast Asia". World Bank Policy Research Working Paper WPS4297. Washington, D.C.: World Bank, 2007.

Ravenhill, John. "Is China an Economic Threat to Southeast Asia?". *Asian Survey* XLVI, no. 5 (Sept./Oct. 2006): 653–74.

Saw Swee-Hock, ed. *ASEAN-China Economic Relations*. Singapore: Institute of Southeast Asian Studies, 2007.

Tham, Siew-Yean. "Can Malaysian Manufacturing Compete with China in the WTO?". *Asia-Pacific Development Journal* 8, no. 2 (Dec. 2001): 1–25.

Tran Van Tho. "The Pattern of Trade Specialization Economic Integration in East Asia: Problems of the Late Comers". <http://www.esri.go.jp/jp/prj-2004_2005/forum/060123/01-3-R.pdf>.

World Tourism Organization (WTO). *China: The Asia and the Pacific Intra-regional Outbound Series*. Madrid: WTO, 2006.

Wu, Friedrich, T. S. Poa, H. S. Yeo, K. K. Puah. "Foreign Direct Investments to China and Southeast Asia: Has ASEAN been Losing Out?". *Economic Survey of Singapore*, Third Quarter, 2002.

Yang Jisheng. *Political Struggles During the Era of China's Reform*. Hong Kong: Excellent Culture Press, 2004. (in Chinese). <http://www.thaksinomics.com/>.

10

WHEN OLD REGIONALISM MEETS NEW REGIONALISM
Taiwan and China in East Asian Regional Integration

Chin-Ming Lin

Although there were no formal commercial agreements amongst East Asian countries prior to the mid-1990s, the region's rapid economic growth contributed to a dramatic increase in intra-regional trade flows. This is manifested in rapidly increasing regionalized investment and production.

The old notion of regionalism emerged as a response to regionalization. National and local governments in East Asia have implemented numerous policy initiatives to facilitate increased transnational economic relationships by opening their national economic space and encouraging regionalization. Taiwan is one of the economies in East Asia that has been engaging regionalization from the beginning, thereby providing an explanation to the development of (old) regionalism. On the other hand, with the emergence of new regionalism, which may be understood as a state strategy to respond simultaneously to national political pressures and the internationalized structure of the global political economy, Taiwan is now destined to engage in deeper regionalization with other major East Asian economies and, especially, with China.

This chapter will explore similarities and differences between old and new regionalisms from Taiwan's vantage point. As economies of East Asia are developing various forms of regional integration, the chapter posits that old regionalism sometimes reappears and is intermingled with new regionalism.

Furthermore, given the fact that the Chinese economy is largely dependent on investments from and trade with the rest of the region, particularly in the form of components from Taiwan and others for the production of exports, Taiwan is in a position to share its experience with China in dealing with old regionalism. In so doing, this study hopes to shed new light on new regionalism.

In East Asian economies, there is still a correlation between formal economic regionalism and informal economic regionalization in East Asia, particularly between Taiwan and China. This chapter will also show that a large proportion of Taiwan's trade with China (more than 60 per cent of Taiwan's exports and more than 70 per cent of Taiwan's outward investment are centred in China) derives from the fact that the process of East Asian regionalization of production is based on a complex web of relationships built on a hierarchy of asymmetric dependencies. The implication of that complex web of asymmetrical dependencies for the region is really worth pondering.

In the following sections, we will show how Japanese capital and domestic industrial restructuring initiated outward investment and production projects beginning in the mid-1980s, which in turn culminated in increasing East Asian regionalization. The second section delves into the replication of Japan's outward development by newly industrialized economies (NIEs) as a kind of subordinate regionalization as well as its implications for other actors in East Asia. The third section examines the impact of the rise of East Asia's new regionalism as well as Taiwan's position vis-à-vis its current intra-regional relationships. The final section concludes with a brief discussion on intra-firm trade between Taiwan and China.

JAPANESE CAPITAL-INITIATED EAST ASIAN REGIONALIZATION

National and local governments across the world have implemented numerous policy initiatives to facilitate and increase transnational economic relationships so as to open their national economic space and to encourage regionalization. The basis for the dynamics of regional integration in East Asia lies in Japan's rising capitalism.

Japan recovered its economy to pre-War levels in the mid-1950s. It built its accumulation model around exports with labour productivity rising higher than real wages. At first, Japan's exports were primarily light-industrial products such as textiles, toys and simple electrical appliances, with radios becoming Japan's leading export by the early 1960s. By the mid-1960s however, output growth and rising employment began to drive up wages, especially of female workers, making it increasingly difficult for Japanese capital to maintain international competitiveness. This development, along with growing trade frictions, especially with the United States, eventually triggered Japan's first post-War industrial restructuring, which lasted from the mid- to late 1960s to the first oil shock in October 1973.

Production of cotton textiles was moved to East Asia (NIEs and ASEAN countries) beginning in the mid-1960s, followed shortly by synthetic textiles.[1] Later on, the production of labour-intensive consumer electronics, including radios, TVs, and tape recorders was relocated to countries in East Asia.[2] The new domestic industrial structure built up during this period centred on heavy and chemical industries, which processed imported raw materials and exported iron and steel, ships, chemicals and petroleum products.[3] This shift led to the creation of a new industrial core and also enabled some light industries to continue producing in Japan — especially those working as subcontractors (e.g., parts manufacturers) for core industrial corporations. "Domestically, these years represented the high point in the development of heavy industry, which symbolized the 'Japanese miracle' and brought unheard of wages and conditions to the male labour aristocracy. However, it also saw a massive influx into temporary and part-time jobs by mainly married women."[4]

The country's second phase of industrial restructuring was triggered by the 1973 rise in prices of oil and other primary commodities and lasted until the 1985 Plaza Accord. The oil shock created massive problems for Japan's newly established, import-dependent, core industries. Japanese capital, in collaboration with the Japanese government, responded with a gradual displacement of the heavy and chemical industries to Asia and the domestic expansion of a new set of machinery industries: general machinery (including office machinery), electrical machinery (including TV and radio receivers, tape recorders, and semiconductors), transport machinery (including motor vehicles), and precision machinery. Table 10.1 shows the growing importance of these industries by highlighting the changing composition of Japanese exports.

With the second phase's running down and relocation of heavy and chemical industries, and the need to control labour costs to ensure the profitable expansion of the new core of machinery production in phase 2, domestic purchasing power became more and more incapable of supporting the growth in productive capacity. However, Japan's growing reliance on machinery industry exports proved problematic. More than 40 per cent of all Japanese machinery exports during the 1985–87 period were sold in North America, mostly in the United States; this included more than 90 per cent of Japan's motor vehicle exports.[5] Japan's export success in such

TABLE 10.1
Composition of Japan's Commodity Exports, 1960–85
(Percentage)

Industry	1960	1970	1975	1980	1985
Textiles	30.2	12.5	6.7	4.9	3.6
Chemicals	4.5	6.4	7.0	5.2	4.4
Metals and metal products	14.0	19.7	22.4	16.4	10.5
Machinery and equipment	22.8	46.3	53.8	62.8	71.8
Other	28.5	15.1	10.1	10.7	9.7

Source: Steven, *Japan's New Imperialism*, p. 17.

key, high value-added products was seen by many U.S. analysts as the main factor explaining growing U.S. trade deficits and the deindustrialization of the U.S. economy. The result was a major escalation of trade tensions between the United States and Japan at the beginning of the late 1970s and early 1980s. The negotiations surrounding these tensions culminated in the September 1985 Plaza Accord, which tried to use exchange rate adjustments to bring about more balance in trade. The Group of Five countries agreed to support a fall in the U.S. dollar and a rise in Japanese yen. But the resulting appreciation of the yen by more than 46 per cent against the dollar during the 1985–88 period threatened Japan's export competitiveness so much so that it triggered the "high-yen crisis" (*endaka fukyo*) and Japan's third round of industrial restructuring.[6] Phase 3 is especially important insofar as it explains the explosive increases in manufacturing FDI in, and manufactured exports from, the ASEAN countries.

The sharp appreciation of the yen hit Japanese producers hard, but the resulting recession did not last long; production resumed its upward trend in 1987. In spite of the recovery, and in sharp contrast to the strategy employed during each of the first two rounds of industrial restructuring, Japanese planners and corporations made no serious attempt at establishing a new industrial core to replace the large portion of the motor vehicle and consumer electronics industries relocated abroad. During the first five years of the high-yen era, Japanese firms invested some US$600 billion — more than those invested by all U.S.-based corporations during the same period.[7] The major focus of investment was modernization of facilities for manufacturing producer goods, in particular machinery and advanced components. As a result, the intended market was other enterprises (often located overseas), not the ultimate consumers (especially domestic ones).

Besides booming domestic investment, Japanese foreign investment, totalling some US$47 billion over the years 1981 to 1985, grew to more than $170 billion in the following five years.[8] While the foreign investment boom was driven largely by the Japanese strategy of relocating production of goods most vulnerable to the high yen and ongoing trade tensions with the United States, foreign expansion in the areas of finance, real estate, and commercial activities also played a major role.[9]

Specifically, the post-1985 manufacturing FDI involved a two-part overseas investment programmes. The first part was a major push to locate production of advanced consumer products such as automobiles in core target markets such as Western Europe and especially the United States. The other part was a significant investment flow into Asia, relocating the production of mass consumer electronics goods and less-advanced industrial components to lower-wage countries. Thus, the majority of new foreign investment went to other advanced countries. Nevertheless, Japanese FDI in the developing world — especially Asia — rose significantly after 1985. For example, Japanese direct investment in South Korea, Taiwan, and Hong Kong during the years 1986–91 was (in U.S. dollars) more than 70 per cent of the amount of the 1951–91 period. Even though the same share was only 56 per cent for the ASEAN countries as a whole, it is roughly three-quarters of Japanese FDI in Malaysia over the years 1951–91 as occurred in 1986–91, while the share for Thailand exceeded 86 per cent.[10] In fact, ever since Japan's ASEAN-bound investment overtook NIE-bound investment in 1988 the gap has been widening.[11] This post-1985 wave of Japanese investment in the NIEs and ASEAN countries was weighted towards manufacturing. During the years 1986–90, manufacturing subsidiaries made up 50.4 per cent of all new Japanese subsidiaries established in the NIEs and 59.1 per cent of those in ASEAN countries — compared to 30.2 per cent in Europe, and 41.3 per cent worldwide.[12]

The third phase of industrial restructuring did not make the Japanese economy less export-dependent. In order to respond to recession beginning in 1990, Japanese enterprises endeavoured to cut production costs, especially by holding down workers' wages. But its suppressing effects on domestic wage-based demand, in turn increased the dependence of Japan's growth on net exports.[13] The increasing outward FDI was creating three regional operating zones in North America, Europe and Asia, with production, finance and trade increasingly integrated over the advanced and developing countries within *and* across these zones.[14] Asia appears to play a crucial role in regionalized production by Japanese capital, especially in manufacturing. For example, while Japanese manufacturing FDI in Asia was 31 per cent of the amount that went to North America over the years 1986–89, it rose to 45 per cent in 1990 and to 88 per cent in 1993.[15] Moreover, this new investment in Asia is not only oriented towards production for Asian markets and/or towards exports to the United States and Europe, both of which also reduce the export role of Japan itself. Increasingly, Japanese firms in other Asian countries are beginning to take advantage of low production costs to re-export Asian production back to Japan.[16]

Another noteworthy aspect of the Japanese foreign investment is the shifting locational focus of Japanese FDI within Asia from ASEAN to China and its low-wage labour, which stimulates interests of capitalists not only from Japan and other advanced countries, but also from the Asian NIEs and ASEAN countries. This reorientation of Japanese FDI is ominously significant for the ASEAN countries as well as the Asian NIEs. Due to the continued refocusing of Japan's economic activities, the ability of the ASEAN countries in particular to continue their export-led growth could be jeopardized not only directly (insofar as their exports are based on Japanese FDI) but also indirectly (due to intensified trade competition from China and other emerging export countries).

The industrialization patterns of Asian NIEs, especially South Korea and Taiwan, are shaped by the restructuring of Japanese industries. Furthermore, the NIEs' own processes of industrial restructuring also helped shape the environment for the ASEAN countries' export-led "miracle". South Korean and Taiwanese firms greatly increased their foreign investment beginning in the late 1980s, following the expansion of Japanese FDI. South Korean firms invested more than US$1 billion abroad in 1990, and 40 per cent in developing countries. Taiwanese firms invested far more, more than US$6 billion. However, only US$1.2 billion of the total amont was officially registered. A favourite target was Southeast Asia where the average wage rate stood at one-third to one-half that in Taiwan.[17] With the exception of Thailand (where Japan maintained FDI leadership), the NIEs invested more in the ASEAN countries during the 1989–92 period than either the United States or Japan (see Table 10.2). The outflow of investment from both South Korea and Taiwan continues at record levels. South Korean businesses increased their FDI to approximately US$3 billion in 1995 and Southeast Asia was among the most attractive locations.[18]

SUBORDINATE REGIONALIZATION OF NIE ENTERPRISES

The expansion of FDI from the NIEs was a replay of Japan's earlier domestic industrial restructuring and foreign investment activities. The post-1985

TABLE 10.2
FDI in ASEAN Countries: Totals and
Selected Origin-Country Shares, 1989–92

	Indonesia	Malaysia	Thailand	Philippines
Totals for year (in US$ millions)				
1989	4,719	1,255	7,996	804
1990	8,750	2,367	8,029	961
1991	8,778	2,255	4,987	783
1992	10,313	2,298	10,021	286
1989–92[a]	32,560	8,175	31,003	2,834
NIE shares[b] (percentage)				
1989	25.4	43.3	25.2	40.0
1990	29.7	42.3	33.6	40.0
1991	22.6	45.0	31.7	8.7
1992	25.7	15.0	9.4	22.7
1989–92[a]	25.9	35.5	23.3	29.6
Japan's shares (percentage)				
1989	16.3	31.3	44.1	19.5
1990	25.6	27.8	34.3	31.8
1991	10.6	23.5	35.3	26.8
1992	14.6	13.4	19.6	25.2
1989–92[a]	16.7	23.1	32.3	26.3
U.S. shares (percentage)				
1989	7.4	3.7	6.9	13.8
1990	1.7	2.9	13.6	6.1
1991	3.1	7.4	22.7	11.1
1992	8.9	9.7	12.3	21.7
1989–92[a]	5.2	6.2	12.9	11.3

Notes: [a] Cumulative totals or cumulative shares.
[b] Republic of Korea, Taiwan, Hong Kong and Singapore.
Source: Steven, *Japan's New Imperialism*, p. 97.

Japanese and NIE foreign direct investment waves were largely triggered by common forces. As mentioned above, the U.S. government negotiated the 1985 Plaza Accord in an attempt at solving the country's trade and industrial problems through depreciation of the dollar relative to the yen. The appreciation of the yen initially improved the competitiveness of South Korea and Taiwan, and they took advantage by greatly increasing their exports to the United States as well as Japan in 1986–88. However, their resulting trade surpluses led the U.S. government to demand that they follow Japan's lead and revalue their currencies and further open their markets.[19] South Korean and Taiwanese capital soon faced a challenge similar to that faced only a few years earlier by Japanese firms: sustaining export-led growth in a situation of appreciating currency, rising wages and trade frictions with the United States. The response was similar; they engaged in FDI to protect profits by focusing increasingly on ASEAN countries and China.

However, the regionalization of NIE capital is qualitatively different from the regionalization of Japanese capital. NIE capital and NIEs themselves are being regionalized in subordinate fashion as part of an emerging Japanese-dominated system of production and investment in East Asia. The subordinate status of NIE capital becomes clearer when one considers the *"interconnections between* Japanese and NIE capital regionalization".[20]

One such interconnection is the direct competition between Japanese and NIE enterprises. By combining their advanced technology with cheap ASEAN labour, Japanese firms place less technologically advanced South Korean and Taiwanese enterprises still producing in their own home countries at a decisive competitive disadvantage. For instance, the establishment of electronics production in ASEAN countries had competitively displaced much NIE production from the Japanese market. Imports of colour TVs from South Korea and Taiwan, for example, fell from 1.6 to 1.3 million units in the years 1989–91. In the same period, imports from Malaysia rose from 2,000 to 385,000 units. By the latter date, Malaysia had replaced Taiwan as Japan's second most important source of imports of this product and was also the single largest supplier of radio cassette recorders to the Japanese market.[21]

A second interconnection stems from the fact that many NIE firms operate as subcontractors for Japanese producers. Thus, shifts in Japan's regional production and investment strategies naturally require corresponding regional shifts on the part of NIE enterprises. Here the response of NIE firms to rising costs and trade frictions are often conditioned and constrained by the regional production strategies of Japanese enterprises rather than the requirements for continuation of the NIEs' national projects of export-led growth and industrialization.

From the Japanese standpoint, it would be inexpedient to destroy all competitors by establishing a regionalized production network in ASEAN and the rest of East Asia. Instead, Japanese firms are trying to incorporate potential competitors into a regional production structure that is supportive of Japanese interests. This requires the integration of NIE and ASEAN firms into hierarchical production and investment systems that allow Japanese enterprises to use their technological, financial and marketing dominance to set the terms for maximum profit creation and their distribution among competing enterprises on different levels of the hierarchy. Once integrated in this regional production network, NIE and ASEAN firms may try to renegotiate the terms on which they participate, but they will not be able to question the hierarchy itself.

What does the regionalized hierarchical competition in East Asia imply for the NIEs? They were gradually experiencing premature industrial hollowing out, growing trade pressures, rising inequality and intensified competitiveness pressures on their labour whose work and living conditions remain far below core standards. NIE industries churn out products not as technologically advanced as Japanese and U.S. goods, and yet they have higher labour and logistics costs than rising Southeast Asian nations. This poses great challenges to the still relatively underdeveloped technological and marketing capabilities of NIE enterprises and the corresponding dependence of the NIEs on imports of advanced economy-controlled components, technologies and services required for continued growth.

Like Japan before them, South Korea and Taiwan tried to develop their domestic economies using a combined export-promotion and import-substitution approach based on industrial planning and trade controls.[22] They made considerable progress in aggregate growth, but their development situations call into question the ability of their domestic growth strategy to survive a regionalized accumulation process. Of course, the strongest South Korean and Taiwanese corporations may profitably participate in this regional process through their subordinate positions vis-à-vis Japanese enterprises and their advanced positions vis-à-vis ASEAN enterprises. Nevertheless, NIE industries have not succeeded in technologically replicating the successes of the Japanese core innovative industries. Thus, about 90 per cent of Taiwanese imports from Japan are components, machinery and parts.[23]

Japanese firms developed their own technology by absorbing and improving the work of others and also created their own advanced marketing networks based on brand recognition. In contrast, South Korean and Taiwanese enterprises continue to rely heavily on original equipment manufacturing (OEM), in which they produce goods according to specification which are then marketed under foreign brand names.

TOWARDS EAST ASIAN NEW REGIONALISM

The term "new regionalism" had first been used in the urban studies literature to refer to substantial regional processes.[24] The wide use of the term in international relations literature owes much to the publications emerging from the UNU WIDER project on new regionalism.[25] Given the relatively large corpus of literature on new regionalism, it is difficult to construct a single understanding of what the approach actually means. One of the key difficulties in generalizing it lies in the fact that there is no attempt to find a "once and for all" explanation or theory. In this respect, it is not a theory but a framework — a framework which not only allows for diversity, but also emphasizes the fact that there is no single answer; no single set of relationships; no single simple understanding.

It is now broadly accepted in the literature that there is a distinction between regionalism and regionalization. Regionalism is largely considered to refer to formalized regions with officially agreed upon membership and boundaries emerging as a result of intergovernmental dialogues and treaties. While such formal regions necessarily necessitate some form of institutionalization, no specific form/type/amount of institutionalization is required to qualify as a "proper" region. Rather, the interest lies in the factors determining the wide variation in the institutional level of regions.[26]

While regionalism refers to the form, regionalization refers to the processes by which societies and economies become integrated — particularly, but not only, in the economic sphere. Such regionalization and economic integration in particular can occur without the creation of formal political regionalism. They are "regions without prescribed or proscribed borders",[27] based on "transnational flows and networks"[28] rather than cartography and political borders. Here, the example of economic integration in East Asia is particularly important, as regionalization not only occurred prior to the mid-1990s, as mentioned above, but has also been relatively unhindered by political conflicts between China and Japan and across the Taiwan Strait.

Clearly, regionalism and regionalization are not necessarily mutually exclusive. Indeed, "old regionalism" scholars saw the emergence of regionalism as a response to regionalization. As economic regionalization occurs, states often move towards cooperation to find regional solutions to common problems. In topics on "regionalization", the focus of attention moves to the role of non-state actors, particularly the investment and trade decisions of enterprises. Economic integration, and possibly the formal regional projects that flow from such integration, are seen as largely driven by the market, rather than by states. Nevertheless, while enterprises might drive regionalization through investment and trade flows, states play an essential role in creating the environment in which enterprises can pursue their interests. The findings of a German Bundestag report on globalization rather than regionalization are particularly relevant here. The report concluded that the hard infrastructure necessary for the physical transportation of goods is usually funded by governments rather than the private sector and that "the growing worldwide integration of economies came not by any law of nature — it has been the result of active and deliberate policies".[29]

New regionalism should be understood as a state strategy responding simultaneously to national political pressures and the international structure of the global political economy (and, in particular, internationally mobile finance capital). Nevertheless, it is enterprises that decide whether to respond or not, and where they are going to invest. As Walter Mattli argues, allowing enterprises to get on with economic activity is essential if economic regionalization is going to occur — either as a precursor to, or as a result of, regionalism.[30]

The financial crises that hit, to greater or lesser extents, East Asia, Russia and Latin America led many policy-makers as well as academics to rethink the legitimacy, validity and efficiency of the post-Washington consensus regime. The financial crises propelled renewed emphasis on the agency of state and enterprises in directing, managing, perhaps mitigating the impact of specific types of global economic activity that dominated the 1990s. As such, regions can be perceived as a mediating layer of governance between national and global economies.[31]

Despite the fact that the European regional project has been characterized by the evolution of a single European Union, Wallace argues that within the EU, there are different locations of governance and multiple layers and levels of integration.[32] Furthermore, many other new regionalism scholars also reject the necessary and inevitable spillover into an EU-style form of regional governance. At the lower level, much of the real integration existent between economies is not between economies of two or more nation states. Rather, it often occurs between sub-national entities across national boundaries. Thus, in the case of integration between parts of southern China and Hong Kong, it can be argued that parts of China are more integrated with external economies than they are with the domestic Chinese economy. At the higher level, the coexistence of different forms of regions at different levels has resulted in overlapping regional membership. For example, if APEC is conceived as a regional organization, then its wide geographic reach means that its member states are all simultaneously members of smaller, more discrete regional organizations.

China's re-engagement with the global economy has played a key role in configuring both the regional economy as a whole and the individual economies of regional states. Investment that once might have gone to Thailand, Indonesia or Malaysia is now largely centred in the cheaper production costs in China. Rather than producing exports for the rest of the world, many regional economies are increasingly dependent on selling components and materials to China. But at the same time, the Chinese economy is itself dependent on investment from and trade with the rest of the region (particularly in the form of components from the region to produce exports). The process of regionalization of production is thus based on a complex web of relationships built on a hierarchy of asymmetric dependencies. It is a process that is driven by the investment and trade decisions of enterprises, and the governmental policies put in place in regional states to facilitate private economic flows.

Crucially, this regionalization is contingent on what happens outside the region. A key issue for regional formation remains the pivotal role of extra-regional actors in promoting the regional economic interaction whereby regional initiatives are at least in part addressed. Without external demand, the formation of a region of production centred on manufacturing in China would have taken on a very different form and moved at a different pace. Furthermore, East Asian investment statistics demonstrate that the region remains heavily dependent on technology and financial capital from outside the region (and also from Japan).

Viewed from the "market positioning" argument, a country desirous of locating its production and exports in the fastest-growing markets has to move into technology-intensive activities and upgrade its technology structure. It can enter the assembly stage, but has to upgrade within the system at a later stage so as to move into manufacturing, design, development and regional service activities. However, export dynamism and success in technology-intensive exports are very highly concentrated, both by region and by country. According to Sanjaya Lall's study, East Asia now accounts for about 75 per cent of developing country total manufactured exports, and about 90 per cent of high-technology exports.[33] The drivers of technological success in export activity differ by country. In all countries except South Korea and Taiwan, high-technology exports are driven by transnational corporations (TNCs) relocating the final labour-intensive stages of production to low-wage countries. Such assembly operations have various beneficial learning and spill-over effects, but they do not — at least initially — need strong technological capabilities. The risk is that when the initial edge provided by low wages runs out, countries may not be able to move up the value chain ladder because they have not built their skills, information, technology and supplier base to the demanding levels needed.

As an illustration, let us look at the concentration of the revelant countries' manufactured exports. Figure 10.1 shows the nine leading developing Asian economies in manufactured exports in 1985 and 1998. These economies, together with Mexico, Brazil and India, account for about 90 per cent of developing country exports, and their dominance has been rising over time. Levels of concentration rise by technology levels, with the highest rise for technology-intensive products. Thus, liberalization and globalization are leading to *higher* rather than *lower* barriers to entry for new competitors in

FIGURE 10.1
Value of Manufactured Exports by Asian Developing Countries, 1985 and 1998
(In US$ million)

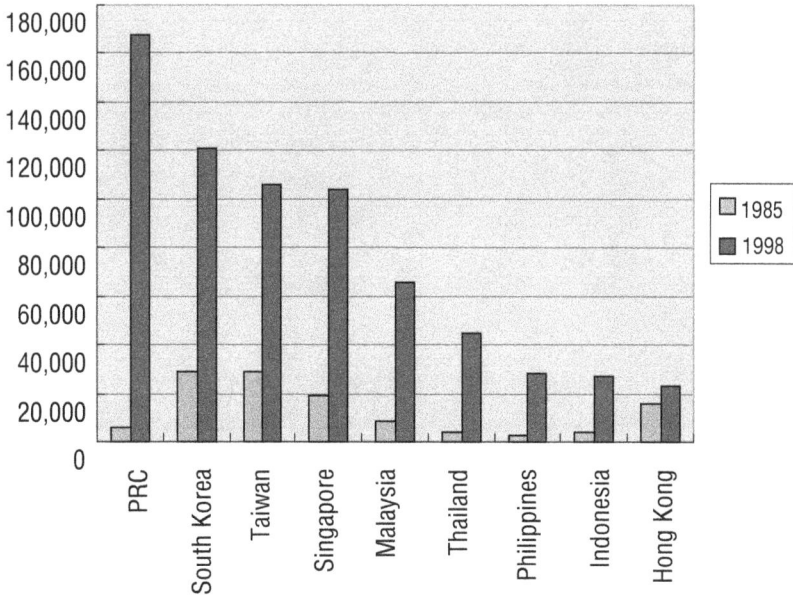

Source: Reproduced from Lall, "New Technologies, Competitiveness, and Poverty Reduction", Figure 5.4, p. 116.

advanced activities. This is consistent with the "old regionalism" fashion in which regional boundaries become narrower with increasing regionalization of investment and production.

On the other hand, there is also increasing regionalized trade in Asia. With rising regionalized production and integration, East Asian countries have gradually shifted an increasingly sizeable proportion of their exports towards other countries in the region rather than to European and North American markets. The intra-regional export ratios of Taiwan, South Korea and Singapore increased from 41.4 per cent in 1991 to 57.2 per cent in 2005. Japan's intra-regional export ratio also increased from 32.1 per cent to 46.8 per cent during the same period (see Table 10.3). This reflects a phenomenon characterized by Oman as "the ongoing development ... of post-Taylorist 'flexible' approaches to the organization of production within and between firms"[34] that had facilitated the ongoing de-territorialization of

TABLE 10.3
Intra-Regional Export Ratios of East Asian Countries
(Percentages)

	1986	1991	2000	2003	2005
East Asian countries	31.0	42.0	46.7	49.8	50.1
Taiwan, S. Korea and Singapore	29.7	41.1	49.3	52.7	57.2
ASEAN-4[a]	52.8	52.3	51.5	54.1	54.0
China and Hong Kong	45.0	54.8	48.5	48.2	45.8
Japan	22.7	32.1	39.9	46.0	46.8

Note: [a] Indonesia, Malaysia, the Philippines and Thailand.
Source: Ruey-Bin Hung, "Taiwan's Economic Development in Globalization", paper presented to the conference on "Japan and East Asia under Globalization", Taipei (November 3, 2007), p. 13.

production. There are growing regional projects and processes in developing Asian states to actively participate in the global economy, in particular the regional economy.[35] In terms of regionalism, this manifests the desire of those countries to access large markets, even adopting the quid pro quo step of gaining membership by introducing domestic economic liberalization.

In this regionalized trade regime, East Asian countries' exports are increasingly dependent on the markets of China and Hong Kong rather than the Japanese market. With the rising role of China in the East Asian industrial value chain, regional economies have seen their export dependence ratio on China increased to 21.9 per cent, while that on Japan declined to 8.9 per cent.[36] In Table 10.4, Taiwan, along with South Korea and Singapore, is shown to have increased its export ratio to China and Hong Kong more than five times in the past two decades. Nevertheless, despite increasing dependence on China and Hong Kong markets, there are higher export ratios to Japan for the ASEAN-4 countries. China's retention of a stable export ratio to Japan (somewhat declined in 2006) during that period is noteworthy. Until the mid-1990s, Japanese-controlled operations in ASEAN countries produced very little in the way of return flows of manufactured goods back to Japan. However, the progressive hollowing out of Japan's productive structure under the influence of industrial restructuring has tended to increase the role of ASEAN (and China) in serving the Japanese market.[37]

As may be seen in Figure 10.2, Taiwan is running increasingly large trade deficits with Japan. On the export side, Taiwan will be hard pressed to maintain past growth rates given the likely intensification of competition from overproduction of Japan, and even other Asian countries, which

TABLE 10.4
Export Dependencies of East Asian Countries on China/Hong Kong and Japan
(Percentages)

	Dependence ratios on China and Hong Kong				Dependence ratios on Japan			
	1986	1991	2000	2006	1986	1991	2000	2006
Taiwan, S. Korea and Singapore	6.8	11.3	17.8	28.2	12.3	12.9	10.4	7.0
Taiwan	7.3	16.3	24.0	39.8	11.4	12.1	11.2	7.3
Singapore	9.0	8.6	11.8	19.9	8.6	8.7	7.5	5.5
South Korea	4.9	8.0	17.0	27.2	15.6	17.2	11.9	8.2
ASEAN-4	4.5	5.8	7.7	13.3	28.3	22.9	16.1	13.8
Japan	8.1	7.9	12.0	19.9	—	—	—	—
China and Hong Kong	—	—	—	—	10.1	9.1	11.7	8.3

Source: Hung, "Taiwan's Economic Development under Globalization", p. 15.

FIGURE 10.2
Taiwan's Trade Balances with China/Hong Kong and Japan
(In US$ billion)

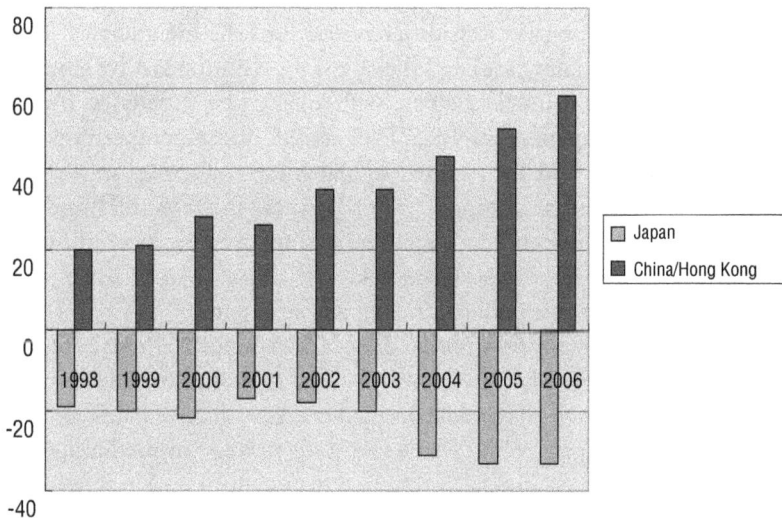

Source: Reproduced from Hung, "Taiwan's Economic Development under Globalization," p. 16.

proceeds among export powerhouses new and old. Insofar as Taiwanese capital is increasingly orienting itself towards other Asian markets by relocating production to them (partly in response to competitiveness pressures), this strategy could end up exacerbating overall trade-balance pressures. Indeed, overall trade-balance pressures may even be greater on the import side.

On the other hand, Taiwan is running larger and larger trade surpluses with China (and Hong Kong). This is inevitable given the increasing integration of Taiwanese and Chinese enterprises into hierarchical production and investment systems. This also allows enterprises of more advanced countries such as Japan to use their technological dominance to distract a certain share of the production output. In other words, there are larger volumes of intra-firm trade between Taiwanese home firms and their overseas affiliates in China. This then will be discussed in the concluding section.

CONCLUDING REMARKS

In this chapter, we have explored how Japan revived export and output growth in the pre-Plaza Accord period. We have also shown how the post-1985 wave of Japanese investment in the NIEs and ASEAN countries (and later in China) has created a regionalized production network. Due to industrial restructuring in Japan, its firms agreed to share new manufacturing processes and product designs with smaller firms in NIEs in exchange for a predetermined share of their output, they set the terms for maximum profit creation and its distribution among competing enterprises on different levels of the hierarchy.

The NIE capital later emulated their Japanese counterpart by employing FDI in other Asian countries, albeit with qualitative difference from the regionalization of Japanese capital. They faced direct competition from, and are conditioned and constrained by, Japanese enterprises in a regional production structure that is supportive of Japanese interests. NIE industries have not succeeded in technologically replicating Japanese innovations, and thus, have fallen into larger and larger trade deficits with Japan by importing a large proportion of components, machinery and parts.

East Asian regionalization initiated by Japan's industrial restructuring in the mid-1980s triggered responses from within as well as outside the region which the (old) regionalism scholars deemed necessary for the states concerned to play some facilitating roles. While the state strategy of mediating cross-border interactions stays crucial in the new regionalism era, it is now up to private enterprises to decide whether or how to respond, and where they are going to invest. Taiwan has been going through these two phases, as it is unable to escape the status of subordinated regionalization. Furthermore, along with other Asian economies, Taiwan is increasingly more dependent on the Chinese market for exports of goods, with the latter gradually becoming the centre of a regionalized production network. Viewed from Taiwan's large trade surpluses with China (and Hong Kong), it seems that we need to be more scrupulous about trade structures between the two sides.

There are no detailed studies on cross-Strait trade structures, especially on trade patterns related to overseas affiliates. From relevant studies on Japan, it appears that the large *cross-border* trade surpluses Japan is running with many countries belies the fact that it is actually in deficit in terms of *cross-national* trade. That is, if we exclude those transactions between domestic and overseas Japanese nationals, then Japan's exports to foreigners are, in many cases, less than its imports.[38] Thus, a large proportion of Japan's foreign trade, especially in manufactured goods, is engaged between Japan's home firms and its foreign affiliates as well as among those affiliates in different countries. As mentioned in the first section, relocation of investment by Japanese enterprises is not only oriented towards exports to the United States or Europe, but also for re-exporting Asian production back to Japan.

What is the extent to which cross-Strait trade is accounted for by intra-Taiwanese transactions? If it is large, as in the case of Japan, would Taiwan's export surpluses with China have some other implications than revealed in the statistical figures? If it is small and deviates from Japan's pattern, then we need to be more concerned with the possibility that East Asia may fall into the vicious circle of technology (non)progress than subordinate regionalization (see section 2). All in all, we really need to conduct more cautious and detailed analyses on cross-Strait trade patterns.

Notes

1. R. Steven, *Japan's New Imperialism* (Armonk, NY: M.E. Sharpe, 1990), p. 70.
2. Shigeto Tsuru, *Japan's Capitalism: Creative Defeat and Beyond* (New York: Cambridge University Press, 1994), pp. 197–98.
3. Steven, *Japan's New Imperialism*, p. 9.
4. Ibid., p. 14.
5. See, for example, Scott Callon, *Divided Sun: MITI and the Breakdown of Japanese High-tech Industrial Policy, 1975–1993* (Stanford: Stanford University Press, 1995).
6. Callon, *Divided Sun*.
7. James Fallows, *Looking at the Sun: The Rise of the New East Asian Economic and Political System* (New York: Vantage Books, 1994), p. 260.
8. R. Steven, *Japan and the New World Order: Global Investment, Trade, and Finance* (New York: St. Martin's Press, 1996), p. 73.

9. Kyoko Sheridan, "Japan's Direct Investment, Its Development Pattern and Future Direction", *Journal of Contemporary Asia* 25 (1995): 478.

10. Chia Siow Yue, "Foreign Direct Investment in ASEAN Economies", *Asian Development Review* 11 (1993): 82–83.

11. H. Hitoshi, "Investment in Asia", *AMPO Japan-Asia Quarterly Review* 24 (1993): 22; cited in Martin Hart-Landsberg and Paul Burkett, "Contradictions of Capitalist Industrialisation in East Asia: A Critique of 'Flying Geese' Theories of Development", *Economic Geography* 74 (April 1998): 94.

12. Hitoshi, "Investment in Asia", p. 24; cited in Hart-Landsberg and Burkett, "Contradictions of Capitalist Industrialisation in East Asia", p. 94.

13. Steven, *Japan and the New World Order*, p. 68.

14. Ibid.

15. Ibid., pp. 78–79.

16. Ibid., p. 194.

17. Walden Bello, *People & Power in the Pacific: The Struggle for the Post-Cold War Order* (London: TNI/Pluto Books, 1992), pp. 89–90.

18. L. Nakarmi, "Seoul Yanks the Chaebol's Leash: A Sudden Policy Shift Could Slow Investment Abroad", *Business Week* (30 October 1995): 58.

19. S. Cho, *The Dynamics of Korean Economic Development* (Washington, D.C.: Institute for International Economics 1994), pp. 164–70.

20. Hart-Landsberg and Burkett, "Contradictions of Capitalist Industrialisation in East Asia", pp. 97–98.

21. Mitchell Bernard and John Ravenhill, "Beyond Product Cycles and Flying Geese: Regionalization, Hierarchy, and the Industrialization of East Asia", *World Politics* 47 (January 1995): 198.

22. Alice H. Amsden, *Asia's Next Giant: South Korea and Late Industrialization* (New York: Oxford University Press, 1989); John Brohman, "Postwar Development in the Asian NICs: Does the Neoliberal Model Fit Reality?", *Economic Geography* 72 (April 1996): 107–30.

23. Fallows, *Looking at the Sun*, pp. 398–99.

24. For a good critique of this literature with an emphasis on the relationship between regionalism and globalization, see Allen J. Scott and Michael Storper, "Regions, Globalization, Development", *Regional Studies* 37 (2003): 579–93.

25. Björn Hettne, Andras Inotai and Osvaldo Sunkel, eds., *National Perspectives on the New Regionalism in the North* (Basingstoke: Macmillan, 2000); Björn Hettne, Andras Inotai and Osvaldo Sunkel, eds., *National Perspectives on the New Regionalism in the Third World* (Basingstoke: Macmillan, 2000); Björn Hettne, Andras Inotai and Osvaldo Sunkel, eds., *Comparing Regionalism: Implications for Global Development* (Basingstoke: Palgrave, 2001); Björn Hettne, Andras Inotai and Osvaldo Sunkel, eds., *Globalism and the New Regionalism* (New York: St. Martin's Press, 1999); and Björn Hettne, Andras Inotai and Osvaldo Sunkel, eds., *The New Regionalism and the Future of Security and Development* (Basingstoke: Palgrave, 2000).

26. Andrew Hurrell, "Explaining the Resurgence of Regionalism in World Politics", *Review of International Studies* 21 (1995): 332.

27. Ash Amin, "Regions Unbound: Towards a New Politics and Place", *Geografiska Annaler B* 86 (2004): 34; as cited in Shaun Breslin, "Theorising East Asian Regionalism(s)", in Melissa G. Curley and Nicholas Thomas, eds., *Advancing East Asian Regionalism* (London and New York: Routledge, 2007), p. 29.

28. Amin, "Regions Unbound", p. 31; cited in Breslin, "Theorising East Asian Regionalism(s)", p. 29.

29. German Bundestag Study Commission (Select Committee), *Globalisation of the World Economy — Challenges and Responses* (2001) <http://www.bundestag. de/gremien/welt/ welt_zwischenbericht/zwb003_vorw_einl_engl.pdf>.

30. Walter Mattli, *The Logic of Regional Integration: Europe and Beyond* (Cambridge: Cambridge University Press, 1999).

31. Helen Wallace, "Europeanisation and Globalisation: Complementary or Contradictory Trends?", in *New Regionalism in the Global Political Economy*, edited by Shaun Breslin et al. (London and New York: Routledge, 2002), p. 149.

32. Wallace, "Europeanisation and Globalisation", pp. 144–45.

33. Sanjaya Lall, "New Technologies, Competitiveness, and Poverty Reduction", in Christopher M. Edmonds, ed., *Reducing Poverty in Asia: Emerging Issues in Growth, Targeting, and Measurement* (Cheltenham, UK: Edward Elgar, 2003), pp. 114–15.

34. Charles Oman, "Globalization, Regionalization, and Inequality", in *Inequality, Globalization and World Politics*, edited by Andrew Hurrell and Ngaire Woods (Oxford: Oxford University Press, 1999), p. 36.

35. Paul Bowles, "ASEAN, AFTA and the 'New Regionalism'", *Pacific Affairs* 70 (1997): 225.

36. Ruey-Bin Hung, "Taiwan's Economic Development in Globalization", paper presented to the conference on "Japan and East Asia under Globalization", Taipei (3 November 2007), p. 14.

37. Steven, *Japan and the New World Order*, p. 193.

38. See, for example, Yao-Ting Jen and Chin-Ming Lin, *A Study on Trade in Services: An FATS Approach*, a project report to the Council on Economic Planning and Development (Taipei, 2007).

11

LANGUAGE POWER: RELATIONAL RHETORIC AND HISTORICAL TACITURNITY
A Study of Vietnam-China Relationship

Chan Yuk Wah

INTRODUCTION

This chapter examines Vietnamese strategies in maintaining a normal diplomatic relationship with China through the concept of "language power". This notion of "language power" comprises both relational rhetoric and taciturnity, and can be applied both on state and non-state levels. Most previous literature on Vietnam-China relationships focus on the themes of persistent Vietnamese resistance against Chinese dominance and the Vietnamese fighting spirit. This chapter argues that besides resistance, Vietnam is also adept in crafting diplomacy to pacify the ambition of its giant neighbour and maintain a relatively peaceful and harmonious relationship. Since the normalization of the China-Vietnam diplomatic relations in 1991, both Vietnam and China have undertaken a pragmatic interactive strategy with an eye to the economic benefits that stability and peace may bring. The language power analysed in this chapter demonstrates that such an effort enlisted by the Vietnamese particularly since 1999 has been part of the normalized diplomatic rituals in both official and civil spheres.

The chapter will firstly relate Vietnam to China in terms of its cultural and political relationships. It will dilate the arguments of the previous literature and point out that some of these views have been mistaken. In the second half of the chapter, the concept of "language power" will be elaborated. Part of this language power engages routinized intimacy and friendship rhetoric painstakingly displayed by state actors as well as laypeople. In contrast to the tactical display of the relational rhetoric in different social and political interactive spaces with the Chinese, the Vietnamese also employ the power of "silencing" on historical conflicts. Language power does not merely enlist the power of speeches, it also takes on the action of taciturnity. Silence can be power.

To illustrate this analytical space, I rely heavily on the border as both a geo-historical and metaphoric plane to explore the theme of "language power". The "border" as a conceptual and geographical space has generated lots of conflicts as well as intimacy between China and Vietnam. It is a metaphoric space for imagining the cultural and power politics involved in Vietnam-China interactions which seek to bring about the maintenance of a harmonious relationship. On the one hand, the Vietnamese have refrained from mentioning the 1979 border war and removed exhibits of border conflicts. On the other hand, there has been enormous ritualistic display of an intimate border/neighbourly relationship. The interplay of amplified "relational rhetoric" and "historical taciturnity" has become a major Vietnamese interactive strategy in both diplomatic and social spheres for maintaining the status quo of normalcy.

VIETNAM'S CULTURAL RELATIONSHIP TO CHINA

One persistent theme in the Vietnamese historical and cultural studies is Vietnam's deep entanglement in terms of Vietnamese historical and cultural identity with China. Not only is this due to the fact that Vietnam had been under Chinese rule for more than ten centuries (from 111 B.C. to 939 A.D.), it is also related to different Vietnamese dynastic regimes which were keen to borrow and adapt China's statecraft, Confucianism, familial structure and values as well as Chinese language and literature. A highly sinicized culture has always made Vietnam fall into an ambiguous position of being half-way Southeast Asia and half-way East Asia. As Woodside (1971, p. 1) has pointed out, "One of the arts of Vietnamese studies lies in being able to artificially disentangle the Chinese or Sino-Vietnamese characteristics of Vietnamese history and society from the Southeast Asian characteristics". However, the discussions on distinguishing Vietnamese "Chinese" and "Southeast Asian" cultural attributes have been problematic, since such discussions assume a distinct Southeast Asian culture and a distinct Chinese culture. What is Southeast Asia after all? Is there really "a" Chinese culture?

Emmerson (1984) has elaborated on the constructed notion of the term "Southeast Asia". Rather than representing a unified and homogeneous entity, Emmerson argues that the term should be seen as a product of a constructive process through diplomatic policies, historical events and world politics. Like Emmerson, Watson (1997) also queries the notion of a unified Southeast Asia. Reynolds (1995) contends that the origin of the interest of contemporary Western historiography in searching for a distinct "Southeast Asia" is a Western post-colonial project motivated by the intention to authenticate Southeast Asia as a region and a field of study.

Scholars arguing against China's chauvinistic cultural hegemony over Vietnam have often opted for a notion of an indigenous Southeast Asian base for Vietnamese culture, creating a non-sinitic part of the Vietnamese culture. Such an attempt runs parallel to the state-sponsored Vietnamese nationalistic discourse. For example, the discovery of a four-thousand-year-old Dong Son culture has been promoted by the Vietnamese state as a base for Vietnam's indigenous origin. Scholars have pooled their efforts to single out bits of historical and cultural elements in Vietnam that are not very "Chinese" to represent its Southeast Asian identity. These elements generally include a higher status of women (O'Harrow 1995), the local creation of *nom* words and *nom* literature (Nguyen Dinh Hoa 1987),[1] and hybrid cultural elements drawn from the Chams and the Khmers (Wolters 1999, p. 22).

Indeed, the efforts in bestowing Vietnam with a distinctive local culture different from China inevitably assumes a counter object — a static and unified Chinese culture. As Evans (2002) argues in an article summarizing the theoretical development in the study of Southeast Asia, including Vietnam, in light of the many findings of regional cultural diversity of peoples, cultural interaction and borrowing within the Chinese empire itself, "the counter-position of a hybrid Vietnam to an allegedly pure 'China' becomes less and less convincing" (2002, p. 154). Refraining from using cultural models, Evans concludes that cultural region is still a useful concept for making comparative studies and Vietnam belongs to the East Asian (rather than Southeast Asian) cultural region.

A number of historians and anthropologists have taken note of the internal development of Chinese culture as a fluid and diversifying process (see Watson and Rawski 1988; also see Faure 1996). Different regions (peripheral regions in particular) within China proper, like Vietnam, had undergone different periods of sinicization. Some of these acculturation processes happened even much later than the Vietnamese one. As Woodside (1971, p. 7) has pointed out, "Vietnamese people were sinicized centuries before Chinese culture had even been definitely consolidated in areas that are today considered part of

China proper." David Faure (1996) has written about the acculturation of the Cantonese people. He suggests that not until the Ming dynasty did the Cantonese lineage families begin to acculturate themselves into the larger Confucian cultural system of imperial China. FitzGerald (1972) has compared the cases of Yunnan and Vietnam:

> The kings of Nanchao sought to increase their power by seizing parts of the empire; the kings of Vietnam turned on their non-Vietnamese neighbors to the south and despoiled them of their possessions. The result of the Nanchao policy was ultimately to undermine the distinct character of the state as a non-Chinese country, and prepare the way for full Chinese authority; the result of Vietnamese policy was to advance the frontiers of Vietnam, bringing Chinese culture as the advance proceeded, and to create a situation where the Vietnamese people gained a national identity which made further Chinese intrusion improbable, rare, and finally wholly discontinued. Cultural penetration therefore produced opposite political results in two countries. (1972, p. 213)

The case of Vietnam's sinicization has made essentialist cultural and identity arguments intriguingly problematic. If one were to argue for Vietnam's distinct identity by stressing its cultural differences with China, one is blind to the giant web of China's cultural diversity. Scholarly representation of Vietnam's Southeast Asian features may mirror some local traditions of the peripheral regions of China, such as a gender tradition in Guangdong area which distinctly diverged from the Confucian ideal (see Evans 2002). FitzGerald's comparison of Yunnan and Vietnam also puts forth an interesting issue. Vietnam has been sinicized much deeper and earlier than Yunnan, but it had never willingly accepted a Chinese identity and had maintained its own distinct Vietnamese identity. On the contrary, the Yunnanese, being less learned and cultured within the Chinese cultural world, became totally assimilated, to the extent that they would not accept that they were not fully Chinese (FitzGerald 1972, p. 213).

One impression I had during the time when I studied the Vietnamese language in a Southeast Asian language institute was that the many examples used by the teacher to assert the indigenous nature of the Vietnamese language vis-à-vis the Chinese influences on the language are based on an assumption of a "unified" Chinese language. The Vietnamese teacher distinguished Vietnamese words into two categories: the Sino-Vietnamese (*Han-Viet*) and Vietnamese (*Viet*). Words that sounded like Mandarin (*Putonghua*) are classified *Han-Viet*, while the remaining are Vietnamese. However, a number of these supposed indigenous words actually sound like Cantonese or Teochiu[2] dialect to me.

When I made this suggestion to the teacher, he was obviously disturbed. He believed that Mandarin represents the Chinese linguistics. But he was now told there are still many other varieties of the Chinese linguistics. To attenuate his uneasiness and weariness, I uttered out of a thrust of involuntary wit, "Who says Cantonese is Chinese?" Such a casual comment made an impression on me too. When did Cantonese become Chinese? Should Cantonese (*Yueh*) be part of the larger Vietnamese language family or should Vietnamese be part of the *Yueh* language family? These questions about language boundaries can be applied to culture. Did Cantonese and Vietnamese culture both belong to a larger *Yueh* culture, which had already been there before a clear concept of Chinese culture came into existence?

Reaching this point, there is no easy way to answer the question what "a" Chinese culture is and how far Vietnamese culture falls into the orbit of Chinese culture. A shrewder way to compare Vietnamese culture and Chinese culture is to downsize China into distinct regional and dialectic culture (such as Cantonese) so that we know what we are comparing.

VIETNAM'S POLITICAL RELATIONSHIP TO CHINA

Previous literature on Sino-Vietnamese relations has mostly stressed Vietnam's resistance against Chinese political dominance. As SarDesai (1989, p. 33) noted, "One of the most persistent themes throughout Vietnamese history is the existence of a love-hate relationship between China and Vietnam. While the Chinese culture was appreciated, admired, and adopted, Chinese political domination was despised, dreaded, and rejected." David Marr (1971, p. 9) also remarks, there has been "the subtle interplay of resistance and dependence which appeared often to stand at the root of historical Vietnamese attitudes toward the Chinese". Joseph Buttinger (1968) has also elaborated on the same theme:

> The more they [Vietnamese] absorbed of the skills, customs, and ideas of the Chinese, the smaller grew the likelihood of their ever becoming part of the Chinese people. In fact, it was during the centuries of intensive efforts to turn them into Chinese that the Vietnamese came into their own as a separate people with political and cultural aspects of their own. (1968, p. 29)

From the 1980s to the 1990s, the thesis of Vietnamese historical struggles and resistance against Chinese domination has been emphasized and reemphasized. This academic focus in fact runs parallel to Vietnam's official effort in building nationalistic consciousness of independence. The discourse on the

Vietnamese resistant spirit against external threats was particularly glorified in the historical writings of post-war Vietnam. As elaborated by Pelley (1995), "The 1950s and 1960s have witnessed official histories cultivating among the Vietnamese an understanding of the national past that revolved around the central thematic of resistance to foreign aggression" (1995, p. 233). In order to rescue Vietnam from China's shadow, scholars of Vietnamese studies have also helped reiterate such a theme.

The unified efforts of scholars and the Vietnamese state in conceptualizing Vietnamese history as a process of continuous struggles against foreign threats and invasion are summarized under themes as "spirit of resistance". These "themes" are tantamount to infusing mythical ordination to the Vietnamese national spirit, erecting a coherent Vietnamese past and historical identity. In the mid-1990s, some historians reflected such official manipulation as well as academic appropriation of historical discourses. A number of historical texts have also been restructured to serve the state's ideological needs. Such awareness was accompanied by reflection on scholarly obsession in championing Vietnamese historical identity and continuity, which has worked in line with the Vietnamese nationalistic sentiment in constructing a coherent Vietnamese past (Taylor and Whitemore 1995).

Taylor, once joined the effort in building the theme of Vietnamese independence consciousness, has come to reflect on the selective use of historical materials, "texts do not particularly lead to the 'past'... but possibilities for many pasts... these pasts mirror our desires to understand in particular ways" (Taylor 1995, p. 5). In order to move away from the stranglehold of Vietnam's nationalistic discourses, historians, Taylor and others pressed for a multiple interpretation of the Vietnamese pasts. Taylor himself has pledged for more historical discontinuity with the concept of "surface orientations". It understands history and culture as discontinuous contingencies rather than as unified and continuous patterns and models. Allowing "the surfaces of times and places" in history to emerge is to enable history itself to negotiate between discourses formulated by different historical agents. Surface orientation stresses the importance of the choices made by different historical actors at different historical planes of space and times, which in turn significantly influence the course of historical development. By emphasizing "surface orientations", Taylor opposes the making of historical models. Referring particularly to the Sino-Vietnamese relationship, he stresses that there is no such a thing as "a single definable model of engagement; dynasties and governments have through time entertained a succession of relationships that cover the full spectrum between war and amity" (1998, p. 971). He summarizes his argument thus:

If we can clear our minds of "Vietnamese" as the object of our knowledge and instead look carefully at what the peoples we call Vietnamese were doing at particular times and places, then we begin to see that beneath the veneers of shared fields of sounds and marks, or of however one may refer to mutually intelligible languages and writings, lay quite different kinds of peoples whose views of themselves and of others was significantly grounded in the particular times and terrains where they dwelled and in the material and cultural exchanges available in those times and terrains. If we speak of these peoples as oriented toward the surfaces of their times and places rather than as oriented toward an imagined unifying depth, we will shift the effects of our ideological intent upon the archive away from the figurations both of univocal national narratives and of multivocal regional narratives contextualized by the nation. (1998, p. 949)

In a recent publication, Brantly Womack (2006) suggests using an "asymmetric model" to analyse Sino-Vietnamese relationship. Although it appears as a single model, such "asymmetry" is a multifaceted one. By delving deep into Vietnam-China political history, Womack (2006) captures the Sino-Vietnamese interactions with a spectrum of "structural asymmetries" through different historical periods. He argues that while the relationship has always been asymmetric, with China being the dominant one and Vietnam the weaker, it does not necessarily lead to a breakdown of relations, nor is Vietnam always more vulnerable. According to Womack, an effort is needed to maintain the normalcy of such asymmetrical imbalance. Rather than focus on conflicts and hostility, he asks how equilibrium can be achieved. Many asymmetric international relations have been able to maintain equilibrium despite the existence of tensions and differences of interests. In the case of China-Vietnam interactions, the key issue for the players is how to manage the imbalanced power dynamics in such a way that a "normalized asymmetry" can be maintained. To manage normalcy, Womack suggests that routinized diplomatic rituals and historically produced commonsense and expectations are both important (2006, pp. 90–91). I will use Womack's asymmetric model to further analyse the concept of "language power" and show how this power has actually assisted Vietnam in managing the process of normalcy.

LANGUAGE POWER: THE POWER OF RHETORIC AND SILENCE

There is no denying that Vietnam is one of the world's most experienced nations in fighting Chinese dominance. However, it is also a nation with the most experience in taming China's ambition, and tackling complex relations with China. Besides times of wars and conflicts, Vietnam has been practising a relatively peaceful relationship with China throughout history. After its independence from China in the tenth century, it constantly kept tributary and advice-seeking relationships with China to pacify China for gaining economic benefits. Vietnam's skilled strategies and flexibility in patching up with China's desire as a huge and masterly neighbour are, however, not sufficiently examined.

Since its reparation of diplomacy with China in 1991, Vietnam has been working on a "language power" to sustain good neighbourly relations. Such power was constructed both of relational rhetoric and taciturnity. Not only has Vietnam been keen to build and sustain packages of intimacy rhetoric, it has also striven to keep silent on the border conflict in 1979 and all sorts of historical military struggles in general. Voiceless is not always powerless. The power of language lies not merely in speeches, but also in silence. A tactful use of silence has often brought practical political results in the studies of political rhetoric. In the case of Vietnam, the interplay of the amplified friendship rhetoric and controlled silence on historical conflicts has tactfully highlighted historical familiarity and at the same time downplayed historical tension. Language power as such has so far been successful in maintaining diplomatic normalcy with China.

POWER OF RHETORIC: FRIENDSHIP AND INTIMACY RHETORIC

On 10 November 1991, China and Vietnam announced together the official normalization of the bilateral relationship and asserted that "normalized relations between the two countries suits the basic and long term interests of the people of the two sides and will contribute to peace, stability and development of the region" (quoted from Nguyen 2001, p. 115). Since then, the two governments have conducted frequent official exchange visits in which state and party leaders are able to become more familiar with each other. These visits have also produced a number of joint communiqués and declarations (in 1992, 1993, 1994, 1995, 1999, 2000, 2001, 2004 and 2005) (Do 2006). The summit meeting in 1999 declared the significant "sixteen-word guideline", setting the basic tone for orienting future Sino-Vietnamese relationships. The guideline includes four basic principles: "comprehensive cooperation, long-term stability, friendly and harmonious neighbourliness, and future-oriented vision" (Do 2006, p. 131). The two nations issued a joint declaration and communiqué in 2000 and 2004 respectively, both of which stressed again the spirit of the sixteen-word guideline.

Peace, stability, friendship and cooperation are the catchwords in the guideline. The former two are the objectives and the latter two are strategies. These catchwords have become ingredients for the Vietnamese to cook up a package of relational rhetoric emphasizing friendship and intimacy. The friendship and intimacy rhetoric has come to frame the ongoing interactions between the Vietnamese and Chinese on both the state and civil levels.

There are also numerous semi-official and unofficial exchanges between the Vietnamese and Chinese peoples. Mutual visits organized by social and cultural units, mass organizations, enterprises, academic, educational and media institutes have marked a friendly, interactive and mutually benefiting era. An official of the Chinese Consulate in Vietnam once told me that the Embassy has been confronted with countless requests of visits to China each year since the normalization, and it has been really hard for the Embassy staff to cater to all the requests. While I was in Vietnam doing my field research, I participated in a number of academic seminars and business fairs between Chinese and Vietnamese. Almost all of the speeches I heard from the Vietnamese presenters, including state officials, scholars, and students, began with similar friendship rhetorical magic lines:

> "China and Vietnam are neighbourly nations with traditional friendly relations with a thousand-year-old history."
> "The two countries are linked together like mountains linking mountains, rivers joining rivers."
> "We are related to each other with generations of friendship, cooperation, and harmonious neighbourly relationship."

Similar rhetoric was practised by traders and businesspeople. I observed Vietnamese and Chinese businessmen toasting each other without saying anything substantial, but reminding each other of their intimate relation with simple words like "good friends" and "intimate friends". Between Vietnamese tour guides and Chinese tourists, the use of friendship and intimacy rhetoric, such as "mountains linking mountains, rivers joining rivers" and good brotherhood is also commonplace. Upon being challenged by his Chinese guests why there was war between the good friends, one tour guide said out of his intuitive rhetorical wit, "It is not fighting, but quarrelling. Brothers sometimes quarrel, it's common." The relational rhetoric had immediately turned an international war into a familial issue. Though it sounds euphemistic, he did succeed in calming the negative emotions of the Chinese guests, bringing a potentially destructive debate back to the track of discursive intimacy.

In January 2008, after a series of relational hurdles stirred up by China's unilateral action around the Spratly Islands and the subsequent protests of the Vietnamese people, the Vietnamese Deputy Foreign Minister, Vu Dung during a visit to Beijing announced that the Steering Committee for Vietnam-China Bilateral Cooperation had worked on the problem and both sides had agreed not to further provoke the situation. In his speech, Vu Dung repeated most of the relational rhetorical catchwords; the word "friendship" appeared four times while "cooperation" appeared more than ten times. He reiterated the following objectives with the strategic rhetorical catchwords:

> Maintaining and further strengthening the friendship and comprehensive cooperation between the two Parties and the two countries are of essential benefits for both Vietnam and China and it is also in line with the trend of peace, stability and cooperation for mutual development in the region and the world.

Although both China and Vietnam have stressed friendship rhetoric, both Vietnamese state and non-state actors are much more attentive to using such rhetoric. Womack (2006) has made note of the politics of over-attention paid by the less powerful side within an asymmetry. As the weaker one within such a relationship, Vietnam's leaders and lay people during their interactions with the Chinese have to make more efforts in crafting ritualistic rhetoric for pacifying China. They are also more sensitive and nervous about any reactions of China (2006, pp. 82–83).

By sealing the interactions with the familiar rhetorical "magic" lines, the Vietnamese are particularly consistent in practising the "language power" in public, semi-public and private speeches. Such rhetorical formality, whether in the public or private space, has become part of everyday ritual (Goffman 1959) and is like a talisman used to lubricate the magical space of the Vietnamese-Chinese interaction and cast off tension.

In the following, I will turn to the "border" to illustrate how Vietnam has strategized on "silence" for keeping a normal relationship. The border is taken as a geo-historical as well as metaphoric plane to illustrate how the Vietnam-China relationship has swung from extreme intimacy to extreme hostility. Border issues often get on China's and Vietnam's nerves, and border tensions often require diplomatic negotiations. When negotiations fail, military actions may break out.

THE TROUBLED BORDER

Borderline Demarcation

Demarcation of frontiers was a sign of modern statecraft which emphasizes a clearly marked national territorial boundary. The physical frontier line between

Vietnam and China had never been clearly marked before the late nineteenth century. It was only after the 1884–85 Sino-French War and the signing of the Sino-French Treaty that China agreed to demarcate the Sino-Vietnam borderline. Demarcation negotiations were extended from July 1886 to June 1897 and lasted a total of twelve years (HZRZ 1997, p. 19).

Before the formal demarcation of the frontier, land administration at many places at the border areas was left to local chieftains (*tusi* in Chinese) who were the indigenous leaders of those places (HZRZ 1997, p. 23). Through negotiations, the Chinese and the French established many border steles which were used to mark the whereabouts of the frontier. By imagining a line linking these steles, an imaginary borderline was thus drawn. However, in reality, many places along the imagined borderline are part of the land without any lines or borders.

From 1885 to 1987, there were three committees negotiating the demarcation of the Sino-Viet borderline. The three committees were responsible for the three parts of the border areas: Guangdong-Vietnam, Guangxi-Vietnam and Yunnan-Vietnam. In 1893, the Guangdong-Vietnam Border Agreement was signed, and a total of thirty-three border steles were established. In 1894, the Guangxi-Vietnam Border Agreement was signed, and 207 steles were established. In 1896, the Yunnan-Vietnam Border Agreement was signed, and sixty-five steles were established (Huang, Xiao and Yang 1988, pp. 469–588). The construction of these steles was supposed to end disputes at the troubled border. In reality, they became sources of further troubles. Along the 2,000-kilometres-long borderline, there were rivers, mountains, villages, forests, and deserted lands.

As quoted in Huang, Xiao and Yang (1988), the French and Chinese agreed to set up border steles at strategic places.

> Steles established at rivers and gullies between two countries should be constructed at sites where people pass by, or at villages, or at important sites, or at river banks. At deserted places, the steles should be constructed at sites where they can be easily found.... one side of the stele should be written *daqing*,[3] while the other side Vietnam. (Huang, Xiao and Yang 1988, p. 473)

However, from one border stele to the other, there were still many spaces of interstices where many disputes occurred. Instead of eliminating fights over land administration, the demarcation had in fact created more territorial conflicts and power struggles. The demarcation arbitrarily divided many natural villages of the same ethnic groups into two parts (Zhang 1999; Fan 2000). One part was assigned to China and the other half to Vietnam.

Moreover, the exact position of the steles had been a constant source of disputes over the years. I cite some of the land dispute examples as follows (HZRZ 1997, pp. 23–24).

Xiaosanmeng land struggle:
Before the demarcation, this piece of land belonged to China's *Linan fu*, and was administered by the designated *tusi*. After China agreed to put it under French administration, the *tusi* would like to continue to collect tax from the twenty villages within the region. Between 1910–45, there were territorial disputes every year between the *tusi* and the French. Among these disputes, five were armed struggles.

Qincai land struggle:
This was a piece of land inhabited by two villages of the Miao people. In 1924, some Miao people on the China side went to cut trees in the nearby forest, but were prohibited by the Vietnamese who claimed that the trees were within the Vietnamese territory. In 1940, the same thing happened, eight Chinese men were arrested. In 1949, the French army ransacked one of the Miao villages, and claimed that the village was under French administration. The French refused to compensate the villagers. In 1971, this piece of land continued to create disputes. The Vietnamese authority claimed that the whole piece of land should belong to Vietnam and started to register all the villagers. From 1976 to 1977, China and Vietnam negotiated over the identity of this piece of land forty-two times.

From the aforementioned incidences, one can take a glimpse at the nature of land disputes and struggles. Border demarcation and landmark planting was supposed to help solve disputes. But in reality, it had created new sources of power struggles between more political actors. At some points, the steles actually became a source of conflict, especially when the diplomatic relationship between China and Vietnam turned bad. I was told by a renowned Chinese scholar, a specialist on Vietnam, that both Vietnamese and Chinese border police were very sensitive about the exact positions of the border landmarks. When one side "discovered" that the border stele was pushed inward into one's territory, the border police would take no delay in moving it back to the "right" position.

The problem of land border demarcation has lingered till today. In July 2007, the two countries' leadership met to reaffirm the progress of the borderline demarcation. After a number of negotiations, Vietnam and China are currently making efforts to speed up the process of establishing landmarks along the borderline. Such negotiations necessitated the use of the "language power" again to overcome differences. In January 2008, leaders of both sides vowed to accomplish the process by the end of the year.

The Border War

During the first half of the twentieth century, the revolutionary leadership of Vietnam and China were simultaneously consolidating their own national strength for fighting against foreign invasions, colonialism and imperialism. Fraternity and comradeship flourished among the new socialist leadership of the two countries and created unprecedented solidarity and intimacy between China and Vietnam. After the Republic of China was established, China and Vietnam formally established diplomatic relations in 1950, and promised not to interfere in each other's internal affairs and respect each other's territorial integrity.

Ho Chi Minh, Vietnam's most revered leader in the revolution, once described this period in the China-Vietnam relationship as one of "comradeship and brotherhood". From the 1950s to 1975, before the relationship between China and Vietnam formally deteriorated, there were many mutual visits between central leaders as well as provincial and county officials. In the borderlands, mutual visits were especially popular. There were forty-four visits and celebrations between the local authorities of Honghezhou of Yunnan and Lao Cai province of Vietnam from 1957 to 1975 (HZRZ 1997, p. 17). As recorded by the Honghezhou Gazette, "There was a long solidified period in which China and Vietnam cooperated with each other. They enjoyed happiness and bitterness together. They supported and encouraged each other. The relationship was very close. The Sino-Vietnam border is a peaceful and friendly border. Both the people and the officials had enjoyed intensive interaction" (HZRZ 1997, p. 17).

A "peaceful and friendly border" could, however, easily turn hostile. The souring of the Sino-Vietnam relationship in fact started in the late 1960s and the early 1970s. In the first place, China and Vietnam had both suspected and accused each other of trying to establish hegemony in Indo-China. Diplomatic and ideological clashes between China and the Soviet Union had also led to a disruption of solidarity within the socialist bloc. All diplomatic moves of the Soviet Union within the region would bring about China's suspicion. In 1969, China made an attempt to repair diplomacy with the United States, which finally led to Nixon's visit to China in 1972. During the Vietnam-American War, China continued to provide Vietnam with military and material assistance to fight against the Americans. In so doing, Beijing's diplomatic policy of reconciling with the United States upset Vietnam who also began to lean towards the Soviet Union. Vietnam's military action in Cambodia in December 1978 made clear to China that Vietnam, backed by the USSR, had an expansion ambition in the region.

Besides the above conflicts, China also blamed Vietnam for purging the ethnic Chinese in Vietnam. In 1978, it was estimated that there were 1.2 million ethnic Chinese in Vietnam, 200,000 of whom lived in the north (Chen 1992, p. 141). The treatment that the ethnic Chinese in Vietnam received often acted as "an important barometer of the nationalist psychologies" (Woodside 1979, p. 389), which work behind the scenes of China and Vietnam relationships. In times of difficult relations, this also served to polarize Sino-Vietnamese antagonism. Towards the end of the Vietnam War, Vietnam-China relationship continued to deterioriate, while the ethnic Chinese in Vietnam also felt the pressure.

The ethnic Chinese in the borderlands were often the immediate victims bearing the brunt of Vietnam-China conflicts. The Chinese in the borderland began to flee in 1977. From 1977 to 1979, it was reported that 45,750 people were forced out of Vietnam and escaped to Hekou and Ginping.[4] Beijing had accused Vietnam of running a policy of "purifying the border areas by expelling the Chinese settlers in the border provinces" (Chen 1992, p. 142). Chinese sources (XHSJZ 1978, p. 112) estimated that by July 1978, 160,000 Chinese refugees had crossed the Sino-Vietnam border into China. Beijing withdrew from Vietnam its aid projects and technical personnel (Chen 1992, p. 141). In March 1978, Hanoi launched an anti-capitalist campaign in the country. The new policy was supposed to clear out all capitalist elements in the country and to apply to all people, regardless of nationality. However, it was felt that in reality the policy was directed towards the Chinese communities, particularly the wealthy Chinese in Ho Chi Minh City who controlled a large part of the commercial capital and activities (Chen 1992, p. 141). Some of these Chinese "capitalists" were sent to the new economic zones in remote areas. Such a policy threatened many ethnic Chinese, and subsequently led to a mass exodus from the south.

In antagonistic diplomatic relations, the border became a hot spot for further conflicts. The oppression against the ethnic Chinese was not the only source of hostility in the borderlands. As noted above, there had often been territorial disputes along the borderline, which, in times of difficult relations, would contribute to immense distrust and disrespect. In 1973, 179 armed clashes took place along the Sino-Vietnamese border and in 1974, there were 121 clashes. Each side accused the other of provoking such border skirmishes (Qiang 2000, p. 210). On 18 March 1975, Beijing suggested that the two countries should negotiate to settle the issue. But Hanoi, being preoccupied with the liberation war in the south, replied that the local authorities on the two sides were responsible for resolving the problem (Qiang 2000, p. 210). On 25 August 1978, an incident occurred at the Friendship Pass at the Guangxi-Lang Son borderlands. Hanoi maintained that Chinese soldiers entered Vietnam territory and attacked Vietnamese border officials, while Beijing alleged that 200 Vietnamese soldiers herded 2,000 Chinese refugees across the border and had killed four Chinese citizens and attacked Chinese officers with stones. Besides land disputes in the borderland areas, China was also upset about Vietnam's occupation of some islands in the South China Sea in 1975 and asserted that the Spratly Islands (Nansha) belonged to China (Chen 1992, p. 130). Territorial and border disputes and accusations did not end until both sides dragged each other to the brink of war (Ross 1988, p. 203). As Chen Min (1992) describes:

> By mid-1978, both China and Vietnam had embarked on a military buildup along the common border… China was building up its military forces along its border in Guangxi and Guangdong provinces, where military strength was estimated at over 150,000 with an unknown number of lightly armed frontier guards… Vietnam had begun preparing for war with China in the mid-1970s… build fortresses and defense works against the perceived possible Chinese invasion. The Vietnamese had reportedly installed barbed-wires fences, land mines, trenches, and anti-aircraft machine guns along the border. (1992, p. 144)

Vietnam began to receive Soviet military equipment, such as military ships, aircrafts, and munitions in the later half of 1978. In November and December 1978, China started to reiterate the reasons for war. Proclamations were made in the *People's Daily* to warn Vietnam not to make further border provocations, which clearly served the "Soviet big-power hegemonism in Southeast Asia and Vietnamese regional hegemonism in Indochina" (Ross 1988, p. 205). China claimed that it had reached the limit of its forbearance and would act with force if Vietnam kept on stretching its hands into the Chinese territory (Ross 1988, p. 205). All such rhetorical discourses served as warnings for the course of war which "was only a defensive, limited, and brief operation to retaliate against Vietnamese-instigated incidents along the Chinese border" (Chen 1992, p. 153).

On 17 February 1979, China's border army marched into Vietnam's northern territory. The war lasted for around two weeks and the war casualties were estimated to be around 50,000 killed and wounded for Vietnam and 20,000 for China (*New York Times*, 3 May 1979, quoted in Chen 1988, p. 171).[5] Acting in a "big-brother" manner, China's self-professed reason for going to war was "to teach Vietnam a lesson"; Vietnam was treated like a misbehaving younger brother. After the war, the border was slammed shut and the diplomatic relationship was abruptly cut off for more than a decade. The border war crystallized both the contemporary power struggle and the ancient mistrust between the two nations. Though short, it has cast long memories and created immense unease in the Sino-Vietnam relationship.

POWER OF SILENCE: AIRBRUSHING THE UNTOUCHABLE HISTORY

During the war, the two sides had fiercely accused each other of starting the war. In Vietnam, the media (BHLS 1979) described the Chinese instigators of the war as "the Chinese reactionary group" (*bon phan dong Trung Quoc*) and cartoons in the newspapers sarcastically accused China of being both an invader and a hypocrite. However, both sides talked very little about the war after it lapsed. Once the fighting was over, Vietnam turned its focus to rebuilding the economy. Rarely was the war mentioned again. China's official interpretation of the border war is a "self-protection retaliation attack". To Vietnam, however, it is an invasion like many of those incidents involving Chinese military incursion into Vietnamese territory. Neither side will agree with the other on their views of this conflict. Therefore, silence prevails. A prominent historian in Hanoi told me that it was hard to talk about this particular episode in Vietnam-China history, since there was no politically correct tone to describe the related events without provoking uneasy feelings from both sides. Thus, in his book on the contemporary Chinese history and Vietnam-China relationship, the border war episode has been omitted. "If I write about the war, no publisher would be willing to publish the book", he said. Indeed, any miscalculated comment or wording may plunge a writer into controversy and bring unpleasant political consequences, including protests from China.

Instead of using words like "war", the 1979 fighting and the border shutdown aftermath is officially marked by both sides as "a period of abnormal Victnam-China relations". Chinese writings about Vietnam have also avoided this period (Wang and Liu 1992; Yu and Zhang 1998). In Vietnam, this episode is carefully crafted. In the book *Vietnam Diplomatic Relationship 1945–2000* published by the Vietnamese National Political Publishers in 2002, the period from the late 1970s to the 1980s is summarized in the section titled "Abnormal Vietnam-China Relationship: Vietnam has insisted in reviving friendship and good neighbourly relationship with China" (NXBCT 2002, p. 310). The first paragraph says, "Vietnam and China are two countries connected by land

and sea. The people of Vietnam and the people of China are related to each other in traditional long-term friendship and have united in supporting each other in their revolutionary struggles. There are many similarities between the two countries" (NXBCT 2002, p. 310). In the few paragraphs that follow, the narrative rests heavily upon the effort that Vietnam had made to bring about solutions to the differences between the two countries. The war is, however, described in three lines:

> On 17 February 1979, China sent a troop of 600,000 to attack Vietnam's territory in the northern provinces of Vietnam. On 1 March 1979, China suggested to hold negotiations of prime ministerial level to restore peace and security at the border and to solve territorial disputes. On 14 March 1979, China withdrew its army from Vietnam. (NXBCT 2002, p. 311)

The three-volume history textbooks published by the Education Publishers in 2006 have included a brief account of the 1979 border war in the second to last chapter of the third volume. The war is mentioned in relation to Vietnam's military action in Cambodia. It begins like this:

> The action of fighting against Vietnam of the Pol Pot group had been supported by America and some other countries. China is Vietnam's intimate neighbour. In the process of our revolutionary struggles, the people of the two countries had developed very intimate relations, solidarity and mutual support. But during the period when the gang of Pol Pot fought against Vietnam, a few people within China's leadership had supported Pol Pot. There were even actions that hurt the feelings of the people of the two countries. For example, China had instigated incursions at the northern border of Vietnam, cut its assistance to Vietnam, repatriated its experts and made United Nations and some other countries do the same thing. All these created immediate difficulties for Vietnam. More seriously, starting from 17 February, China sent thirty-two armies, 550 tanks, 480 artilleries, 1260 rifles to launch an attack on our country along the northern border (from Mong Cai, Quang Ninh to Phong Tho, Lai Chau) of over 1000 km.
>
> To protect the territory of the nation, our people's armies, the soldiers of the six border provinces, were prepared to fight. Because of our high fighting spirit for independence, freedom of the people and the army, and the strong opposition from our country and from the world, China had to announce the repatriation of its armies from our country. The repatriation started from 5 March 1979 and ended on 18 March 1979. (Le, Tran and Nguyen 2006, pp. 306–07)

The author had a chance to discuss with a group of university students about the general taboos about Vietnam-China military conflicts. When I asked why people were able to talk openly about the American-Vietnamese war, but not the Chinese-Vietnamese war, a student majoring in History replied that Asian ways of thinking were different from the Western since the Asians were supposed to be less direct and inward-looking. "Since the Americans are Westerners, we don't need to worry about them." The student cautiously added that perhaps the historians in Vietnam had not yet researched deep enough into the border event, so that they could not talk much about it.

Besides manipulating history-writing, Vietnam has also gradually appropriated its museum exhibitions. In the Military Museums in Ho Chi Minh City and Hanoi, the exhibits about the 1979 border war have been removed. There was not any official explanation about the removal. But alert citizens were well aware of possible underlying reasons. To the Vietnamese, removing such historical memories from exhibition halls is to exchange history for friendship. Chinese tourists, being asked why they thought there was no mention of the 1979 military operations, were quite ready to provide analyses of their own. One tourist from Shangdong said, "Aren't China and Vietnam already good friends now? What is the point to put those things here?". Another young man from Jiejiang said, "Didn't you see all these Chinese tourists here?". Indeed, besides within museums, the border war has become a taboo in tourist activities. Some tourist companies have made it a rule that tour guides should avoid any mention of the border conflict.

In place of the history of military conflicts, Vietnam has installed "friendly" exhibitions. Walking up the stairs that lead to the main exhibition hall of the Ho Chi Minh Museum in Hanoi, visitors will not fail to see the eye-catching red flags of China and Vietnam at the entrance of a side hall with an exhibition entitled "President Ho Chi Minh and China: Archival Exhibition". The exhibition displays many photos showing Ho's visits to China and his intimate hugs and handshakes with different Chinese revolutionary leaders.

In Vietnam and China, the border war and the subsequent grudge have been treated like a kind of "untouchable" history, and have been airbrushed from public discourses by the technology of silencing (Sider and Smith 1997). Such technology of appropriating history is, however, not uncommon. In many cases, history-writing is manipulated by the state (Anagnost 1997; Watson 1994). Burke (1989) sees history as social memory and explains that the use of social amnesia in history is often to "officially erase memories of conflict in the interests of social cohesion" (1989, p. 108). In the above case of Vietnam and China, historical amnesia is used for smoothing inter-state relations rather than for enhancing internal social cohesion. Climo and Cattell (2002) have also elaborated on the theme of history and memory.

> [M]emory, whether individual or collective, is constructed and reconstructed by the dialectics of remembering and forgetting, shaped by semantic and interpretive frames, and subject to a panoply of distortions... [W]ho is to be the master of memory and, with it, the master of meaning? For the masters of memory and meaning also control much else. (2002, pp. 1–2)

The language power of silencing history is actually a power controlling public memory. As such, history is being put aside to make way for making a new relationship and thus new history.

CONCLUSION

To the Vietnamese, a large part of their ancient as well as contemporary histories has been woven into a tapestry of being on good and bad terms with the Chinese. Since 1991, both China and Vietnam have been striving for more pragmatic diplomacy with an eye to bringing both nations to a stable and harmonious relationship. It is hoped that through trials and errors, a more reliable/mature normalcy (Womack 2006) can be achieved.

To the Vietnamese, China is always part of their history and Vietnamese history would not be complete without its correlation to China. Thus, in the Vietnamese historical consciousness, a giant China is always present. A large part of the previous literature of the China-Vietnam relationship has stressed Vietnam's consistent resistance against China. But besides fighting and resistance, the Vietnamese people are actually experts in managing a relatively peaceful relationship with the Chinese. They have enough experiences and knowledge about China to make sure about what should be avoided and what must be stressed, especially when there is not another giant backing them up.

The enormous use of a routinized relational rhetoric and historical taciturnity has shaped a ritualistic formality for Vietnamese-Chinese interactions, meant to lubricate any awkward interactive space. Those two skills — one of silencing (on the border war and conflicts in general), and another of amplifying (friendship and traditional intimacy) — are at present widely utilized by the Vietnamese both at state and non-state levels. The analysis of the oscillation between these two spaces, one loud and one soundless, is for illuminating the thesis of the diplomatic "language power" and should be illustrative for examining the power and cultural dynamics in ongoing Vietnam-China interactions.

Notes

1. *Chu nom* (southern characters) appeared in Vietnam around the eleventh century as a native script or demotic system of writing. It involves combinations or deconstruction of Han characters to create new words. It was used in private documents, deeds, contracts, poetry and verses, until its demise in the early twentieth century (see Nguyen 1987, p. 22).
2. My mother and father were both from Teochiu (Chaozhou), Guangdong. When I grew up in Hong Kong, they used Teochiu dialect at home. Though I cannot speak Teochiu fluently, I can understand most of it.
3. This Mandarin word means "the Great Ching/Qing court".
4. Another border region between Honghezhou of China and Lai Chau of Vietnam.
5. There are different estimates for war casualties. Some estimate that there were 26,000 Chinese people killed and 37,000 wounded, and 30,000 Vietnamese people killed and 32,000 wounded (see Cheung et al. 1993, p. 35).

References

Anagnost, A. *National Past-Times: Narratives, Representation and Power in Modern China*. London: Duke University Press, 1997.

BHLS (*Bao Hoang Lien Son*, Hoang Lien Son News). Feb–April 1979.

Burke, P. "History as Social Memory". In *Memory: History, Culture and the Mind*, edited by T. Butler, pp. 97–114. New York: Basil Blackwell, 1989.

Buttinger, J. *Vietnam: A Political History*. New York: Praeger, 1968.

Chen, M. *The Strategic Triangle and Regional Conflicts: Lessons from the Indochina Wars*. Boulder: Lynne Rienner Publishers, 1992.

Cheung, W. M. et al. *Zhongyue Zhanzheng Milu* [The Secret Report on China-Vietnam Border War]. Hong Kong, 1993.

Climo, J. and M. Cattell, eds. *Social Memory and History: Anthropological Perspectives*. Walnut Creek, CA: Alta Mira Press, 2002.

Do, T. S. "Vietnam-China Relations: Present and Future". In *China's Development and Prospect of ASEAN-China Relations*, edited by Centre for ASEAN and China Studies, pp. 130–40. Hanoi: The Gioi Publishers, 2006.

Emmerson, D. "Southeast Asia: What is in a Name?". *Journal of Southeast Asian Studies* 15, no. 1 (1984): 1–21.

Fan, H. G. *Tonggensheng de Minzu* [People of the Same Roots]. Beijing: Guangming Ribao Chubanshe, 2000.

Faure, D. "Becoming Cantonese: The Ming Dynasty Transition". In *Unity and Diversity: Local Cultures and Identities in China*, edited by Tao Tao Liu and David Faure, pp. 37–50. Hong Kong: Hong Kong University Press, 1996.

Fitzgerald, C. P. *The Southern Expansion of the Chinese People*. New York: Praeger Publishers, 1972.

Goffman, E. *The Presentation of Self in Everyday Life*. New York: Doubleday, 1959.

Huang, G., D. H. Xiao, and L. B. Yang, eds. *Jindai Zhongyue Guanxishi Ziliao Xuanpian* [Selected Essays on The Contemporary China-Vietnam Relationships]. Guangxi: Guangxi People's Publishers, 1998.

HZRZ (Honghe Zizhizhou Renmin Zhengfu, government of the autonomous region of Honghezhou). *Honghezhou Hanizu Zizhizhou Zhi* [The Gazette of Honghe Prefecture]. Beijing: Sanlian Publishers, 1997.

Le, M.H., B.D. Tran, and V.T. Nguyen. *A Summary of the History of Vietnam* [Dai Cuong Lich Su Viet Nam], 3rd vol. Hanoi: The Education Publishers, 2006.

Marr, D. *Vietnamese Anti-Colonialism, 1885–1925*. Berkeley: University of California Press, 1971.

NXBCT (Nha Xuat Ban Chinh Tri, National Political Publishers). *Vietnam Diplomatic Relationship 1945–2000* [Quan He Ngoai Giao Viet-Trung 1945–2000]. Hanoi: Nha Xuat Ban Chinh Tri, 2002.

Nguyen, D. H. "Vietnamese Creativity in Borrowing Foreign Elements". In *Borrowing and Adaptation in Vietnamese Culture*, edited by Truong B. L., pp. 22–44. Honolulu: Southeast Asia Program, Centre of Asian and Pacific Studies, University of Hawaii at Manoa, 1987.

Nguyen, M. H., ed. *Vietnam-China Border Trade: History, Present Situation, and Future Prospects* [Buon Ban Qua Ben Gioi Viet-Trung]. Hanoi: Social Science Publishers, 2001.

O'Harrow, S. "Vietnamese Women and Confucianism: Creating Spaces from Patriarchy". In *"Male" and "Female" in Developing Southeast Asia*, edited by Wazir Jahan Karim, pp. 161–80. Oxford: Berg Publishers, 1995.

Pelley, P. "The History of Resistance and the Resistance to History in Post-Colonial Construction of the Past". In *Essays into Vietnamese Pasts*, edited by K. Taylor and J. Whitemore, pp. 232–45. New York: Southeast Asia Program, 1995.

Qiang, Z. *China and the Vietnam Wars 1950–1975*. Chapel Hill: The University of Carolina Press, 2000.

Reynolds, C. "A New Look at Old Southeast Asia". *Journal of Asian Studies* 54, no. 2 (1995): 419–46.

Ross, R. *The Indochina Tangle: China's Vietnam Policy, 1975–1979*. New York: Columbia University Press, 1988.

SarDesai, P. *Southeast Asia: Past and Present*. 3rd ed. Boulder: Westview Press, 1989.

Taylor, K. W. "Surface Orientations in Vietnam: Beyond Histories of Nation and Region". *Journal of Asian Studies* 57, no. 4 (1998): 949–78.

―――. "Preface". In *Essays into Vietnamese Pasts*, edited by K. Taylor and J. Whitemore, pp. 5–8. New York: Southeast Asia Program, Cornell University, 1995.

Taylor, K. W. and J. Whitemore, eds, *Essays into Vietnamese Pasts*. New York: Southeast Asia Program, Cornell University, 1995.

Wang, S.L. and Z. Liu, eds. *Dandai Yuenan* [The Contemporary Vietnam]. Sichuan: Sichuan People's Publishers, 1992.

Watson, B. "The Unity of Southeast Asia: Historical Approaches and Questions". *Journal of Southeast Asian Studies* 28, no. 1 (1997): 161–71.

Watson, R. "Memory, History, and Opposition under State Socialism: An Introduction". In *Memory, History, and Opposition under State Socialism*, edited by R. Watson, pp. 1–20. Sante Fe: School of American Research Press, 1994.

Watson, J. L. and E. S. Rawski, eds. *Death Ritual in Late Imperial and Modern China*. Berkeley: University of California Press, 1988.

Wolters, O.W. *History, Culture and Region in Southeast Asian Perspectives*. Rev. ed. New York: Cornell Southeast Asian Program, 1999.

Womack, B. *China and Vietnam: The Politics of Asymmetry*. New York: Cambridge University Press, 2006.

Woodside, A. "Nationalism and Poverty in the Breakdown of Sino-Vietnamese Relations". *Pacific Affairs* 52, no. 3 (1979): 381–409.

———. *Vietnam and the Chinese Model: A Comparative Study of Nguyen and Ching Civil Government in the First Half of the Nineteenth Century*. Cambridge: Harvard University Press, 1971.

XHSJZ (Xin Hua She Ji Zhe). "What are the Reasons for the Returning of the One Hundred and Sixty Thousand Overseas Chinese?" [Shiliuwan Huaqiao Huiguo Yuanyin Hezai]. In *Guanyu Yuenan Qugan Huaqiao Wenti* [The Problems of Expelling Ethnic Chinese from Vietnam], pp. 112–18. Beijing: Beijing People's Publishers, 1976.

Yu, P. and J. X. Zhang. *Yuenan-Beijing* [Vietnam-Beijing]. Guangxi: Dandai Shijie Chubanshe, 1998.

Zhang, Y. J., ed. *Bianjing Shang de Zuqun* [The Ethnic Groups on the Border]. Guangxi: Guangxi People's Publishers, 1999.

INDEX

www.ingramcontent.com/pod-product-compliance
Lightning Source LLC
Chambersburg PA
CBHW020752300326
41914CB00050B/139